CW00537783

THE
REBEL
PUBLISHING
HOUSE

# THE HIDDEN HARMONY

# OSHO

*Spontaneous talks given to disciples and friends of Osho in Chuang Tzu Auditorium, Poona, India*

# THE HIDDEN HARMONY

*Discourses on the Fragments of Heraclitus*

Editing by Swami Krishna Prabhu
Typesetting by Ma Deva Naveena
Design and Illustration by Ma Krishna Gopa
Photography by Swami Navajata (Salomon), Swami Vijayo
Production by Ma Dhyan Amiyo, Swami Prem Prabhu
Printing by Mohndruck, Gütersloh, West Germany

Published by The Rebel Publishing House GmbH
Venloerstraße 5 - 7
5000 Cologne, West Germany

1075 N.W. Murray Road, Suite 258
Portland, OR 97229, U.S.A.



ISBN 3-89338-110-4

# TABLE OF CONTENTS

# INTRODUCTION

BEFORE YOU READ ANY FURTHER, be warned: What you hold in your hands is not a book, but a bomb. Heraclitus – the Greek mystic of twenty-five centuries ago – and Osho, a contemporary mystic, make a dynamic duo. In the astute wisdom and beauty of these visionaries' words, within the integrity and the unexpected humor, lies a potent brew that is not for the faint hearted.

Seventeen years of listening to Osho – and almost as many years reading and editing His words – and I am touched and amazed all over again when I look through these discourses on Heraclitus' "fragments." Osho has the unfailing knack of introducing people you may have only vaguely heard of – and before you realize it you are captivated. Then you can't recall a time when you didn't know them.

Osho's commentaries – like Heraclitus' own statements – are not intellectual observations wrapped in scholastic verbiage. They are existential. So if you come across seemingly contradictory statements – and you will – and if you were to point them out to Osho, He might well reply: What can I do? Life is such!

The mystics understand that life is not confined to the logical. Not only is life not confined to logic, one is not truly alive unless one can fully embrace life's inherent irrationality. This of course is quite contrary to the whole Western – essentially Aristotelian – value system and way of thinking...quite contrary to the Christian tradition. But for Osho there is no problem, as there is for Christians, in reconciling the coexistence of God and Devil.

"Just think of a world where evil doesn't exist. Do you think good will exist? Just think of a world where there is no sinner. Do you think there will be saints? The saint cannot exist without the sinner – the sinner needs the saint.... God cannot exist without the Devil.... And life is beautiful because of both," Osho points out.

Seditious views, these...not consoling sentiments to soothe the mind, but explosive insights to erase the mind entirely. For the mind – with its clever categorizations, its penchant for pigeon-holing, its dualism and endless dissection and analysis – has created the insanity we call everyday life.

As amoral as it may appear to the majority of mankind, for Osho it is self-evident that God and the Devil are in partnership, not opposition – just as are war and peace, love and hate, light and dark, heat and cold. The creation of a child needs the meeting of a man and woman. In the meeting of the bow as it strikes the strings of a violin is the creation of a melody. All these seeming contradictions are, in Osho's vision, just part of a cosmic "conspiracy."

This conspiracy is what Heraclitus calls "The Hidden Harmony." And in Osho's vision, living both polarities without clinging to either – "watching," "witnessing" – is the essence of this mystical music.

Read and really comprehend just one line of these small fragments of Heraclitus' and you will hear the tune he is trying to convey. For those less perceptive, Osho – liberal with His love for us and, by His own admission, His love of "gossip" as He calls His discourses – speaks over three hundred pages in this volume: a veritable symphony.

If you really get into this book, this book will really get into you. Heraclitus says: You cannot step twice in the same river. Osho might say: You cannot step into this book and submerge yourself in my message even once, and remain exactly who you were.

Ma Prem Maneesha

# *Chapter* 1

THE HIDDEN HARMONY
IS BETTER THAN THE OBVIOUS.

OPPOSITION BRINGS CONCORD.
OUT OF DISCORD
COMES THE FAIREST HARMONY.

IT IS IN CHANGING
THAT THINGS FIND REPOSE.

PEOPLE DO NOT UNDERSTAND
HOW THAT WHICH IS AT VARIANCE WITH ITSELF,
AGREES WITH ITSELF.

THERE IS A HARMONY IN THE BENDING BACK,
AS IN THE CASE OF THE BOW AND LYRE.

THE NAME OF THE BOW IS LIFE,
BUT ITS WORK IS DEATH.

# THE HIDDEN HARMONY

I HAVE BEEN IN LOVE with Heraclitus for many lives. In fact, Heraclitus is the only Greek I have ever been in love with – except, of course, Mukta, Seema and Neeta!

Heraclitus is really beautiful. Had he been born in India, or in the East, he would have been known as a buddha. But in Greek history, Greek philosophy, he was a stranger, an outsider. He is known in Greece not as an enlightened person but as Heraclitus the Obscure, Heraclitus the Dark, Heraclitus the Riddling. And the father of Greek philosophy and of Western thought, Aristotle, thought that he was no philosopher at all. Aristotle said, "At the most he is a poet," but that too was difficult for him to concede. So later on he said in other works, "There must be some defect in Heraclitus' character, something wrong biologically; that's why he talks in such obscure ways, and talks in paradoxes." Aristotle thought that he was a little eccentric, a little mad – and Aristotle dominates the whole West. If Heraclitus had been accepted, the whole history of the West would have been totally different. But he was not understood at all. He became more and more separate from the main current of Western thinking and the Western mind.

Heraclitus was like Gautam Buddha or Lao Tzu or Basho. The Greek soil was absolutely not good for him. He would have been a great tree in the East: millions would have profited, millions would have found the way through him. But for Greeks he was just outlandish, eccentric, something foreign, alien; he

didn't belong to them. That's why his name has remained just on the side, in a dark corner; by and by he has been forgotten.

At the moment when Heraclitus was born, precisely at that moment, humanity reached a peak, a moment of transformation. It happens with humanity just as with an individual: there are moments when changes happen. Every seven years the body changes, and it goes on changing – if you live for seventy years, then your total biophysical system will change ten times. And if you can use those gaps when the body changes, it will be very easy to move in meditation.

For example, at fourteen for the first time sex becomes important. The body goes through a biochemical change, and if at that moment you can be introduced into the dimension of meditation, it will be very, very easy to move because the body is not fixed, the old pattern has gone and the new has yet to come in – there is a gap. At the age of twenty-one, again deep changes happen, because every seven years the body completely renovates itself: all the old cells drop and the new cells come in. At the age of thirty-five again it happens, and this goes on. Every seven years your body comes to a point where the old goes and the new settles – and there is a transitory period. In that transitory period everything is liquid. If you want some new dimension to enter into your life, that is precisely the moment.

In the same way exactly it happens also in the history of humanity as a whole. Every twenty-five centuries there comes a peak – and if you can use that moment, you can easily become enlightened. It will not be so easy in other times because at that peak the river itself is flowing in that direction; everything is fluid, nothing is fixed.

Twenty-five centuries ago there were born in India, Gautam Buddha, Mahavira the Jaina; in China, Lao Tzu, Chuang Tzu; in Iran, Zarathustra; and in Greece, Heraclitus. They are the peaks. Never before were such peaks attained, or if they were attained they are not part of history, because history starts with Jesus.

You don't know what happened these twenty-five centuries ago. Again the moment is coming, we are again in a fluid state: the old is meaningless, the past doesn't have any significance for you, the future is uncertain – the gap is here. And again humanity will achieve a peak, the same peak as there was in Heraclitus' time. And if you are a little aware, you can use this moment – you can simply drop out of the wheel of life. When things are liquid, transformation is easy. When things are fixed, then transformation is difficult.

You are fortunate that you are born in an age when things are again in a state of liquidity. Nothing is certain, all old codes and commandments have become useless. New patterns have not settled in. They will settle soon; man cannot remain forever

unsettled, because when you are unsettled there is insecurity. Things will settle again, this moment will not last for ever; it is only for a few years.

If you can use it, you can reach a peak which will be very, very difficult to reach in other times. If you miss it, the moment is missed for twenty-five centuries again.

Remember this: life moves in a cycle, everything moves in a cycle. The child is born, then comes the age of youth, then old age, then death. It moves just as seasons move: summer comes, then rains follow, then comes winter, and it goes on in a circle. The same happens in the dimension of consciousness: every twenty-five centuries the circle is complete and before the new circle starts there is a gap you can escape through; the door is open for a few years.

Heraclitus is a really rare flowering, one of the most highly penetrating souls, one of those souls who become like Everest, the highest peak of the Himalayas. Try to understand him. It is difficult; that's why he is called Heraclitus the Obscure. He is not obscure. To understand him is difficult; to understand him you will need a different type of being – that is the problem. So it is easy to categorize him as obscure and then forget him.

There are two types of people. If you want to understand Aristotle you don't need any change in your being, you simply need some information. A school can provide some information about logic, philosophy; you can collect some intellectual understanding and you can understand Aristotle. You need not change to understand him, you need only a few more additions to your knowledge. The being remains the same, you remain the same. You need not have a different plane of consciousness; that is not the requirement. Aristotle is clear. If you want to understand him, a little effort is enough; anybody of average mind and intelligence will understand him. But to understand Heraclitus is going to be rough terrain, difficult, because whatsoever you collect as knowledge will not be of much help; just a very, very cultivated head won't be of any help. You will need a different quality of being – and that is difficult – you will need a transformation. Hence, he is called obscure.

He is *not* obscure! You are below the level of being where he can be understood. When you reach that level of being, suddenly all darkness around him disappears. He is one of the most luminous beings; he is not obscure, he is not dark – it is you who are blind. Remember this always, because if you say he is dark you are throwing the responsibility on him, you are trying to escape from a transformation that is possible through encountering him. Don't say that he is dark. Say, "We are blind," or, "Our eyes are closed."

The sun is there: you can stand in front of the sun with closed eyes and you

can say the sun is dark. And sometimes it also happens that you can stand with open eyes before the sun, but the light is so much that your eyes temporarily go blind. The light is too much to bear, it is unbearable; suddenly, darkness. Eyes are open, the sun is there, but the sun is too much for your eyes so you feel darkness. And that is the case – Heraclitus is not dark. Either you are blind, or your eyes are closed, or there is also the third possibility: when you look at Heraclitus, he is such a luminous being that your eyes simply lose the capacity to see. He is unbearable, the light is too much for you. You are not accustomed to such light so you will need to make a few arrangements before you can understand Heraclitus. And when he is talking he looks as if he is riddling, he looks as if he is enjoying riddles, because he talks in paradoxes.

All those who have known always talk in paradoxes. There is something to it – they are not riddling, they are very simple. But what can they do? If life itself is paradoxical, what can they do? Just to avoid paradoxes you can create neat and clean theories, but they will be false, they will not be true to life. Aristotle is very neat, clean; he looks like a man-managed garden. Heraclitus looks like riddles – he is a wild forest.

With Aristotle there is no trouble; he has avoided the paradox, he has made a neat and clean doctrine – it appeals. You will be scared to face Heraclitus because he opens the door of life, and life is paradoxical. Buddha is paradoxical, Lao Tzu is paradoxical; all those who have known are bound to be paradoxical. What can they do? If life itself is paradoxical, they have to be true to life. And life is not logical. It is a logos, but it is not logic. It is a cosmos, it is not a chaos – but it is not logic.

The word logos has to be understood because Heraclitus will use it. And the difference between logos and logic also has to be understood. Logic is a doctrine about what is true, and logos is truth itself. Logos is existential, logic is not existential; logic is intellectual, theoretical. Try to understand. If you see life you will say there is death also. How can you avoid death? If you look at life, it is implied. Every moment of life is also a moment of death; you cannot separate them. It becomes a riddle.

Life and death are not two separate phenomena; they are two faces of the same coin, two aspects of the same coin. If you penetrate deeply you will see that life is death and death is life. The moment you are born, you have started dying. And if this is so, then when you die you will start living again. If death is implied in life, then life will be implied in death. They belong to each other, they are complementary.

Life and death are just like two wings or two legs: you cannot move only with the right leg or the left leg. In life you cannot be a rightist or a leftist, you have to be both together. With doctrine you can be a rightist, you can be a leftist. Doctrine is never true to life and cannot be, because doctrine, of necessity, needs to be clean, neat, clear, and life is not that – life is vast.

Somewhere, one of the greatest poets of the world, Whitman, has said, "I contradict myself because I am vast."

Through logic you will attain to a very tiny mind – you cannot be vast. If you are afraid of contradiction you cannot be vast. Then you will have to choose, then you will have to suppress, then you will have to avoid the contradiction, then you will have to hide it – but by your hiding, can it disappear? By just not looking at death, are you going to not die?

You can avoid death, you can have your back towards it, you can forget completely about it.... That's why we don't talk about death; it is not good manners. We don't talk about it, we avoid it. Death happens every day, everywhere it is happening, but we avoid it. The moment a man dies we are in a hurry to be finished with him. We make our graveyards out of the town so nobody goes there. And there also we make graves with marble and write beautiful lines on them. We go and put flowers on the grave. What are you doing? You are trying to decorate it a little.

In the West, how to hide death has become a profession. There are professionals who help you to avoid it, to make the dead body beautiful, as if it is still alive. What are you doing? – can this help in any way? Death is there. You are headed towards the graveyard; wherever you put it makes no difference – you will reach there. You are already on the way, you are standing in the queue waiting for the moment, just waiting in the queue to die. Where can you escape to from death?

But logic tries to be clear, and just to be clear it avoids. It says life is life, death is death – they are separate. Aristotle says A is A, it is never B. That became the foundation stone of all Western thought: avoid the contradiction – love is love, hate is hate; love is never hate. This is foolish because every love implies hate, has to; that's how nature is. You love a person and you hate the same person, you have to; you cannot avoid it. If you try to avoid it everything will become false. That's why your love has become false: it is not true, it is not authentic. It cannot be sincere, it is a façade.

Why is it a façade? – because you are avoiding the other. You say, "You are my friend and a friend cannot be an enemy. And you are my enemy, you cannot be my friend." But these are two aspects of the same coin – the enemy is a hidden friend,

and the friend is a hidden enemy. The other aspect is hidden, but it is there. But it will be too much for you. If you see both it will be unbearable. If you see the enemy in the friend you will not be able to love him. If you see the friend in the enemy you will not be able to hate him. The whole life will become a riddle.

Heraclitus is called "that Riddler." He is not, he is true to life. Whatsoever it is, he simply reports it. He has no doctrine about life, he is not a system-maker – he is simply a mirror. Whatsoever life is he represents it. Your face changes, the mirror represents it; you are loving, the mirror represents it; next moment you become hateful, the mirror represents it. The mirror is not riddling, it is true.

Aristotle is not like a mirror, he is like a dead photograph. It doesn't change, it doesn't move with life. That's why Aristotle says there is some defect in this man Heraclitus, some defect in his very character. For Aristotle mind should be clear, systematic, rational; logic should be the goal of life and you should not mix the opposites. But who is mixing them? Heraclitus is not mixing them. They are there, mixed. Heraclitus is not responsible for them. And how can you separate them if they are mixed in life itself? Yes, in your books you can try, but your books will be false. A logical statement is basically going to be false because it cannot be a life statement. And a life statement is going to be illogical because life exists through contradictions.

Look at life: everywhere there is contradiction. But nothing is wrong in contradiction, it is just because it is unbearable for your logical mind. If you attain to a mystic insight it becomes beautiful. Really, beauty cannot exist without it. If you cannot hate the same person you love there will be no tension in your love. It will be a dead thing. There will be no polarity; everything will go stale. What happens? If you love a person, in the morning you love and by the afternoon it has become hate. Why? What is the reason for it? Why is it so in life? ...Because when you hate, you separate; the initial distance is again regained. Before you fell in love you were two separate individuals. When you fell in love you became a unity, you became a community.

You must understand this word community. It is very beautiful; it means common unity. You became a community, you attained to a common unity. Community is beautiful for a few moments, but then it looks like slavery. To attain to common unity for a few moments is beautiful, it leads to a height, to a peak – but you cannot live on the peak for ever. Then who will live in the valley? And the peak is beautiful only because the valley is there. If you cannot move to the valley again, the peak will lose all its peakness. It is against the valley that it is a peak. If you make a house there you will forget that this is a

peak – the whole beauty of love will be lost.

In the morning you love, by the afternoon you are filled with hate. You have moved to the valley, you have moved to the initial position where you were before you fell into love – now you are again individuals. To be individual is also beautiful because it is a freedom. To be in the valley is also beautiful, because it is a relaxation. To be in the dark valley is soothing, it helps you to regain balance. Then you are ready again to go to the peak; by the evening you are again in love. This is a process of coming apart, then coming together – and again and again. When you fall in love again after a hateful moment it is a new honeymoon.

If there is no change life is static. If you cannot move to the opposite everything will go stale and it will become boring. That's why people who are too cultivated become boring – because they always go on smiling, they are never angry. You insult them and they smile; you praise them and they smile; you condemn them and they smile. They are unbearable. Their smile is dangerous, and their smile cannot be very deep; it remains just on the lips, it is a face. They are not smiling, they are just following a code. And their smile is ugly.

People who are always in love and never hate, never get angry, you will always find superficial – because if you don't move to the opposite, from where will you gain depth? Depth comes through a movement to the opposite. Love is hate. In fact, we should not use the words love and hate, we should use a single word: lovehate. A love relationship is a lovehate relationship – and it is beautiful!

Nothing is wrong in hate, because it is through hate that you gain love.

Nothing is wrong in being angry, because it is through anger that you come to a silent stillness.

Have you observed? Every morning airplanes pass over here with a loud sound. And when the airplane has passed, a deep silence follows in its wake. It was not so silent before the airplane came, no. When the airplane has gone, it is more silent. You are walking down a street on a dark night, suddenly a car comes. With full speed it passes by you; your eyes are dazzled by the light – when the car has passed it is more dark than before.

Through the opposite, through the tension of the opposite, everything lives – and becomes deeper. Go away so that you can come near; move to the opposite so that you can come closer again.

A love relationship is a relationship of falling again and again into honeymoons. If the honeymoon is over and the thing has settled, it is already dead – anything that is settled is dead. Life remains through an unsettled movement – anything that is secure is already in the grave. Your bank balances are your graveyards; that is

where you have died. If you are totally secure you are no longer alive, because to be alive is basically to move between the opposites.

Illness is not bad: it is through illness that you regain health. Everything fits in the harmony – that's why Heraclitus is called the Riddler. Lao Tzu would have understood him deeply, but Aristotle could not understand him. And, unfortunately, Aristotle became the source of Greek thought. And Greek thought, even more unfortunately, became the whole base of the Western mind.

What is the message of Heraclitus, the deepest message? Understand so you can follow.

He does not believe in things, he believes in processes – process is God to him. And if you watch closely, you will see that *things* don't exist in the world; everything is a process. In fact to use the word "is," is existentially wrong, because everything is becoming. Nothing is in a state of isness, nothing!

You say, "This is a tree." By the time you say it, it has grown; your statement is already false. The tree is never static, so how can you use the word, is? It is always becoming, becoming something else. Everything is growing, moving, in a process. Life is movement. It is like a river – always moving. Says Heraclitus, "You cannot step in the same river twice," because by the time you come to step into it the second time, it has moved. It is a flow. Can you meet the same person twice? Impossible! You were here yesterday morning also – but am I the same? Are you the same? Both rivers have changed. You may be here again tomorrow, but you will not find me; somebody else will be here.

Life is changing. "Only change is eternal," says Heraclitus – only change never changes. Everything else changes. He believes in a permanent revolution. Everything is in revolution. It is how it is there. To be means to become. To remain where you are means to move; you cannot stay, nothing is static. Even the hills, the Himalayas, are not static; they are moving, moving fast. They are born, then they die. The Himalayas is one of the youngest mountain ranges in the world, and it is still growing. It has not reached its peak yet, it is very young – every year it grows one foot. There are old mountains whose peaks have been attained; now they are falling down, old, their backs are bent.

These walls you see around you, every particle of them is in movement. You cannot see the movement because the movement is very subtle and fast. Now physicists agree with Heraclitus, not with Aristotle, remember. Whenever any science reaches nearer to reality, it has to agree with Lao Tzu and Heraclitus. Now physicists say everything is in movement. Eddington has said that the only word which is false is rest. Nothing is at rest, nothing can be; it is a false word, it

doesn't correspond to any reality. "Is" is just in the language. In life, in existence, there is no "is"; everything is becoming. Heraclitus himself, when he says about the river – and the symbol of the river is very, very deep with him – that you cannot step in the same river twice, he also says that even if you do, you are the same and you are not the same. Just on the surface you look the same. Not only has the river changed, you have also changed.

It happened: A man came to Buddha to insult him – he spat on his face. Buddha wiped his face and asked the man, "Have you anything more to say?" – as if he had said something. The man was puzzled, because he never expected this type of response. He went away. The next day he came again – because the whole night he couldn't sleep; he felt more and more that he had done something absolutely wrong, he felt guilty. The next morning he came, fell at Buddha's feet and said, "Forgive me!"

And Buddha said, "Who will forgive you now? The man you spat upon is no more, and the man you were who spat is no more either – so who will forgive whom? Forget about it, now nothing can be done about it. It cannot be undone – finished!...because nobody is there, both parties are dead. What can be done? You are a new man and I am a new man."

This is the deepest message of Heraclitus: everything flows and changes; everything moves, nothing is static. And the moment you cling, you miss reality. Your clinging becomes the problem, because reality changes and you cling.

You loved me yesterday; now you are angry. I cling to the yesterday and I say, "You have to love me, because yesterday you were loving and yesterday you said you would love me always – now what has happened?" But what can you do? And yesterday when you said that you would love me always, it was not false, but it was not a promise either – it was simply the mood, and I believed in the mood too much. At that moment you felt it, that you would love me always and always and always, forever; and it was not untrue, remember. It was true to the moment, that was the mood, but now that mood has gone. The one who said it is no more. And if it is gone, it is gone; nothing can be done. You cannot force love. That's what we are doing – and making much misery out of it. The husband says, "Love me!" The wife says, "Love me because you promised – have you forgotten the courting days?" But they are no longer there. Those persons are no longer there either. A young man of twenty, just remember: are you the same man? Much has passed; the Ganges has flowed too much – you are no longer there.

I have heard: One night Mulla Nasruddin's wife said, "You no longer love me, you no longer kiss, you no longer hug me. Remember when you were courting me?

– you used to bite me and I loved that very much! Can't you bite me once more?"

Nasruddin got out of his bed, started walking. His wife said, "Where are you going?"

He said, "To the bathroom to get my teeth."

No, you cannot step in the same river twice. It is impossible. Don't cling; if you cling you create a hell. Clinging is hell, and a nonclinging consciousness is always in heaven. One moves with the mood, one accepts the mood, one accepts the change; there is no grudge, no complaint about it because this is how life is, things are. You can fight, but you cannot change.

When somebody is young, of course there are different moods because youth has different seasons and moods. How can an old man have the same? And an old man will look very foolish with those moods. How can an old man say the same thing? Everything has changed. When you are young you are romantic, inexperienced, dreamy. When you are old all the dreams have gone. Nothing is bad in it, because when the dreams are gone you are nearer and closer to reality – now you understand more. You are less of a poet because you cannot dream now, but nothing is wrong. Dreaming was a mood, a season – it changes. And one has to be true to the state in which one finds oneself at a certain point.

Be true to your changing self, because that is the only reality. That's why Buddha says there is no self. You are a river. There is no self because there is nothing unchanging in you. Buddha was thrown out of India because the Indian mind, particularly the brahmins, the Hindus, believed in a permanent self, *atma*. They always said that something is permanent, and Buddha said only change is permanent – nothing is permanent.

Why do you want to be a permanent thing? Why do you want to be dead?... because only a dead thing can be permanent. Waves come and go, that's why the ocean is alive. If waves stop, everything will stop in the ocean. It will be a dead thing. Everything lives through change – and change means changing to the polarity. You move from one pole to another; that's how you again and again become alive and fresh. In the day you work hard, and in the night you relax and go into sleep. Again in the morning you are alive and fresh to work. Have you ever observed the polarity?

Work is against relaxation. If you work hard you become tense, tired, exhausted, but then you fall into the deep valley of rest, a deep relaxation. The surface is far away, you move to the center. You are no more the identity you are on the surface, no more the name, the ego; nothing from the surface is carried. You simply forget who you are, and in the morning you are fresh. This forgetfulness is good, it makes you fresh. Just try for three weeks not to sleep – you will go mad, because you have forgotten to move to the opposite.

If Aristotle is right, then if you don't sleep at all, if you don't move to the opposite, then you will become an enlightened man. You will be *mad*. And it is because of Aristotle that there are so many mad people in the West. If they don't listen to the East, or to Heraclitus, sooner or later the whole West is going to be mad. It is bound to be so because you have lost the polarity. Logic will say something else. Logic will say rest the whole day, practice rest the whole day, so that in the night you can go into a deep sleep – this is logical. This is logical: practice rest! This is what rich people do: they rest the whole day, then they have insomnia and they say, "We cannot sleep." And they are practicing the whole day – lying on their beds, lying on their easy chairs, resting and resting and resting. And then in the night, suddenly they find that they cannot sleep. They have followed Aristotle, they are logical.

One day Mulla Nasruddin went to his doctor. Coughing, he entered. The doctor said, "It sounds better."

Nasruddin said, "Of course, it has to sound better – because I practiced it the whole night."

If you practice rest the whole day, in the night you will be restless. You will change sides again and again: that is just an exercise the body is doing so that some rest becomes possible. No – in life you cannot find a man more wrong than Aristotle. Move to the opposite: work hard in the day and you will go into a deeper sleep in the night. Go deeper in sleep, and in the morning you will find you are capable of doing tremendous work, infinite energy you have. Through rest one gains energy; through work one gains rest – just the opposite.

People come to me and they say, "We have insomnia, we cannot sleep, so tell us some way to relax" – they are Aristotelian.

I tell them, "There is no need for you to relax. Just go for a walk, a long walk, run madly – two hours in the morning, two in the evening, and then rest will follow automatically. It always follows! You don't need techniques of relaxation; you need techniques of active meditation, not relaxation. You are already too relaxed; that's what insomnia is showing, that you are already too relaxed – there is no need."

Life moves through one opposite to another. And Heraclitus says this is the secret, the hidden harmony; this is the hidden harmony. He is very poetic, he has to be. He cannot be philosophic because philosophy means reason. Poetry can be contradictory; poetry can say things which philosophers will be ashamed

to say – poetry is truer to life. And philosophers just go around and around: they never hit the point in the center, they beat around and around the bush. Poetry simply hits directly.

If you want any parallels to Heraclitus in the East, then you will find them in Zen masters, Zen poets, particularly in the poetry known as haiku. One of the great masters of haiku is Basho. Basho and Heraclitus are absolutely close, in a deep embrace; they are almost one. Basho has not written anything in a philosophical way; he has written in small haikus, just three-line, seventeen-syllable haikus, just small pieces. Heraclitus has also written fragments; he has not written a system like Hegel, Kant; he is not a systematizer – just oracular maxims. Each fragment is complete in itself, just like a diamond; each cut to its perfection in itself, no need to be related to another. He has spoken in an oracular way.

The whole method of the oracular maxim has disappeared from the West. Only Nietzsche wrote in the same way again: his book, Thus Spake Zarathustra consists of oracular maxims – but since Heraclitus, only Nietzsche. In the East, everybody who has been enlightened has written in that way. That is the way of the Upanishads, the Vedas, Buddha, Lao Tzu, Chuang Tzu, Basho: just maxims. They are so small that you have to penetrate them, and just by trying to understand them you will change and your intellect cannot cope with them. Says Basho in a small haiku:

Old pond frog jump
in water
sound

Finished! He has said everything. Pictorial: you can see an ancient pond, a frog sitting on the bank, and...the jump of the frog. You can see the splash, and the sound of water. And, says Basho, everything has been said. This is all life is: An ancient pond...a jump of the frog, the sound of water – and silence. This is what you are; this is what everything is – and silence.

The same way Heraclitus talks in his river fragment. First he uses the sounds of a river – *autoisi potamoisi;* before he says something he uses the sounds of the river, and then he gives the maxim: You cannot step twice in the same river. He is a poet, but no ordinary poet – a poet Hindus have always called a *rishi*. There are two types of poets. One who is still dreaming and creating poetry out of his dreams – a Byron, a Shelley, a Keats. Then there is another type of poet, a rishi, who is no longer dreaming – he looks at the reality, and out of the reality poetry is born. Heraclitus is a rishi, a poet who is no longer dreaming, who has encountered existence. He is the first existentialist in the West.

Now, try to penetrate his oracular maxims.

*The hidden harmony*
*is better than the obvious.*

Why? Why is the hidden harmony better than the obvious? – because the obvious is on the surface, and the surface can deceive and the surface can be cultivated, conditioned. At the center you are existential, on the surface you are social. Marriage is on the surface, love is at the center. Love has a hidden harmony, marriage has an obvious harmony.

Just go to some friend's house. If you look through the window and the husband and wife are fighting, their faces ugly, the moment you enter everything changes: they are so polite, they are talking to each other so lovingly. This is a harmony that is obvious, a harmony that is on the surface. But deep down there is no harmony, it is just a mannerism, it is just for display. A real man may appear unharmonious on the surface, but he will always be harmonious in the center. Even if he contradicts himself, in his contradictions there will be a hidden harmony. And a person who never contradicts himself, who is absolutely consistent on the surface, will not have the real harmony.

There are consistent people: if they love they love, if they hate they hate – they don't allow opposites to mingle and meet. They are absolutely clear who their enemy is and who their friend is. They live on the surface and they create a consistency. Their consistency is not real consistency: deep down inconsistencies are boiling; on the surface they are somehow managing. You know them because you are them! On the surface you manage, but this won't help. Don't be bothered too much with the surface. Go deeper – and don't try to choose between the opposites. You will have to live both. And if you can live both, nonattached, unattached to either, if you can live both – if you can love and remain a witness, and you can hate and remain a witness, that witnessing will be the hidden harmony. Then you will know that these are climates, changes in season, moods that just come and go – and you will see the gestalt in them.

This German word gestalt is beautiful. It says there is a harmony between the figure and background. They are not opposites, they *appear* opposites. For example: in a small school you see the blackboard, and the teacher writes with white chalk on the blackboard. Black and white are opposites. Yes, for Aristotelian minds they are opposites: black is black and white is white – they are the polarities. But why is this teacher writing with white on black? Can't she write with

white on white? Can't she write with black on black? She can, but it will be useless. The black has to be the background and the white becomes the figure on it: they contrast, there is a tension between them. They are opposites and there is a hidden harmony. The white looks whiter on black; that's the harmony. On white it will simply disappear because there is no tension, no opposition.

Remember, Jesus would have disappeared if Jews had not crucified him. They made it a gestalt: the cross was the blackboard, and Jesus became whiter on it. Jesus would have completely disappeared; it is because of the cross that he has remained. And it is because of the cross that he has penetrated people's hearts more than a Buddha, more than a Mahavira. Almost half of the world has fallen in love with him – it is because of the cross. He was a white line on a black board. Buddha is a white line on a white board. The contrast is not there, the gestalt is not there; the background is just the same as the figure.

If you simply love and can't hate, your love will not be worthwhile, it will simply be useless. It will have no intensity in it, it will not be a flame, it will not be a passion; it will be simply cold. It becomes a passion – and passion is a beautiful word because passion has intensity. But how does it become a passion? – because the same man is capable of hate also. Compassion has an intensity if the same man is capable of anger also. If he is simply incapable of anger, then his compassion will be just impotent – just impotent! He is helpless, that's why compassion is there. He cannot hate, that's why he loves. When you love in spite of hate, there is passion. Then it becomes a figure and background phenomenon, then there is a gestalt.

And Heraclitus is talking of the deepest gestalt. The obvious harmony is no harmony really, the hidden harmony is the real harmony. So don't try to be consistent on the surface; rather, find a consistency between the deep inconsistencies, find a harmony between the deepest opposites.

*The hidden harmony*
*is better than the obvious.*

That is the difference between a religious man and a moral man. A moral man is just harmonious on the surface; a religious man is harmonious at the center. A religious man is bound to be contradictory; a moral man is always consistent. You can rely on a moral man; you cannot rely on a religious man. A moral man is predictable; a religious man, never. How Jesus will behave nobody knows – even his close disciples were not aware, they couldn't predict him. This man is unpredictable. He talks of love and then he takes a whip in the temple and chases the moneychangers out. He talks of compassion, he talks in terms of "love your enemy," and he upsets the whole temple – he is rebellious. A man who talks of love seems to be inconsistent.

Bertrand Russell has written a book, Why I am not a Christian. In that book he raises all these inconsistencies. He says, "Jesus is inconsistent and looks neurotic. Somewhere he says love your enemy, and then he behaves in such an angry way – not only with persons, even with trees – he curses a fig tree. They came near the fig tree and they were hungry, but it was not the season at all for figs to come. They looked at the tree and there were no fruits, and it is said Jesus cursed the tree. What type of man is this? And he talks of love!"

He has a hidden harmony, but Bertrand Russell cannot find it because he is the modern Aristotle. He cannot find it, he cannot understand it. It is good that he is not a Christian – very, very good. He cannot be a Christian, he cannot be a religious man. He is a moralist; each act should be consistent – but with what? With whom? With whom should it be consistent? With your past? My one assertion should be consistent with another – why? It is possible only if the river is not flowing.

Have you watched a river? Sometimes it is going left, sometimes it is going right, sometimes to the south, sometimes to the north, and you will see that this river is very inconsistent – but there is a hidden harmony: it reaches the ocean. Wherever it is going, the ocean is the goal. Sometimes it has to move towards the south because the slope is towards the south; sometimes it has to move just the opposite way, towards the north, because the slope is towards the north – but in every direction it is finding the same goal: it is moving towards the ocean. And you will see that it has reached.

Think of a river which is consistent, which says, "I will always move to the south because how can I move to the north? – people will say I am inconsistent." This river will never reach the ocean. The rivers of Russells and Aristotles never reach the ocean; they are too consistent, too much on the surface. And they don't know the hidden harmony – that through opposites you can seek the same goal. The same goal can be sought through the opposites. That possibility is completely unknown to them – that possibility is there.

*The hidden harmony*
*is better than the obvious.*

...But difficult, you will be in constant difficulty. People expect consistency from you and the hidden harmony is not a part of the society. It is part of the

cosmos, but not of the society. Society is a manmade affair, and society has worked out the whole plan as if everything is static. Society has created moralities, codes, as if everything is unmoving. That's why moralities continue for centuries together. Everything changes and dead rules continue. Everything goes on changing and the so-called moralists always go on preaching the same things which are absolutely irrelevant – but they are consistent with their past. Absolutely irrelevant things go on....

For example: in the times of Mohammed, in Arabian countries there were four times more women than men, because the Arabians were warriors and continuously warring and killing each other, murderers. And women have never been so foolish, so they survived four times more; then what to do? In the whole society, if there are four times more women than men, then you can understand it will be too difficult for any morality to exist there. Many problems will arise. So Mohammed made a rule that every Mohammedan could marry four women...they are still following the rule.

Now it has become an ugly thing, but they say they are consistent with the Koran. Now the whole situation is different, absolutely different: there are not four times more women now – but they follow the rule. And the thing that was a beautiful response in a particular historic situation is now ugly, absolutely ugly. But they will follow it because Mohammedans are very consistent people. They can't change; and they cannot consult Mohammed again, he is not there. And Mohammedans are very, very cunning: they have closed the door for any prophet to come again; otherwise he will do something, make some change. So this Mohammed is the last – the door is closed even if Mohammed himself wants to come. He cannot come because they have closed the door. It always happens. Moralists always close the door because any new prophet will always create trouble, because a new prophet cannot be consistent with old rules. He will live the moment. He will have his own discipline – consistent with the reality now, but what is the guarantee that it will be consistent with the past? There is no guarantee, it is not going to be so. So every moral tradition closes the door.

Jainas have closed their door: they say Mahavira is the last, now no more *tirthankaras*. Mohammedans say Mohammed is the last; Christians say Jesus is the only begotten son of God, now no more – all doors closed. Why do moralists always close the doors? – just as a safety measure, because if a prophet comes, a man who lives moment-to-moment, he will topsy-turvy everything, he will create a chaos. Somehow you get settled: a church, a morality, a code; everything fixed – and you follow the rules. On the surface you attain an obvious harmony. Again a prophet comes and he recreates everything, disturbs everything; he starts creating everything anew again.

A moralist is a man on the surface. He lives for the rules, rules are not for him. He is for the scriptures, scriptures are not for him. He follows the rules, but he doesn't follow awareness. If you follow awareness, witnessing, you will attain to a hidden harmony. Then you are not bothered by the opposite, you can use it. And once you can use the opposite, you have a secret key: you can make your love more beautiful through hate.

Hate is not the enemy of love. It is the very salt that makes love beautiful – it is the background. Then you can make your compassion intense through anger, then it is not the opposite. And this is the meaning of Jesus when he says, "Love your enemies." This is the meaning: Love your enemies, because enemies are not enemies – they are friends, you can use them. In a hidden harmony they fall and become one.

Anger is the enemy – use it, make it a friend! Hate is the enemy – use it, make it a friend! Allow your love to grow deeper through it, make it a soil – it becomes a soil.

This is the hidden harmony of Heraclitus: Love the enemy, use the opposite. The opposite is not the opposite, it is just the background.

*Opposition brings concord.*
*Out of discord*
*comes the fairest harmony.*

Never is Heraclitus surpassed.

*Opposition brings concord.*
*Out of discord*
*comes the fairest harmony.*

*It is in changing*
*that things find repose.*
*People do not understand*
*how that which is at variance with itself,*
*agrees with itself.*

*There is a harmony in the bending back,*
*as in the case of the bow and lyre.*

*The name of the bow is life,*
*but its work is death.*

Of course, to the rationalist he will seem to be speaking in riddles, obscure, dark. But is he? He is so crystal clear if you can see, he is so luminous. But if you are addicted to the rational mind it becomes difficult, because he says that out of disharmony the fairest harmony is born, opposition brings concord, love the enemy.

Life will be absolutely saltless if the opposition is simply destroyed. Just think of a world where evil doesn't exist. Do you think good will exist? Just think of a world where there is no sinner. Do you think all will be saints? The saint cannot exist without the sinner – the saint needs the sinner. The sinner cannot exist without the saint – the sinner needs the saint. There is a harmony, a hidden harmony: they are polarities. And life is beautiful because of both. God cannot exist without the Devil. God is eternal, the Devil is also eternal.

People come to ask me, they say, "Why? If God exists why is there so much misery, evil, bad – why?" It is because God cannot exist without them – that is the background. God alone without the Devil will be just tasteless, just tasteless – you can vomit him, but you cannot eat him – just tasteless, nauseous. He knows the hidden harmony; he cannot exist without the Devil, so don't hate the Devil – use him. If God is using him, why not you? If God cannot exist without him, how can you? So real saints, saints who have an intensity, are just like Gurdjieff.

Alan Watts has written about Gurdjieff: "He is the holiest rascal I have ever known!" And it is so: he is a rascal – but the holiest. God himself is that rascal, the holiest. If you cut out the Devil, simultaneously you have killed God. The game needs two parties.

When Adam was tempted by the Devil it was God himself who was tempting him. It is a conspiracy. The serpent is in the service of God, the Devil also. The very word Devil is beautiful; it comes from a Sanskrit root which means the divine. Divine comes from the same root, *dev*, as Devil; both words come from the same root. It is as if the root is one, only the branches are different: on one branch the Devil, on another branch the divine – but the root is the same: *dev*. There must be a conspiracy, otherwise the game cannot continue. There must be a deep harmony – that is the conspiracy. Here God says to Adam, "You are not to eat from this tree of knowledge." Now the conspiracy starts, the game starts; now, the first rules are being set.

Christianity has missed many beautiful things because it has tried to create

an obvious harmony, and for twenty centuries Christian theologians have been worried about the Devil: "How to explain him?" There is no need, it is simple, Heraclitus knows. It is very simple, no need to explain. But Christians have been worried because if the Devil is, God must have created him; otherwise, how is he there?

If the Devil is there, God must be allowing him to be there; otherwise, how can he be there? And if God cannot destroy him your God becomes impotent; then you cannot call him omnipotent. And if God created the Devil without knowing that he was going to be the Devil, then he is not omniscient, all-knowing. He created the Devil not knowing that this was going to disturb the whole world. He created Adam not knowing that he would eat the fruit of the tree. He prohibited it! – then he is not omniscient, all-knowing. If the Devil is there, then God cannot be omnipresent because who is present in the Devil? Then he cannot be everywhere; at least he is not there in the Devil's heart. And if he is in the Devil's heart, then why condemn the poor Devil?

There is a conspiracy – a hidden harmony. God prohibited Adam from eating just to tempt him. This is the first temptation, because whenever you say, "Don't do this," temptation has entered. The Devil comes only later on – the first temptation is from God himself. Otherwise, in the garden of Eden there were millions of trees, so if Adam had been left to himself it is almost impossible that he would have found the tree of knowledge – almost impossible, unbelievable!

Even up to now we have not been able to find all the trees of this earth. Many trees still remain unknown, uncategorized, many species still have to be discovered. And this earth is nothing – the garden of Eden was God's garden: millions and millions of trees, infinite. Left to themselves, alone, Adam and Eve would never have found it – but God tempted them. This I insist: the temptation comes from God. And the Devil is just the other partner in the game. He tempted, "Don't eat!" – and immediately the tree was known, and then the desire must have come. Why does God prohibit? There must be something to it. And it is not prohibited to God, he himself eats from it; and just for us it is prohibited – the mind has started to function, the game starts. Then, just as a partner in the conspiracy, the Devil comes, the serpent, and he says, "Eat it! – because if you eat, you will be like gods." And that is the deepest desire in the human mind, to be like gods.

The Devil did the trick because he knows the conspiracy. He didn't approach Adam directly, he approached through Eve – because if you want to tempt man, you can tempt him only through woman; otherwise, directly, there is

no temptation. Every temptation comes through sex, every temptation comes through woman. Woman is more important for the Devil to play the game because it is impossible to say no to a woman who loves you. You can say no to the Devil, but to the woman...? And the Devil comes in the form of the serpent. That is just a phallic symbol, a symbol for the sex organ, because there is nothing like the serpent to represent the male sex organ – they are exactly alike. And through woman it comes, because how can you say no to a woman?

Mulla Nasruddin had arranged for his wife to go to the mountains for her asthma. But his wife was not willing, she refused. She said, "I am afraid that the mountain air is going to disagree with me."

Mulla Nasruddin said, "My dear, don't you be worried. There is no mountain air so brave as to disagree with you! Don't be worried."

It is impossible to disagree with a woman you love, so women become easy conspirators with the Devil. Then the temptation entered, and Adam ate the apple on the tree, the fruit of knowledge – and that's why you are out of the garden of Eden...and the game continues.

It is a deep hidden harmony. God cannot function alone. It would be just like electricity functioning with only a positive pole, no negative pole; he would be functioning only with man, no woman. No, he had tried it before – he failed. He first made Adam, but he failed because with Adam alone the game was not going on, there was no go. Then he created woman, and the first woman he created was not Eve. The first woman was Lilith – but she must have believed in the women's liberation movement. She created trouble because she said, "I am just as independent as you." And the first day when they were going to sleep the trouble came because they had only one cot, one bed. So who would sleep on the bed, and who would sleep on the floor? Lilith simply said, "No! You sleep on the floor." This is how the liberation movement goes on. Adam didn't listen and Lilith disappeared. Lilith went to God and she said, "I am not going to play this game."

This is how, in the West, woman is disappearing – Lilith is disappearing – and the beauty and the grace and everything. And the whole game is in trouble, because there are women who say, "Don't love a man."

I was reading a pamphlet. They say, "Kill man! Murder every man! – because if man lives, there can be no freedom for woman." But if you kill man, can you be there? The game needs both.

Lilith disappeared, then the game could not continue, so God had to create a woman. That's why he tried one bone of man himself this time, because to bring a separate woman would again create trouble. So he took a rib out of Adam and

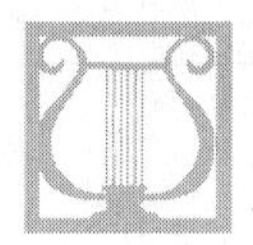

created a woman. Hence, there is a polarity and still a unity. They are two and still they belong to the same body. That is the meaning: they are two, opposites, and still they belong to the same body, deep down the same root; they are one body deep down. That's why when they meet in a deep, loving embrace, they become one body. They come to that state where Adam was, alone; they become one, meet and merge.

There is opposition for the game, but still there is oneness deep within. These two things are needed for the game to continue: opposition, and still harmony. If there is absolute harmony the game will disappear – because with whom will you play? And if there is complete discord, opposition absolute, no harmony, then too the game will disappear.

Harmony in discord, oneness in opposition, is the key of all mysteries.

*It is in changing*
*that things find repose.*

*People do not understand*
*how that which is at variance with itself,*
*agrees with itself.*

The Devil agrees with God, God agrees with the Devil – that's why the Devil exists.

*There is a harmony in the bending back,*
*as in the case of the bow and lyre.*

A musician plays with a bow and a lyre; the opposition is just on the surface. On the surface it is a clash, a struggle, a fight, a discord, but there comes beautiful music out of it.

*Opposition brings concord.*
*Out of discord*
*comes the fairest harmony....*

*The name of the bow is life,*
*but its work is death.*

And death is its work, the ultimate result. Death and life are not two either.

*The name of the bow is life,*
*but its work is death.*

So death cannot be really the opposite – it must be the lyre. If the name of the bow is life, then the name of the lyre must be death. And between these two the fairest harmony of life comes up.

You are just in the middle between death and life – you are neither. So don't cling to life and don't be afraid of death. You are the music between the lyre and the bow. You are the clash and the meeting and the merging, and the harmony, and the fairest that is born out of it.

Don't choose!

If you choose, you will be wrong. If you choose, you will become attached to one, identified with one. Don't choose!

Let life be the bow, let death be the lyre – and you be the harmony, the hidden harmony.

*The hidden harmony is better than the obvious.*

# *Chapter* 2

MEN ARE AS FORGETFUL AND HEEDLESS
IN THEIR WAKING MOMENTS
OF WHAT IS GOING ON AROUND THEM
AS THEY ARE DURING THEIR SLEEP.

FOOLS, ALTHOUGH THEY HEAR,
ARE LIKE THE DEAF;
TO THEM THE ADAGE APPLIES
THAT WHENEVER THEY ARE PRESENT
THEY ARE ABSENT.

ONE SHOULD NOT ACT OR SPEAK
AS IF HE WERE ASLEEP.

THE WAKING HAVE ONE WORLD IN COMMON;
SLEEPERS HAVE EACH A PRIVATE WORLD OF HIS OWN.

WHATEVER WE SEE WHEN AWAKE IS DEATH,
WHEN ASLEEP, DREAMS.

# FAST ASLEEP EVEN WHILE AWAKE

ERACLITUS TOUCHES THE DEEPEST PROBLEM of man: that is – fast asleep even while awake.

You sleep when you sleep, but you also sleep while you are awake. What is the meaning of it? – because this is what Buddha says, this is what Jesus says, this is what Heraclitus says. You look wide awake, but that is only appearance; deep within you the sleep continues.

Even right now you are dreaming within: a thousand and one thoughts continue and you are not conscious of what is happening, you are not aware of what you are doing, you are not aware of who you are. You move as people move in sleep.

You must have known somebody who moves, does this or that, in sleep, and then goes back to sleep again. There is a disease called somnambulism. Many people in the night get up from their beds; their eyes are open, they can move! They can move, they can find the door. They will go to the kitchen, they will eat something; they will come back and they will go to bed. And if you ask them in the morning, they don't know anything about it. At the most, if they try to remember it they will see that they had a dream that night, that they woke up, they went into the kitchen. But it was a dream, at the most; even that is difficult to remember.

Many people have committed crimes; many murderers when in the court say that they don't know, they don't remember ever having done such a thing. It is

not that they are deceiving the court – no. Now psychoanalysts have come to find that they are not deceiving, they are not being untrue; they are absolutely truthful. They did commit the murder – when they were fast asleep they did commit it – as if in a dream. This sleep is deeper than ordinary sleep. This sleep is like being drunk: you can move a little, you can do a little, you can be a little aware also – but drunk. You don't know what is exactly happening. What have you done in your past? Can you exactly recollect it, why you did what you did? What happened to you? Were you alert when it was happening? You fall in love not knowing why; you become angry not knowing why. You find excuses, of course; you rationalize whatsoever you do – but rationalization is not awareness.

Awareness means that whatsoever is happening in the moment is happening with complete consciousness; you are present there. If you are present when anger is happening, anger cannot happen. It can happen only when you are fast asleep. When you are present, immediate, transformation starts in your being, because when you are present, aware, many things are simply not possible. All that is called sin is not possible if you are aware. So, in fact, there is only one sin and that is unawareness.

The original word sin means to miss. It doesn't mean to commit something wrong; it simply means to miss, to be absent. The Hebrew root for the word sin means to miss. That exists in a few English words: misconduct, misbehavior. To miss means not to be there, doing something without being present there – this is the only sin. And the only virtue: while you are doing something you are fully alert – what Gurdjieff calls selfremembering, what Buddha calls being rightly mindful, what Krishnamurti calls awareness, what Kabir has called *surati*. To be there! – that's all that is needed, nothing more. You need not change anything, and even if you try to change you cannot.

You have been trying to change many things in you. Have you succeeded? How many times have you decided not to be angry again? What happened to your decision? When the moment comes you are again in the same trap: you become angry, and after the anger has gone, again you repent. It has become a vicious circle: you commit anger and then you repent, then you are ready again to commit it. Remember, even while you are repenting you are not there; that repentance is also part of sin. That's why nothing happens. You go on trying and trying and you take many decisions and you take many vows, but nothing happens – you remain the same. You are exactly the same as when you were born, not even a slight change has happened in you. Not that you have not tried, not that you have not tried enough – you have tried and tried and tried

and you fail, because it is not a question of effort. More effort won't help. It is a question of being alert, not of effort.

If you are alert, many things simply drop; you need not drop them. In awareness certain things are not possible. And this is my definition, there is no other criterion. You cannot fall in love if you are aware; then falling in love is a sin. You can love but it will not be like a fall, it will be like a rise.

Why do we use the term falling in love? It is a falling; you are falling, you are not rising. When you are aware, falling is not possible – not even in love. It is not possible, it is simply not possible. With awareness, it is impossible; you rise in love. And rising in love is a totally different phenomenon from falling in love. Falling in love is a dream state. That's why people who are in love, you can see it from their eyes: as if they are more asleep than others, intoxicated, dreaming. You can see from their eyes because their eyes have a sleepiness. People who rise in love are totally different. You can see they are no more in a dream, they are facing the reality and they are growing through it.

Falling in love you remain a child; rising in love you mature. And by and by love becomes not a relationship, it becomes a state of your being. Then it is not that you love this and you don't love that, no – you are simply love. Whosoever comes near you, you share with them. Whatsoever is happening, you give your love to it. You touch a rock and you touch as if you are touching your beloved's body. You look at the tree and you look as if you are looking at your beloved's face. It becomes a state of being. Not that you are in love – now you *are* love. This is rising, this is not falling.

Love is beautiful when you rise through it, and love becomes dirty and ugly when you fall through it. And sooner or later you will find that it proves poisonous, it becomes a bondage. You have been caught in it, your freedom has been crushed, your wings have been cut; now you are free no more. Falling in love you become a possession: you possess and you allow somebody to possess you. You become a thing, and you try to convert the other person you have fallen in love with into a thing.

Look at a husband and a wife: they both have become like things, they are persons no more. Both are trying to possess each other. Only things can be possessed, persons never. How can you possess a person? How can you dominate a person? How can you convert a person into a possession? Impossible! But the husband is trying to possess the wife; the wife is trying the same. Then there is a clash, then they both become basically enemies, then they are destructive to each other.

It happened: Mulla Nasruddin walked into the office of a cemetery and complained to the manager: "I know well that my wife is buried here in your cemetery but I can't find her grave."

The manager checked in his register and asked, "What is her name?"

So Mulla said, "Mistress Mulla Nasruddin."

He looked again and he said, "There is no Mistress Mulla Nasruddin, but there is a Mulla Nasruddin." So he said, "We are sorry, it seems something has gone wrong in the register."

Nasruddin said, "Nothing is wrong. Where is the grave of Mulla Nasruddin? – because everything is in my name." Even the grave of his wife!

Possession...everybody goes on trying to possess: the beloved, the lover. This is no longer love. In fact when you possess a person, you hate, you destroy, you kill; you are a murderer. Love should give freedom; love *is* freedom. Love will make the beloved more and more free, love will give wings, and love will open the vast sky. It cannot become a prison, an enclosure. But that love you don't know because that happens only when you are aware; that quality of love comes only when there is awareness. You know a love which is a sin, because it comes out of sleep.

And this is so for everything you do. Even if you try to do something good, you harm. Look at the do-gooders: they always do harm, they are the most mischievous people in the world. Social reformers, so-called revolutionaries, they are the most mischievous people. But it is difficult to see where their mischief lies because they are very good people, they are always doing good to others – that is their way of creating an imprisonment for the other. If you allow them to do something good to you, you will be possessed.

They start by massaging your feet, and sooner or later you will find their hands reach your neck; at the feet they start, at the neck they end – because they are unaware, they don't know what they are doing. They have learnt a trick: that if you want to possess someone, do good. They are not even conscious that they have learnt this trick. But they will do harm because anything, anything that tries to possess the other person, whatsoever its name or form, is irreligious, is a sin. Your churches, your temples, your mosques, they have all committed sins on you because they all became possessors, they all became dominations.

Every church is against religion because religion is freedom. Why does it happen then? Jesus tries to give freedom, wings to you. Then what happens, how does this church come in? It happens because Jesus lives on a totally different plane of being, the plane of awareness; and those who listen to him, those who follow him, they live on the plane of sleep. Whatsoever they hear, interpret, it is

interpreted through their own dreams – and whatsoever they create is going to be a sin. Christ gives you religion and then people who are fast asleep convert it into a church.

It is said that once Satan, the devil, was sitting under a tree, very sad. A saint was passing; he looked at Satan and he said, "We have heard that you never rest, you are always doing some mischief or other somewhere or other. What are you doing here sitting under the tree?"

Satan was really depressed. He said, "It seems my work has been taken over by the priests, and I cannot do anything – I am completely unemployed. Sometimes I have the idea of committing suicide because these priests are doing so well." Priests have done so well because they converted freedom into imprisonments, they converted truth into dogmas – they converted everything from the plane of awareness to the plane of sleep. Try to understand what this sleep exactly is, because if you can feel what it is you have already started to become alert, already – already you are on the way to go out of it. What is this sleep? How does it happen? What is the mechanism? What is its modus operandi?

The mind is always either in the past or in the future. It cannot be in the present, it is absolutely impossible for the mind to be in the present. When you are in the present, the mind is there no more because mind means thinking. How can you think in the present? You can think about the past; it has already become part of the memory, the mind can work it out. You can think about the future; it is not yet there, the mind can dream about it. Mind can do two things: either it can move into the past; there is space enough to move, the vast space of the past – you can go on and on and on. Or the mind can move into the future; again vast space, no end to it – you can imagine and imagine and dream. But how can mind function in the present? It has no space for the mind to make any movement.

The present is just a dividing line, that's all. It has no space. It divides the past and the future; just a dividing line. You can be in the present but you cannot think; for thinking, space is needed. Thoughts need space, they are just like things – remember it. Thoughts are subtle things, they are material; thoughts are not spiritual, because the dimension of the spiritual starts only when there are no thoughts. Thoughts are material things, very subtle, and every material thing needs space. You cannot be thinking in the present; the moment you start thinking it is already the past.

You see the sun is rising; you see and you say, "What a beautiful sunrise!" – it is already the past. When the sun is rising there is not even space enough to say,

"How beautiful!" because when you posit these two words "How beautiful!" the experience has already become past, the mind already knows it in the memory. But exactly when the sun is rising, exactly when the sun is on the rise, how can you think? What can you think? You can be with the rising sun, but you cannot think. For you there is enough space, but not for thoughts.

A beautiful flower in the garden and you say, "A beautiful rose"; now you are not with this rose this moment; it is already a memory. When the flower is there and you are there, both present to each other, how can you think? What can you think? How is thinking possible? There is no space for it. The space is so narrow – in fact there is no space at all – that you and the flower cannot even exist as two because there is not enough space for two, only one can exist.

That's why in a deep presence you are the flower and the flower has become you. You are also a thought – the flower is also a thought in the mind. When there is no thinking, who is the flower and who is the one who is observing? The observer becomes the observed. Suddenly boundaries are lost. Suddenly you have penetrated, penetrated into the flower and the flower has penetrated into you. Suddenly you are not two – one exists.

If you start thinking, you have become two again. If you don't think, where is the duality? When you exist with the flower, not thinking, it is a dialogue, not a duologue but a dialogue. When you exist with your lover it is a dialogue, not a duologue, because the two are not there. Sitting by the side of your lover, holding the hand of your beloved, you simply exist. You don't think of the days past, gone; you don't think of the future reaching, coming – you are here, now. And it is so beautiful to be here and now, and so intense; no thought can penetrate this intensity. And narrow is the gate, narrow is the gate of the present. Not even two can enter into it together, only one. In the present, thinking is not possible, dreaming is not possible, because dreaming is nothing but thinking in pictures. Both are things, both are material.

When you are in the present without thinking, you are for the first time spiritual. A new dimension opens – that dimension is awareness. Because you have not known that dimension Heraclitus will say you are asleep, you are not aware. Awareness means to be in the moment so totally that there is no movement toward the past, no movement toward the future – all movement stops. That doesn't mean that you become static. A new movement starts, a movement in depth.

There are two types of movement. And that is the meaning of Jesus' cross: it shows two movements, a crossroads. One movement is linear: you move in a line, from one thing to another, from one thought to another, from one dream

to another dream; from A you move to B, from B you move to C, from C you move to D. This way you move – in a line, horizontal. This is the movement of time; this is the movement of one who is fast asleep. You can go like a shuttle, back and forth – the line is there. You can come from B to A, or you can go from A to B – the line is there. There is another movement which is in a totally different dimension. That movement is not horizontal, it is vertical. You don't go from A to B, from B to C; you go from A to a deeper A: from A1 to A2, A3, 4, in depth – or in height.

When thinking stops, the new movement starts. Now you fall into depth, in an abyss-like phenomenon. People who are meditating deeply, they come to that point sooner or later; then they become afraid because they feel as if an abyss has opened – bottomless, you feel dizzy, you become afraid. You would like to cling to the old movement because it was known; this feels like death. That is the meaning of Jesus' cross: it is a death. Going from the horizontal to the vertical is death – that is the real death.

But it is death only from one side; on the other side it is resurrection. It is dying, to be born; it is dying from one dimension to be born in another dimension. Horizontal you are Jesus, vertical you become Christ.

If you move from one thought to another you remain in the world of time. If you move into the moment, not into thought, you move into eternity; you are not static – nothing is static in this world, nothing can be static – but a new movement, a movement without motivation. Remember these words. On the horizontal line you move because of motivation. You have to achieve something – money, prestige, power, or God, but you have to achieve something; a motivation is there. A motivated movement means sleep.

An unmotivated movement means awareness – you move because to move is sheer joy, you move because movement is life, you move because life is energy and energy is movement. You move because energy is delight – not for anything else. There is no goal to it, you are not after some achievement. In fact you are not going anywhere, you are not going at all – you are simply delighting in the energy. There is no goal outside the movement; movement has its own intrinsic value, no extrinsic value. A Buddha also lives, a Heraclitus lives, I am here living, breathing – but a different type of movement...unmotivated.

Somebody was asking me a few days ago, "Why do you help people in meditation?"

I told him, "This is my delight. There is no why to it – I simply enjoy." Just like a person enjoys planting seeds in the garden, waiting for the flowers, when

you flower I enjoy. It is a gardening. When somebody flowers it is a sheer delight. And I share. There is no goal to it. If you fail, I am not going to be frustrated. If you don't flower, that too is okay, because flowering cannot be forced. You cannot open a bud forcibly – you can, but then you kill it. It may look like a flowering; it is not a flowering.

The whole world moves, existence moves, into eternity; mind moves in time. Existence is moving into the depth and the height, and mind moves backwards and forwards. Mind moves horizontally: that is sleep. If you can move vertically, that is awareness.

Be in the moment. Bring your total being in the moment. Don't allow the past to interfere, and don't allow the future to come in. The past is no more, it is dead. And as Jesus says, "Let the dead bury their dead." The past is no more! Why are you worried about it? Why do you go on chewing it again and again and again? Are you mad? It is no more; it is just in your mind, it is just a memory. The future is not yet. What are you doing thinking about the future? That which is not yet, how can you think about it? What can you plan about it? Whatsoever you do about it is not going to happen, and then you will be frustrated, because the whole has its own plan. Why do you try to have your own plans against it?

The existence has its own plans, it is wiser than you – the whole has to be wiser than the part. Why are you pretending to be the whole? The whole has its own destiny, its own fulfillment. Why do you bother about it? And whatsoever you do will be a sin because you will be missing the moment, this moment. And if it becomes a habit – as it becomes; if you start missing, it becomes a habitual form – then when the future has come again you will be missing it because it will not be a future when it comes, it will be a present. Yesterday you were thinking about today because then it was tomorrow; now it is today and you are thinking about tomorrow, and when the tomorrow comes it will become today – because anything that exists here and now, it cannot exist otherwise. And if you have a fixed mode of functioning such that your mind always looks at tomorrow, then when will you live? Tomorrow never comes. Then you will go on missing – and this is sin. This is the meaning of the Hebrew root of "to sin." The moment the future enters, time enters. You have sinned against existence, you have missed. And this has become a fixed pattern: robotlike, you go on missing.

I have people coming to me from faraway countries. When they are there they think about me and they get very much excited about me, and they read and they think and they dream. When they come here they start thinking about their

homes; the moment they reach they are already going back! Then they start thinking about their children, their wives and their jobs and this and that and a thousand and one things. And I see the whole foolishness. Again they will be back there and then they will be thinking about me. They miss, and this is sin.

While you are here with me, be here with me; be totally here with me so that you can learn a new mode of movement, so that you can move into eternity, not in time.

Time is the world and eternity is God; horizontal is the world, vertical is God. Both meet at a point – that is where Jesus is crucified. Both meet, the horizontal and the vertical, at a point – that point is here and now. From here and now you can go on two journeys: one journey in the world, in the future; the other journey into God, into depth. Become more and more aware, become more and more alert and sensitive to the present.

What will you do? How can it become possible? – because you are so fast asleep that you can make that a dream also. You can make that itself a thinking object, a thinking process. You can become so tense about it that just because of it you cannot be in the present. If you think too much about how to be in the present, this thinking won't help. If you feel too much guilt...if you sometimes move into the past you will; it has been such a long routine and sometimes you will start thinking about the future – immediately you will feel guilty that you have committed a sin again. Don't become guilty; understand the sin but don't become guilty – and this is very, very delicate. If you become guilty you have missed the whole thing. Now, in a new way, the old pattern starts: now you feel guilty because you have missed the present. Now you are thinking about the past because that present is no longer present; it is past and you are feeling guilty about it – you are still missing.

So remember one thing: whenever you remember that you have gone to the past or into the future, don't create a problem out of it; simply come to the present, not creating any problem. It's okay! Simply bring back your awareness. You will miss millions of times; it is not going to happen right now, immediately. It can happen, but it cannot happen because of you. It is such a long, long, fixed mode of behavior that you cannot change it right now. But no worry, God is not in a hurry; eternity can wait eternally.

Don't create a tension about it. Whenever you feel you have missed, come back, that's all. Don't feel guilty; that's a trick of the mind, now it is again playing a game. Don't repent: "I again forgot." Just when you think, come back to whatsoever you are doing: taking your bath, come back; eating your food, come

back; going for a walk, come back. The moment you feel you are not here and now, come back – simply, innocently. Don't create guilt. If you become guilty then you miss the point.

There is sin and there is no guilt – but difficult for you. If you feel there is something wrong, you become immediately guilty. The mind is very, very cunning. If you become guilty the game has started now; on new ground but the game is old. People come to me, they say, "We go on forgetting." They are so sad when they say, "We go on forgetting. We try but we remember only for a few seconds. We remain alert, selfremembering, then again it is lost – what to do?" Nothing can be done. It is not a question of doing at all. What can you do? The only thing that can be done is not to create guilt. Simply come back.

The more you come back...simply, remember, not with a very serious face, not with much effort; simply, innocently, not creating a problem out of it, because eternity has no problems. All problems exist on the horizontal plane; this problem will also exist on the horizontal plane. The vertical plane knows no problems, it is sheer delight; without any anxiety, without any anguish, without any worry, any guilt, nothing. Be simple and come back.

You will miss many times – it is taken for granted. But don't worry about it, that is how it is. You will miss many times but that is not the point. Don't pay much attention to the fact that you have missed many times, pay much attention to the fact that you have regained many times. Remember this. The emphasis should not be that you missed many times, it should be that you regained remembrance many times. Feel happy about it. That you miss, of course, is as it should be. You are human, have lived on the horizontal plane for many, many lives, so it is natural. The beauty is that many times you came back. You have done the impossible; feel happy about it!

In twenty-four hours, twenty-four thousand times you will miss, but twenty-four thousand times you will regain. Now a new mode will start functioning. So many times you come back home, now a new dimension is breaking in by and by. More and more you will be able to stay in awareness, less and less you will go back and forth. The span of going back and forth will be smaller and smaller. Less and less you will forget, more and more you will remember – you are entering the vertical. Suddenly one day, the horizontal disappears. An intensity comes to awareness and the horizontal disappears.

That is the meaning behind Shankara, Vedanta and Hindus calling this world illusory...because when awareness becomes perfect, this world, this world that you have created out of your mind, simply disappears. Another world

becomes revealed to you. Maya disappears, the illusion disappears. The illusion is there because of your sleep, your unconsciousness. It is just like a dream. In the night you move in a dream, and when the dream is there it is so true. Have you ever thought in a dream, "This is not possible"? The impossible happens in a dream, but you cannot doubt it. In a dream you have such faith, in a dream nobody is skeptical, not even a Bertrand Russell. No! In a dream everybody is like a child, trusting whatsoever happens. You see your wife coming in a dream – suddenly she becomes a horse. Not for a single moment do you say, "How can this be possible?"

Dream is trust, it is faith. You cannot doubt in a dream. Once you start doubting in a dream the rules are broken. Once you doubt, the dream starts disappearing. If even once you can remember that this is a dream, suddenly this will become a shock and the dream will shatter and you will be fully awake.

This world that you see around you is not the real world. Not that it doesn't exist. It exists – but you are seeing it through a screen of sleep, an unconsciousness is in between. You look at it, you interpret it in your own way; you are just like a drunkard.

It happened: Mulla Nasruddin came running. He was totally drunk and the man who was operating the elevator was just going to close the door, but he somehow pushed in. It was overcrowded. Everybody became aware that he was very drunk; his breath was smelling. He tried to pretend; he tried to face towards the door, but he couldn't see anything – his eyes, too, were drunk and sleepy. Somehow he was trying to stand, but that was not possible either. And then he felt very much embarrassed, because everybody was looking and everybody was thinking that he was completely drunk; he could feel that. Then he suddenly forgot where he was and he said, "You must be wondering why I called this meeting." Seeing that so many people were around, he thought that he had called a meeting and that the people were wondering why. By the morning he will be okay. He will himself laugh as you are laughing.

All buddhas have laughed when they awaken. Their laughter is like a lion's roar. They laugh, not at you, they laugh at the whole cosmic joke. They lived in a dream, in a sleep, intoxicated completely by desire, and through desire they looked at the existence. Then it was not the real existence, they projected their own sleep on it.

You are taking the whole existence as a screen, and then you project your own mind on it and you see things which are not there, and you don't see things which are there. And the mind has explanations for everything. If you raise a

doubt, the mind explains. It creates theories, philosophies, systems, just to feel comfortable, that nothing is wrong. All philosophies exist to make life convenient, so that everything looks okay, nothing is wrong – but everything is wrong while you are asleep.

One man came to me. He was worried; he is the father of a beautiful daughter. He was very much worried. He said, "Every morning she feels a little sick, and I have been to all the doctors and they say nothing is wrong. So what to do?"

So I told him, "You go to Mulla Nasruddin – he is the wise guy around here and he knows everything, because I have never heard him say, 'I don't know.' You go."

He went. I also followed just to see what Nasruddin would say. Nasruddin closed his eyes, contemplated on the problem, then he opened his eyes and said, "Do you give her milk before she goes to bed at night?"

The man said, "Yes!"

Nasruddin said, "Now, I have found the problem: if you give milk to a child, then the child changes sides the whole night from right to left, from left to right, and through the churning the milk becomes curd. Then the curd becomes cheese, then the cheese becomes butter, then the butter becomes fat, then the fat becomes sugar, then the sugar becomes alcohol – and, of course, in the morning she has a hangover."

This is what all the philosophies are: some explanations of things; some explanation of things which cannot be explained; pretending to know about something which is not known. But they make life convenient. You can sleep better, they are like tranquilizers.

Remember, this is the difference between religion and philosophy: philosophy is a tranquilizer, religion is a shock; philosophy helps you to sleep well, religion brings you out of sleep. Religion is not a philosophy – it is a technique to bring you out of your unconsciousness. And all philosophies are techniques to help you to sleep well; they give you dreams, utopias.

Religion takes all dreams from you, all utopias. Religion brings you to the truth, and the truth is possible only when you are not dreaming. A dreaming mind cannot see the true. A dreaming mind will convert the truth also into a dream.

Have you ever observed: you set an alarm; in the morning you want to get up at four o'clock, you have to catch a train. Then in the morning the alarm goes off, and your mind creates a dream: you are sitting in a temple and the bells of the temple are tolling – then everything is explained. The alarm is no longer a problem, it cannot awaken you, you have explained it away – immediately! Mind is subtle.

And now psychoanalysts are very much worried as to how it happens, how the mind creates immediately, so immediately. It is so difficult! – the mind must project it beforehand. How, suddenly, do you find yourself in a church or in a temple where the bells are tolling? The alarm goes off – immediately you have an explanation within the dream. You are trying to avoid the alarm; you don't want to get up, you don't want to get up on such a cold winter night. The mind says, "This is not the alarm, this is a temple you are visiting." Everything explained, you fall asleep.

This is what philosophies have been doing, and that's why there are so many philosophies – because everybody needs a different explanation. The explanation that helps somebody else to go into sleep will not help you. And this is what Heraclitus says in this passage.

Now try to understand him. He says:

*Men are as forgetful and heedless*
*in their waking moments*
*of what is going on around them*
*as they are during their sleep.*

In sleep you are not aware of what goes on around you, but in your waking hours are you aware of what goes on around you?

Much research has been done. Ninety-eight percent of messages coming to you your mind never allows to enter – ninety-eight percent. Only two percent is allowed to enter, and that two percent mind also interprets. I say something, you hear something else. I say something else, you interpret it in such a way that it doesn't disturb your sleep. Your mind immediately gives you an interpretation. You find a place in your mind for it and the mind absorbs it; it becomes part of the mind. That's why you go on missing Buddhas, Christs, Heraclituses, and others. They go on talking to you; they go on saying they have found something, they have experienced something, but when they say it to you, you immediately interpret it. You have your own tricks.

Aristotle was very much disturbed by Heraclitus. He found out that this man must have some defect in his character – finished! You have categorized because he doesn't suit you, he disturbs you. Heraclitus must have been very heavy on Aristotle's mind – because Aristotle moves on the horizontal, he is the master of that, and this man is trying to push you into the abyss. Aristotle moves on the plain ground of logic and this man is trying to push you into the mystery. Some explanation is needed. Says Aristotle, "This man has some defect, some

biological, physiological, 'characterological' – some defect is there. Otherwise, why should he insist on paradox? Why should he insist on mystery? Why should he insist that there exists a harmony – between the opposites? Opposites are opposites. There is no harmony. Life is life and death is death. Be clear about it, don't mix things – this man seems to be a muddler."

Lao Tzu also felt the same. Lao Tzu said, "Everybody seems to be wise except me. Everybody seems to be very clever except me – I am a fool!" Lao Tzu is one of the greatest, one of the most wise persons ever born, but he feels amidst you that he is a fool. Lao Tzu says, "Everybody seems to be so clear a thinker, I am muddle-headed." What Aristotle says to Heraclitus, Lao Tzu says about himself.

Lao Tzu says, "When somebody listens to my teaching without the mind, he becomes enlightened. If somebody listens to my teaching through the mind, then he finds his own explanations – which have nothing to do with me. And when somebody listens, not listening at all – there are people who listen without listening – when somebody listens as if he is listening without listening, then he laughs at my foolishness." And the third type of mind is the majority. And says Lao Tzu, "If the majority doesn't laugh at you, you must be aware that you must be saying something wrong. If the majority laughs, only then are you saying something true. When the majority thinks you are a fool, only then is there some possibility of your being a wise man; otherwise, there is no possibility."

Heraclitus looks muddle-headed to Aristotle. It will look so to you also because Aristotle has captured all the universities, all the colleges of the whole world. Now everywhere you are taught logic, not mystery. Everywhere you are taught to be rational, not mystic. Everybody is being trained to be clearcut. If you want to be clearcut you have to move on the horizontal; there, A is A, B is B, and A is never B. But in the mysterious abyss of the vertical, boundaries meet and merge into each other: man is woman, woman is man; right is wrong, wrong is right; dark is light, light is dark; life is death, death is life. All boundaries meet and merge. Hence, God is a mystery, not a syllogism. Those who give proofs for God are simply doing the impossible; no proof can be given for God. Proofs exist on the horizontal.

That is the meaning of trust: you fall into the abyss, you experience the abyss, you simply disappear in it...and you know. You know only when the mind is not, never before.

*Fools, although they hear,*
*are like the deaf;*

*to them the adage applies*
*that whenever they are present*
*they are absent.*

Wherever you are present, that is exactly the place where you are absent. You may be somewhere else, but not there where you are. Wherever you are, there you are not.

It is said in old Tibetan scriptures that God comes many times to you, but he never finds you there where you are. He knocks at your door, but the host is not there – he is always somewhere else. Are you in your house, at your home, or somewhere else? How can God find you? No need to go to him, just be at home and he will find you. He is in search of you just as you are in search of him. Just be at home so when he comes he can find you. He comes, he knocks, millions of times, waits at the door, but you are never there.

Says Heraclitus:

*Fools, although they hear,*
*are like the deaf;*
*to them the adage applies*
*that whenever they are present*
*they are absent.*

This is the sleep: being absent, being not present to the present moment, being somewhere else.

It happened: Mulla Nasruddin was sitting in the coffee-house and talking about his generosity. And when he talks he goes to the very extreme as everybody does, because he forgets what he is saying. Then somebody said, "Nasruddin, if you are so generous why do you never invite us to your home? Not even for a single meal have you invited us. So what about it?"

He was so excited he forget completely about his wife. So he said, "Come on, right now!" The nearer he reached home, the more sober he became. Then he remembered his wife and then he became afraid – thirty persons coming. Just outside the house he said, "You wait! You all know I have a wife. You also have wives so you know. Just wait. Let me first go and persuade her, then I will call you in." So he went and disappeared.

They waited and they waited and they waited and he did not come, did not come, so they knocked. Nasruddin had told his wife exactly what had happened, that he was talking too much about generosity and he had been caught. His wife

said, "But we don't have anything for thirty persons, and nothing is possible at this late hour in the night."

So Nasruddin said, "You do one thing: when they knock you simply go and tell them that Nasruddin is not at home."

So when they knocked the wife came and she said, "Nasruddin is not at home."

They said, "This is surprising because we came with him, and he went in and we have not seen him go out, and we are waiting on the step, thirty persons – he must be in. You go in and find him. He must be hiding somewhere."

His wife went in. She said, "What to do?"

Nasruddin became excited. He said, "Wait!" He came out and said, "What do you mean? He could have gone out by the back door!"

This is possible, this is happening every day to you. He forgot himself completely; that's what happened – in the logic he forgot himself. The logic is right, the argument is right, but what do you mean: "You are waiting at the front door; he could have gone by the back door"? The logic is right but Nasruddin has completely forgotten that he himself is saying it.

You are not present. You are neither in the present to the world, nor to yourself. This is the sleep. Then how can you hear? Then how can you see? Then how can you feel? If you are not present here and now, then all doors are closed. You are a dead person, you are not alive. That's why Jesus again and again says to his hearers, listeners: "If you have ears, hear me; if you have eyes, see me!"

Heraclitus must have found many people who listen but don't hear; who see but can't see because their homes are completely empty. The master is not at home; eyes are looking, ears are hearing, but the master is not present inside. Eyes are just windows; they can't see unless you see through them. How can a window see? You have to stand at the window, only then can you see. How? – it is just a window, it cannot feel. If you are there then it becomes totally different.

The whole body is like a house and the mind is traveling, the master is always traveling somewhere else and the house remains empty. And the life knocks at your door – you may call it God, or whatsoever you like, the name doesn't matter; call it existence – it knocks at the door, it is already knocking continuously, but you are never found there. This is the sleep.

*One should not act or speak*
*as if he were asleep.*

Act, speak, with full awareness and then you will find a tremendous change in you. The very fact that you are aware changes your acts. Then you cannot

commit sin. Not that you have to control yourself, no! Control is a poor substitute for awareness, a very poor substitute; it doesn't help much. If you are aware, you need not control anger; in awareness anger never arises. They cannot exist together; there is no coexistence for them. In awareness jealousy never arises. In awareness many things simply disappear, all the things which are negative.

It is just like a light: when the light is in your house how can darkness exist there? It simply escapes out. When your house is lighted, how can you stumble? How can you knock at the wall? The light is there, you know the door; you simply reach the door, you get out or in. When there is darkness you stumble, you grope, you fall. When you are unaware you grope, you stumble, you fall. Anger is nothing but stumbling; jealousy is nothing but groping in dark. All that is wrong is wrong, not because of itself but because you are living in darkness.

If a Jesus wants to be angry, he can be; he can use it. You cannot use it – you are being used by it. If Jesus feels that it will be good and helpful, he can use anything – he is a master. Jesus can be angry without being angry. Many people worked with Gurdjieff, and he was a terrible man. When he was angry he would be terribly angry, he would look like a murderer; but that was just a game, just a game, just a situation to help somebody. And immediately, not a single moment's gap would be there, he would look at another person and he would be smiling. And he would look again at the same person towards whom he had been angry, and he would be angry and terrible looking.

It is possible. When you are aware you can use everything. Even poison becomes elixir when you are aware; and when you are asleep even elixir becomes poison – because the whole thing depends on your being alert or not. Acts don't mean anything. Acts do not matter. You, your awareness, your being conscious, mindful, is what matters. What you do is not the concern.

It happened: There was one great master, a Buddhist master, Nagarjuna. A thief came to him. The thief had fallen in love with the master because he had never seen such a beautiful person, such infinite grace. He asked Nagarjuna, "Is there some possibility of my growth also? But one thing I must make clear to you: I am a thief. And another thing: I cannot leave it, so please don't make it a condition. I will do whatsoever you say, but I cannot stop being a thief. That I have tried many times – it never works, so I have left the whole sport. I have accepted my destiny, that I am going to be a thief and remain a thief, so don't talk about it. From the very beginning let it be clear."

Nagarjuna said, "Why are you afraid? Who is going to talk about your being a thief?"

The thief said, "But whenever I go to a monk, to a religious priest or to a religious saint, they always say, 'First stop stealing.'"

Nagarjuna laughed and he said, "Then you must have gone to thieves; otherwise, why? Why should they be concerned? I am not concerned!"

The thief was very happy. He said, "Then it is okay. It seems that now I can become a disciple. You are the right master."

Nagarjuna accepted him. He said, "Now you can go and do whatsoever you like. Only one condition has to be followed: Be aware! Go, break into houses, enter, bring things, steal; do whatsoever you like, that is of no concern to me, I am not a thief – but do it with full awareness."

The thief couldn't understand that he was falling into the trap. He said, "Then everything is okay. I will try."

After three weeks he came and said, "You are tricky because if I become aware, I cannot steal. If I steal, awareness disappears. I am in a fix."

Nagarjuna said, "No more talk about your being a thief and stealing. I am not concerned, I am not a thief. Now you decide! If you want awareness then you decide. If you don't want it, then too you decide."

The man said, "But now it is difficult. I have tasted it a little, and it is so beautiful – I will leave anything, whatsoever you say." The thief said, "Just the other night for the first time I was able to enter the palace of the king. I opened the treasure. I could have become the richest man in the world – but you were following me and I had to be aware. When I became aware, suddenly – no motivation, no desire. When I became aware, diamonds looked just like stones, ordinary stones. When I lost awareness the treasure was there. And I waited and did this many times. I would become aware and I became like a buddha, and I could not even touch it because the whole thing looked foolish, stupid – just stones, what am I doing? Losing myself for stones? But then I would lose awareness; they would become again beautiful, the whole illusion. But finally I decided that they were not worth it."

Once you have known awareness, nothing is worth it – you have known the greatest bliss of life. Then, suddenly, many things simply drop; they become stupid, become foolish. The motivation is not there, the desire is not there, the dreams have fallen.

*One should not act or speak*
*as if he were asleep.*

This is the only key.

*The waking have one world in common;*
*sleepers have each a private world of his own.*

Dreams are private, absolutely private! Nobody can enter into your dream. You cannot share a dream with your beloved. Husbands and wives, they sleep on one bed but dream separately. It is impossible to share a dream because it is nothing – how can you share a nothing? Just like a bubble, it is absolutely nonexistential; you cannot share it, you have to dream alone.

That's why, because of sleepers, so many sleepers, there exist so many worlds. You have your own world; if you are asleep you live enclosed in your own thoughts, concepts, dreams, desires. Whenever you meet another, two worlds clash; worlds in collision – this is what the situation is. Watch!

Look at a husband and a wife talking; they are not talking at all. The husband is thinking about the office, the salary; the wife is thinking about her dresses for Christmas. Inside they have their own private worlds, but their private worlds meet somewhere – clash rather – because the wife's dresses will depend on the salary of the husband, and the husband's salary has to provide for the wife's dresses. The wife says, "Darling," but behind the word darling are dresses; she is thinking about them. The "darling" doesn't mean that which is written in the dictionary, because every time a woman says "darling" this is now just a façade and the husband immediately becomes afraid. He does not show it, of course, because when someone says "darling" you cannot show it. He says, "What is it, dear? How are you?" But he is afraid because he is thinking of his salary, and he knows Christmas is coming and there is danger.

Mulla Nasruddin's wife was saying to him, "What has happened? Lately I even cry and weep and tears roll down my face and you don't even ask, 'Why are you weeping?' "

Nasruddin said, "Enough is enough! – it costs too much to ask. And in the past I have committed that mistake so many times, because those tears are not just tears – dresses, a new house, new furniture, a new car, many things are hidden behind those tears. Those tears are just a start." No dialogue is possible because there are two private worlds inside. Only conflict is possible.

Dreams are private, truth is not private. Truth cannot be private – truth cannot be mine or yours, truth cannot be Christian or Hindu, truth cannot be Indian or Greek. Truth cannot be private. Dreams are private. Whatsoever is private, remember, it must belong to the world of dreams. Truth is an open sky, it is for all, it is one.

That's why when Lao Tzu speaks, the language may be different; Buddha talks, the language is different; Heraclitus talks, the language is different – but they mean the same, they indicate towards the same. They don't live in a private world. The private world has disappeared with their dreams, desires – with the mind. Mind has a private world but consciousness has no private worlds. The waking have one world in common.... All those who are waking, they have one world in common – that is existence. And all those who are asleep and dreaming have their own worlds.

Your world has to be dropped; that is the only renunciation I require of you. I don't say leave your wife, I don't say leave your job, I don't say leave your money; leave your anything, no! I simply say leave your private worlds of dreams. That is sannyas for me. The old sannyas was leaving this world, the visible. One goes to the Himalayas, leaves the wife and children; that is not the point at all. That is not the world to leave. How can you leave it? Even the Himalayas belong to this world. The real world which has to be renounced is the mind, the private dreaming world. If you renounce it, sitting in the market you are in the Himalayas. If you don't renounce it, in the Himalayas also you will create a private world around you.

How can you escape yourself? Wherever you go you will be with yourself. Wherever you go you will behave in the same way. Situations may be different but how can you be different? You will be asleep in the Himalayas. What difference does it make whether you sleep in Poona or you sleep in Boston or you sleep in London or in the Himalayas? Wherever you are you will be dreaming. Drop dreaming! Become more alert. Suddenly dreams disappear, and with dreams all miseries disappear.

*Whatever we see when awake is death,*
*when asleep, dreams.*

This is really beautiful: whenever you are asleep you see dreams, illusions, mirages; your own creation, your own private world. When you are awake what do you see? Says Heraclitus, "When you are awake you see death all around." Maybe that's why you don't want to see. Maybe that's why you dream and create a cloud of dreams around you, so that you are not required to face the fact of death. But remember, a man becomes religious only when he encounters death, never before.

When you encounter death, when you see it face to face, when you don't avoid, when you don't dodge, when you don't escape, when you don't create a

cloud around you, when you face it, encounter it, the fact of death, suddenly you become aware that death is life. The deeper you move into death, the deeper you move in life because, Heraclitus says, the opposites meet and mingle, they are one.

If you are trying to escape from death, remember, you will be escaping from life also; that's why you look so dead. This is the paradox: escape death and you remain dead; face, encounter death and you become alive. At the moment when you face death so deeply, so intensely, that you start feeling that you are dying – not only around, but within also, you feel and touch death – the crisis comes. That is the cross of Jesus, the crisis of dying. At that moment, from one world you die – the world of the horizontal, the world of the mind – and you resurrect into another world.

Jesus' resurrection is not a physical phenomenon. Christians have been unnecessarily creating so many hypotheses around it. It is not a resurrection of this body, it is a resurrection into another dimension of this body; it is a resurrection into another dimension of another body that never dies. This body is temporal, that body is eternal. Jesus resurrects into another world, the world of the truth; the private world has disappeared.

In the last moment Jesus says he is worried, troubled. Even a man like Jesus dying is worried, it has to be so. He says to God, he cries, "What are you doing to me?" He would like to cling to the horizontal, he would like to cling to life – even a man like Jesus.

So don't feel guilty about yourself; you would also like to cling. This is the human in Jesus, and he is more human than Buddha, Mahavira. This is the human: the man comes to face death and he is troubled, and he cries, but he doesn't go back, he doesn't fall. Immediately he becomes aware of what he is asking. Then he says, "Thy will be done!" – relaxes, surrenders. Immediately the wheel turns – he is no more in the horizontal; he has entered the vertical, the depth. There he is resurrected into eternity.

Die to time so that you are resurrected into eternity.

Die to mind so you become alive in consciousness.

Die to thinking so that you are born into awareness.

Says Heraclitus, "Whatever we see when awake is death...." That's why we live in dreams, sleeps, tranquilizers, narcotics, intoxicants – in order not to face the fact. But the fact has to be faced. If you face it, the fact becomes the truth; if you escape, you live in lies. If you face the fact, the fact becomes the door for the truth. The fact is death; that has to be faced. And the truth will be life,

eternal life, life in abundance, life which never ends.

And then death is not death. Then life and death are both one, like two wings – this is the hidden harmony.

# *Chapter* 3

IT PERTAINS TO ALL MEN
TO KNOW THEMSELVES
AND TO BE TEMPERATE.

TO BE TEMPERATE IS THE GREATEST VIRTUE.

WISDOM CONSISTS IN SPEAKING AND ACTING THE TRUTH,
GIVING HEED TO THE NATURE OF THINGS.

LISTENING TO ME BUT NOT TO THE LOGOS,
IT IS WISE TO ACKNOWLEDGE
THAT ALL THINGS ARE ONE.

WISDOM IS ONE –
TO KNOW THE INTELLIGENCE BY WHICH
ALL THINGS ARE STEERED THROUGH ALL THINGS.

WISDOM IS ONE AND UNIQUE;
IT IS UNWILLING AND YET WILLING
TO BE CALLED BY THE NAME OF ZEUS.

# WISDOM IS ONE AND UNIQUE

A FEW THINGS BEFORE WE enter these sutras of Heraclitus.

First: to know oneself is the most difficult thing. It should not be so. It should be just the opposite, the most simple thing. But it is not – for many reasons. It has become so complicated, and you have invested so much in self-ignorance that it seems almost impossible to turn back, to return to the source, to encounter oneself.

Your whole life, as it is, as it is approved by the society, by the state, by the church, is based on self-ignorance. You live without knowing yourself, because the society doesn't want you to know yourself. It is dangerous for the society. A man who knows himself is bound to be rebellious.

Knowledge is the greatest rebellion – selfknowledge I mean, not knowledge gathered through scriptures, not knowledge found in the universities, but knowledge that happens when you encounter your own being, when you come to yourself in your total nudity, naked; when you see yourself as God sees you, not as the society would like to see you; when you see your natural being in its total wild bloom – not a civilized phenomenon, conditioned, cultured, polished.

Society is concerned with making a robot of you, not a revolutionary, because it is helpful. It is easy to dominate a robot; it is almost impossible to dominate a man of selfknowledge. How can you dominate a Jesus? How can you dominate a Buddha or a Heraclitus? He will not yield, he will not follow dictates. He will move through his own being. He will be like the wind, like the clouds; he will

move like rivers. He will be wild – of course beautiful, natural, but dangerous to the false society. He will not fit. Unless we create a natural society in the world, a Buddha is going to remain always a misfit, a Jesus is bound to be crucified.

The society wants to dominate; the privileged classes want to dominate, to oppress, to exploit. They would like you to remain completely unaware of yourself. This is the first difficulty. And one has to be born in a society. The parents are part of the society, the teachers are part of the society, the priests are part of the society. The society is everywhere, all around you. It seems really impossible – how to escape? How to find a door back to nature? You are enclosed from every side.

The second difficulty comes from your own self – because you would also like to oppress, to dominate; you would also like to possess, to be powerful. A man of selfknowledge cannot be made a slave, and he cannot make a slave of anybody else either. You cannot oppress a man of knowledge, and a man of knowledge cannot oppress anybody. He cannot be dominated and he will not dominate. Domination simply disappears from that dimension. You cannot possess him and he will not possess anybody. He will be free and he will help others to be free. This is an even deeper difficulty than the first. You can avoid society, but how to avoid your own ego? You are afraid – because a man of knowledge simply doesn't think in terms of possession, domination, power. He is innocent like a child. He would like to live totally free, and he would like others also to live totally free.

This man will be a freedom here in your world of slavery. Would you like not to be exploited? Yes, you will say, you would like not to be exploited. Would you like not to be made a prisoner? Yes, you would like not to be made a prisoner. But would you like the other thing also: not to make a prisoner of anybody else? not to dominate, not to oppress and exploit? not to kill the spirit, not to make a person into a thing? That is difficult. And remember: if you want to dominate, you will be dominated. If you want to exploit, you will be exploited. If you want somebody else to be a slave to you, you will be enslaved. They are both aspects of the same coin. This is the difficulty in selfknowledge; otherwise, selfknowledge should be the most simple thing, the most easy. There should not be any need to make any efforts.

Efforts are needed for these two things; they are the barriers. Just watch and see these two barriers, and start by dropping your own. First stop dominating, possessing, exploiting, and suddenly you will become capable of getting out of the trap of the society.

The ego is the problem; that's why you cannot know yourself. The ego gives

you certain false images of yourself, and if you carry those images for a long time, you become afraid. The fear enters that if your image falls, then your identity will be broken. You create a false face and then you become afraid: if this false face falls, who will you be? You will go mad. You have invested too much in it. And everybody thinks about himself in such lofty terms, in such false terms; nobody agrees with him, nobody approves, but then your ego thinks that everybody is wrong.

I used to know an old man, a very old man. He lived in a country town for almost half a century in one house, never went outside the town, in fact never went inside the town either. He always remained in the house, a very isolated, introverted type of man: no friends, never got married, a permanent bachelor; no children, parents dead – alone. People thought that he was a little eccentric, a little crazy. Nobody ever came to see him, and he never went to see anybody. Then suddenly he surprised the whole town and the neighborhood: he was moving into the house next door. The neighbors gathered and they asked, "Why?" For half a century he had lived in the same house, why so suddenly?...

The man said, "Boys, it seems that it is the gypsy in me."

That is his image. Whether you agree or not, that is not the point, but he thinks that he is a gypsy. And this is how you are all carrying your own images.

The first problem arises: if you want to know yourself you have to drop your false images, you have to see yourself as you are – and that is not very beautiful, that is the trouble. That is not very beautiful, that's why you have created beautiful images – to hide. If you see yourself in total nakedness it is not going to be a very beautiful scene. Then you will see anger, then you will see jealousies, then you will see hatred, and then you will see millions of wrong things all around you. You think yourself a great lover – and there is jealousy and possessiveness and hatred and anger and all sorts of negativities. You think yourself a very, very beautiful person – but when you enter yourself, ugliness is encountered. Immediately you turn your back.

That's why for thousands of years buddhas have been always teaching: "Know thyself," but nobody listens to them. To know oneself seems to be such a difficult thing. Why? – because you have to encounter ugly phenomena. They are there, one has to pass through them. You have a beautiful being within you, but that beautiful being is not on the periphery, it is at the center. And to reach the center you have to pass through the periphery. And you cannot escape, there is no way to escape, one has to pass through it. You have to pass through all the ugliness, all the negativity, hatred, jealousy, violence, aggression, and if

you are ready and mature enough to pass through the periphery, only then will you reach the center. Then the scene changes.

At the center you are God.

At the periphery you are the world – and the world is ugly. At the periphery you are nothing but a miniature society, and the society is ugly. At the periphery you are a Napoleon, a Hitler, a Genghis Khan, a Tamerlane, and all the politicians, and all the mad people of the world. At the periphery you are a miniature of all that; you are the whole history of aggression, violence, oppression, slavery. At the periphery, remember, you are the history that belongs to this world. Everything is involved; it has to be so because mind is not your own, it is a social product. Mind carries all the germs of the past, all the diseases of the past, all the ugliness of the past, because mind belongs to the collective. There are certain moments when you can see and watch your own Genghis Khan, your own Hitler. There are certain moments when you can see that you would like to murder and kill and destroy the whole world.

You have to be very courageous to pass through the periphery, to be a witness. And if you can enter this periphery, this society, the history, then at the center you are God himself. Then there is infinite beauty – but that infinite beauty is untouched by the society, it is not the periphery. Then you are innocent like a newborn baby, fresh as the dewdrop in the morning, uncontaminated. But to reach that, you have to pass through all the ugliness. The whole history of man has to be crossed. You cannot simply avoid it.

That's what you have been doing. That's why selfknowledge has become difficult – you want to avoid it. The only way to avoid is: close your eyes, don't see. Create a private dream against it. Look at yourself as you would like yourself to be – all ideals, utopias, beautiful images. Make a small niche near the periphery – beautiful, decorated – and don't look at the periphery, just keep your back to it.

And then Heraclitus says "Know thyself!" because that is the only wisdom. You become afraid to come out of your decorated part because just near it is the volcano – it will erupt any moment. So people talk about selfknowledge, they discuss it, they write about it, they create systems about it, but they never try it. Even those who talk continuously about knowing the self, they just talk about it, argue about it, discuss it, but they never try it in actual fact. And selfknowledge is an existential experience, it is not theory. Theories won't help. Theories will also be just part of your decoration. They will not break the ice. They will not break the periphery. They will not lead you to the center.

You listen to people: if they say that you are God, you feel very happy; if they

say you are eternal souls, you feel very, very happy. But these theories also you will paint, decorate. They will also be the same trick, escapes – they will not help. Go around India: everybody knows that everybody is part of God, everybody is brahman – and look at their life and the ugliness of it! The people who talk about God, look at their lives and you will not find even a particle, not even an atomic part of what they are saying. They are saying it not to convince you, they are saying it to convince themselves. But they remain on the periphery and they are also afraid to move.

The fear is there. This fear has to be dropped. Remember, before you attain to the ultimate bliss you will have to pass through long suffering. Before you attain to the infinite, the eternal, you will have to pass through the temporal, the whole history of man. It is inbuilt, it is in every cell of your body, every cell of your mind and brain – you cannot avoid it. The whole past is there with you, it is in you, it has to be passed through. It is a nightmare, it is a very, very long nightmare, millions of years, but one has to pass through it – that is the difficulty.

Suffering has to be suffered; that is the meaning of Jesus on the cross. Through suffering he attains to the resurrection; through suffering you will attain to selfknowledge. So don't try to avoid it – there is no way to avoid it. The more you avoid it, the more you are losing opportunities. Face it! There is nothing that can be done except to face it. And the more you face it, the more it disappears. A moment comes when you are absolutely ready to face it, whatsoever it is – you drop all the images. In a single moment even, of intense alertness, you can reach the center. But in that single moment you will have to suffer the whole past of humanity, the whole history; you will have to suffer all that has happened.

It is said, you must have heard, that if people drown in water in the sea or in a river, in a single fragment of a moment they remember their whole past from the very birth, the pangs of birth – in a single moment, a flash, and the whole life passes. This is true. And the same happens when you reach the moment of *samadhi*, the ultimate death, when the ego dies completely. This happens! But in a single moment you suffer the whole past of humanity, not your own. This is the cross. You suffer the whole past of humanity because now you are transcending humanity. You have to pass through all that humanity has lived. You will have to suffer it. It is tremendous – the anguish is absolute. And only then do you reach the center and bliss becomes possible.

Selfknowledge is difficult because you are not ready to pass through any suffering. You think of selfknowledge in terms of tranquilizers; you think selfknowledge

is a tranquilizer. People come to me and they say, "Give us peace, silence." If somebody promises to give you silence and peace without suffering, he is befooling you – and you will be caught in the trap very easily, because that's what you would like to have. That is the appeal of Maharishi Mahesh Yogi type people in the West. They are not giving you meditation in fact, they are giving you tranquilizers. ...Because a meditation is bound to pass through suffering; it is not a play.

You have to move through fire, and only in that fire will your ego drop. Looking at the whole ugliness of it, it drops automatically.

But Maharishi Mahesh Yogi and others, they say there is no need to suffer: "I will give you a technique – just do it for ten minutes in the morning and in the evening and it will tranquilize your being. You will feel infinite peace and everything will be okay, and just in a few days you will become enlightened."

Not so easy – it is arduous. Tricks won't help. Don't waste your time on tricks. Just by chanting a mantra for ten minutes, how can you become enlightened?

You have passed through history, and you have come to a point, here, to this moment you have come; you have passed through millions of years – who will pass back? ...Because meditation means returning to the source. You have come up to this point in time; you will have to go back, you will have to regress, you will have to reach the original point from where the journey started. Just by chanting a mantra for ten minutes in the morning, you are thinking you will attain to it?

Whom do you think you are befooling? You are befooling yourself. It is not by chanting mantras that you have come up to now. Humanity has lived, and lived in millions of wrong ways – wandered, missed, committed sin, murdered; war, exploitation, oppression, domination. You have been a part of it, you are responsible for it. Just by chanting a mantra for ten minutes you think all responsibility is gone, you have transcended? You call this chanting transcendental meditation? Whom do you think you are befooling?

Transcendence is possible, but not through such easy tricks. Transcendence is possible only through the cross. Transcendence is possible only through suffering. And if you are ready you can suffer the whole past in a single moment – but it is going to be an intense nightmare. That's why a master is needed – because you can go completely mad. It is moving through dangerous terrain. Selfknowledge is the greatest thing, and selfknowledge is the greatest danger also. You can miss a step and you will go mad. That's why buddhas are not listened to. You also know that this is dangerous. Moving into oneself *is* dangerous! A master is needed to

watch every step; otherwise you will fall into an abyss, you will get dizzy and the mind will simply crack, and it will be difficult to repair it.

These are the problems, and this is why man listens to Heraclitus, to Lao Tzu, to Buddha, to Jesus, but never tries. Only a few try it. If you are ready to try it, you have to be aware of what it means. Just a desire to be happy won't help – a desire to know the truth, not a desire to be happy, because a man who wants to be happy will be in search of tranquilizers, narcotics. Meditation also will be a narcotic to him. He wants to sleep well, he wants not to bother about what is happening. He would like to have a private world of his own dreams – of course beautiful dreams, not nightmares. That's all he wants.

But a man who is in search of truth does not think in terms of happiness. His happiness, or unhappiness, that is not the point. "I must know the true. Even if it is painful, even if it leads to hell, I am ready to pass through it. Wheresoever it leads, I am ready to go to it."

There are only two types of people. One is in search of happiness; he is the worldly type. He may go into a monastery, but the type doesn't change: there also he is asking for happiness, pleasure, gratification. Now in a different way – through meditation, prayer, God – he is trying to become happy, more and more happy. Then there is the other type of person – and only two types exist – who is in search of truth. And this is the paradox: the one who seeks happiness will never find it, because happiness is not possible unless you attain to the true. Happiness is just a shadow of truth; it is nothing in itself – it is just a harmony.

When you feel one with the truth, everything fits together, falls together. You feel a rhythm – that rhythm is happiness. You cannot seek it directly.

Truth has to be sought. Happiness is found when truth is found, but happiness is not the goal. And if you seek happiness directly you will be more and more unhappy. And, at the most, your happiness will be just an intoxicant so that you can forget unhappiness; that's all that is going to happen. Happiness is just like a drug – it is LSD, it is marijuana, it is mescaline.

Why has the West come to drugs? It is a very, very rational process. It has to come to it because searching for happiness one has to reach LSD sooner or later. The same has happened in India before. In the Vedas they reached soma, LSD, because they were seeking happiness; they were not really seekers of truth. They were seeking more and more gratification – they came to soma. Soma is the ultimate drug. And Aldous Huxley has named the ultimate drug, when it is to be found somewhere in the twenty-first century, he has called it soma again.

Whenever a society, a man, a civilization, seeks happiness, it has to come somewhere to drugs – because happiness is a search for drugs. The search for happiness is a search to forget oneself; that's what a drug helps you to do. You forget yourself, then there is no misery. You are not there, how can there be misery? You are fast asleep.

The search for truth is just the opposite dimension: not gratification, not pleasure, not happiness, but "What is the nature of existence? What is true?" A man who seeks happiness will never find it – at the most he will find forgetfulness. A man who seeks truth will find it, because to seek truth he will have to become true himself. To seek truth in existence, first he will have to seek the true in his own being. He will become more and more selfremembering.

These are the two paths: self-forgetfulness, the way of the world; and self-remembrance, the way of God. The paradox is that one who seeks happiness never finds it; and one who seeks truth and doesn't bother about happiness has always found it.

Heraclitus says this is the first thing to be understood: selfknowledge must be the only search, selfknowledge must be the only goal because if without knowing yourself you know everything else, it is meaningless. You may come to know everything except yourself, but what does it mean? It cannot carry any significance – because if the knower himself is ignorant, what can his knowledge mean? What can his knowledge give? When you yourself remain in darkness you may gather millions of lights around you, but they will not make you filled with light. You will remain in darkness in spite of them. You will live in darkness, you will move in darkness. That type of knowledge is science. You know a million and one things, but you don't know yourself.

Science is all knowledge but selfknowledge, minus selfknowledge; the seeker himself remains in darkness. It is not of much use. Religion is basically selfknowledge. You should be lighted within, the darkness should disappear from within, then wherever you move your inner light falls on the path. Wherever you go, whatsoever you do, everything is illuminated by your inner light. And this movement with the light gives you a rhythm, a harmony, which is happiness. Then you don't stumble, then you don't clash, then there is no conflict. Then you move easily, then your steps have a dance to them, then everything is a fulfillment. Then you don't ask for something extraordinary to happen. Then you are happy. You are simply happy in your ordinariness.

And unless you are happy in your ordinariness, you will never be happy.

You are happy just to breathe, you are happy just to be; you are happy just to

eat, just to go to sleep again. You are happy. Now happiness is not derived from anything – it is you. A man who knows himself is happy not because of any reasons; his happiness is uncaused. It is not a thing that happens to him, it is his whole way of being. He is simply happy. Wherever he moves he takes his happiness with himself. If you throw him into hell, he will create a heaven around him there, a heaven will enter with him. As you are, ignorant of yourself, if you could be thrown into heaven you would create a hell there because you carry your hell with you. Wherever you go it will not make much difference, you will carry your own world around you. That world is within you, your darkness.

This inner darkness should disappear – that is what is meant by selfknowledge.

The second thing Heraclitus says is that this will become easy to attain if you are aware not to move to the extremes. Remain in the middle – the golden mean...what Buddha calls *majjhim nikaya,* the middle way. Remain in the middle, don't move to the extremes, because when you move to the extremes you think you are going to the opposite, but the opposite is not exactly the opposite, it is a complementary whole. That is his whole teaching.

Watch people and watch yourself. One person indulges too much in sex: indulgence brings boredom, excitement is lost, he is simply bored. Then he starts thinking of celibacy because he is finished with indulgence. Now he is not interested in sex at all; he would like to become a monk, he would like to move to a monastery, take a vow of *brahmacharya.* This is going to the extreme; this is again indulgence. The extreme is indulgence. Sex is not indulgence, the extreme is indulgence. There is only one indulgence: to indulge in the extreme. He indulged in one extreme, now he is moving to the other; that too is indulgence. Sooner or later he will be fed up. Catholic monks are fed up now, so they are entering into marriage. They have done too much. One must know where to stop, and the middle is the way.

If you can remain in the middle, mind disappears – because mind lives in extremes. You eat too much, then you fast, then you go on fasting. The first was stupid; this too is stupid. The body doesn't need too much food and doesn't need fasting either. It needs just a midpoint; the right quantity of food it needs. First you eat too much, you fill the body too much, the body becomes a burden. To carry it becomes a burden to you; it is not a bliss to be in the body. Then you move to the other extreme. Now you fast; that too is destructive. Why can't you be in the middle? Why can't you eat the right quantity of food and the right type of food? Why can't you remain in the middle? If you remain in the middle, the mind disappears.

With the extreme the mind exists – because the mind has to think again and again. When you eat too much, you think about fasting; when you fast, you will think about food. But when you are just in the middle, balanced, what is there to think about? A man who is in the middle has nothing to think of. He is hungry, he eats – finished! He is sleepy, he sleeps – finished! What is there to think about? But you don't sleep, then you think about sleeping; then sleeping becomes a cerebral phenomenon, the mind gets into it. You don't eat, or eat too much, then you have to think about it; it goes into the mind. Either you indulge too much in sex, or you become a *brahmacharin*. Then in both cases it becomes cerebral. Sex enters into the mind, then the mind goes on thinking around and around.

Thinking exists because of extremes.

Whenever you are simply in the middle, there is no point in thinking; there is nothing to think. In the middle thinking disappears. When you are really harmonious you have attained to a rhythm. You fulfill the needs; you are neither a slave to them nor an enemy to them. You are neither an indulgent one nor one who is ascetic. You simply remain in the middle. Everything becomes peaceful. This Heraclitus calls being temperate, being moderate, being balanced.

In everything balance has to be gained. Through balance you will come nearer to truth, because truth is the ultimate balance. When you are balanced, suddenly the doors open.

Now try to understand these sutras:

*It pertains to all men*
*to know themselves*
*and to be temperate.*

To be temperate is the way to know oneself. Watch your mind and you will always see the mind insists on the extreme; it enjoys the extreme, it indulges in the extreme. When you are just in the middle, the mind is unemployed, unoccupied.

Somebody asked a Zen master, "What is your way?"

He said, "When I feel hungry, I eat; and when I feel sleepy, I go to sleep – this is my way. I never eat when I am not hungry, and I never fast when I am hungry – this is my way!"

The man said, "But this doesn't seem much of a way – we all do this."

The master laughed. He said, "If you all did this, there would be no need to come to me."

Either you eat too much, or you eat too little. And the mind has a tendency

always to find causes for being miserable. It is simply wonderful, the mind is simply wonderful – it is so skilled in finding causes to be miserable! It creates all your miseries – because in a blissful state the mind will die. It is against all bliss. You are in a misery: it will suggest to you that this is not good, do that. And it will suggest just the opposite. Be alert: when the mind suggests just the opposite to you, don't follow it! Always find the golden mean. Don't listen to the mind, know where to stop.

Lao Tzu has said, "Three treasures I give to you. One treasure is love. The second treasure is never go to the extreme. And the third treasure is be natural." And he says everything will take care of itself. Why will everything take care of itself if you follow these simple things? Mind is a perfect expert in creating miseries.

One young man came to me and he said, "I would like to live just on water." Why? Why just on water? He is already miserable. He has been eating too much. Now that has become a hell, now he wants to create another hell – because how can you live just on water? That will be another hell. Then from that hell again you will move to another hell. From hell to hell is the passage of the mind. And somewhere between two hells is heaven, but the mind always bypasses it.

Between two hells is heaven, so know well where to stop. Just in the middle, stop! Don't eat too much, and don't fast. But then you will not be able to become very egoistic about it, because eating too much you can be egoistic.

Mulla Nasruddin goes on talking about his capacity to eat, and many times I have heard him saying: "I can eat ninety-nine *kachoris!*"

So I told him, "Why not make it a hundred?"

He said, "What do you think of me? Am I a liar just for one kachori? Should I lie?" Bragging – people brag about how much they can eat, and then people brag about how much they can fast, but the bragging remains the same. Criminals brag, and your so-called saints also. Both are in the same boat – because bragging is the boat.

I have heard that one criminal entered a prison cell. The other one who was already there asked, "How long do you have to be here?" He was an old master.

The young, new one said, "Just fifteen years."

He said, "Then keep your bed near the door. You will be leaving soon. I am to be here for twenty-five years more."

If you are sentenced for twenty-five years you are a great criminal. But just fifteen? – you are just a beginner, amateur. Even criminals brag about how much they can do, how much they have done. If they commit one murder, they claim

seven. And saints also do the same. Then what is the difference? In India, saints publish how many days they fasted this year.

One man came to me with his wife, and his wife was saying about him, "He is a very, very generous man" – her husband – "he has donated almost one lakh rupees up to now."

The man looked at his wife and corrected her. He said, "Not one lakh – one lakh ten thousand." You give and you don't give – because if the ego is fulfilled through giving, nothing is being given. Ego cannot share. The ego can never be generous; that is not its nature. The ego always fulfills itself by the opposite. Know this trap well.

Says Heraclitus:

*It pertains to all men*
*to know themselves*
*and to be temperate.*

*To be temperate is the greatest virtue.*

Really it is. I have not come across anything greater than being temperate. There is nothing like it. Why? Why is it the greatest virtue? – because it simply destroys your ego, and ego is the only sin. Because of the ego you miss the divine. And just being ordinary, in the middle, what can you claim? Can you claim that you eat the right quantity of food? Can you claim that you move into sex exactly in the middle, just right? Can you claim anything from the middle? No, that's not possible. Indulge in sex and you can claim that even at the age of fifty you can make love thrice a day. Or become a brahmacharin, a celibate, and claim that you are a virgin, never made love to anybody. But just in the middle, what can you claim? Just in the middle there is nothing to claim. And when there is nothing to claim and declare, the ego is not fed. Just be ordinary and in the middle – this is the greatest virtue.

To be ordinary is the greatest virtue – because when you are just ordinary, nothing to claim, of this world or that, the ego disappears. The ego feeds on imbalance, the ego feeds on extremes. The ego lives on the polarities – in the middle it disappears. And in every area, in every direction of life, remember this: just stop in the middle and soon you will find the mind has stopped, the ego has stopped. Nothing to claim, it disappears. And when it disappears you have become virtuous. Now the door is open for the divine. In the middle you meet him; at the extremes you miss.

*Wisdom consists in speaking and acting the truth,*
*giving heed to the nature of things.*

Heraclitus is just like Lao Tzu, exactly the same. He says:

*Wisdom consists in speaking and acting the truth....*

Try, because to know the truth it is going to be a long journey. Much preparation will be needed. Before the truth can descend on you, you will have to become a vehicle, you will have to be completely empty for the guest to come because only your emptiness can become the host. What to do right now? If you are a seeker after truth, then, says Heraclitus, speak and act truth. If you speak truth, there is not much to say; you will become more and more silent automatically.

In a ladies' club it happened: One lady had just left and other ladies were talking about her. Said one, "She seems to be very sweet, but – yakety-yakety-yak...and I couldn't think how she would be able to stop."

Another member of the club said, "But is everything that she says true?"

"I should say not," said the third lady, "because there simply does not exist that much truth!"

If you want to be true you will become silent – because ninety-nine percent of your talk is simply untrue; it will drop automatically. And there are two types of silence: one that you force upon yourself, which is not really silence. You can cut off your tongue, but that will not be the silence. You can close your mouth, that will not be a true silence because inside: yakety-yakety-yak, it goes on and on and on. True silence comes if you start talking truth. Only say that which you know is true; otherwise don't speak. Then what is left to say? – not much...and then a silence descends on you which is totally different. It is not a forced silence. It comes spontaneously because there is nothing to say.

And when you have nothing to say, first you start being silent with people; you talk less and listen more. Then inside also talk stops, by and by, because if you cannot speak untruth to other people, how can you go on talking about it inside? The whole thing becomes absurd. Inside you talk too much because that is just a rehearsal for talking outside. If you can listen to people, not talking much, just the truth – that for which you can vouch, that to which you can say, "I am a witness" – a silence will come to you...a silence not forced, a silence not disciplined, a silence that comes naturally.

Heraclitus says, "Talk the truth and act the truth, and act only in such a way that it comes out of your feeling of truth." In the beginning it will be difficult

because the whole life depends on lies. In the beginning you will feel always out of step with others, but soon everything settles again in a new pattern, a new gestalt arises. The interim period is going to be difficult.

Just first watch in how many ways you lie. You smile and you don't feel like smiling within. It is a lie. Don't smile, because you are being violent to the lips, to the face. And if you go on doing it for long you will completely forget the feeling of a smile, what a true smile is. Only small children know; you have completely forgotten what a true smile is. You simply smile; it is a gesture, false. You smile as a polite mannerism. You smile because people expect you to smile. You smile not knowing what you are doing. Why are you forcing your lips? And if your smile has become false, what else can be true in you? Your tears, they also have become false. You weep when it is required to weep; otherwise you suppress.

Watch in how many millions of ways you have become untrue. You say things you don't mean. You use words completely unconsciously – and then you are trapped through them. You say to someone, "You are beautiful." It may have been just a mannerism with you, but you have touched the other person, you have stirred something in the other person. The other person may start feeling that you feel that way. Now expectations arise, and soon frustrations will follow – because you had said it just by the way, you never meant it. Now you are in a trap: you have to fulfill the expectation. Now you feel burdened.

Be true and you will be less burdened. Be true; don't create false expectations around you, otherwise you will be in a prison, trapped! Say exactly what you mean and always say, "This I mean in this moment. For the next moment I cannot say anything – because who knows what will happen in the next moment? I love you this moment but how can I speak for the next moment?"

Only an enlightened person can say something about the next moment because he has come to a point where everything is eternal. But how can you speak about the next moment? Your moods change. This moment you feel, "I love," and this moment you can say, "I will love you for ever and ever." This is true only in this moment; for the next moment, how can you say anything? Then be alert and make the statement conditional: "This is only for this moment – this is how I feel. Nobody knows about the next moment. I cannot promise."

All your promises are untrue – how can you promise? – because a promise means you have attained to a crystallized center. How can you keep a promise? You say to a woman, "I will love you for ever and ever." How can you keep this promise? And after just a few days you feel the excitement has disappeared, now there is no love – what to do? Now you have to smile falsely. You have to kiss this

woman, you have to make love to this woman – because of the promise. Now everything goes false. You become untrue. Now you feel guilty if you don't fulfill it. If you fulfill it, it is untrue, you are acting. It cannot make you ecstatic – it will create more anxiety and burdens. It cannot be a fulfillment, it will be a frustration. And the more you force yourself to love that woman the more you will take revenge, because this woman has become a rock around your neck. Now you feel: "If she dies it will be good." Now you feel: "Somehow, if she goes away it will be good." Now you will find a way to escape – just because of a promise! A promise that is given in a moment and given for one life is not possible for you. You live in moments. You don't have an eternal center in you yet, you have just a wheel-like periphery that moves. And this is how you are trapped.

You cannot love, you cannot laugh, you cannot weep – everything is untrue, and you are in search of truth. No, it is not possible. You have to be true to meet truth, because only the same can meet the same. An untrue person cannot reach the truth; only a true person can reach the truth.

Be alert, don't promise! Just say that this moment it appears so. It will give you a feeling of helplessness, of course; the ego cannot stand. The ego can say, "I will, for ever and ever." You will feel helpless that even this promise you cannot give; but it is being true. And I know that if even for a single moment you can love another person totally, that will change you, that will give you a taste of truth. But be true. Say what you mean. If you don't know, if in a situation you are confused, don't speak – or simply put your confusion out, express it. Before you act, act with full awareness that this is going to give you a truer being. Be authentic!

Millions of things you go on doing that you don't want to do. Who is forcing you? You simply drift – nobody is forcing you to do those things. Why do you do them? You are not aware. It is just a chain: you do one thing, then another arises. One thing leads to another and you go on and on. Then when will you stop? Every moment is the right moment to stop. Just watch and start falling out of the chain of lies that you have created.

Of course, you will feel very, very humiliated, humble, helpless. But that's true – feel it. Weep when you want to weep, when it comes from your heart. Don't stop; don't say, "I am a man, I cannot be a sissy, I cannot behave like a woman." Don't say that. Nobody is so totally a man and nobody can be. Man is woman also, woman is man also; both meet and mingle inside. Weep, because if you cannot weep authentically you cannot smile. Then you will be afraid. When you would like to laugh you will be afraid because tears may come; they

are suppressed there so you cannot laugh. When you cannot laugh, you cannot weep – it becomes a vicious circle. When you are angry, be angry and take the consequences – be truly angry.

And this has been my observation: if you are truly angry, nobody is offended by true anger – nobody! But your anger is impotent, dead. If you are a father and you feel angry with your child, be angry and the child will never feel anything antagonistic towards you. But you are angry and you smile, and the child simply detects it because a child is innocent, he has clear eyes, more clarity than you have. He simply detects the falsity – that you are angry and you are smiling. He will never be able to forgive you because you are untrue. A child never feels so bad about anything as he feels about untruth. Be authentic! If you feel like hitting the child, hit him, but don't be untrue. And when you feel repentance, ask forgiveness also, and be true in that.

A husband who has never said anything in anger to his wife will not be able to love, because everything remains false, on the surface. If you cannot bring deep anger, how can you bring deep love? And if you are so much afraid of being angry, that shows that you are not confident of love. You are afraid that things may fall apart, the relationship may break; that's why you are afraid. But then this relationship is not worth much. If it cannot pass through anger and mature, it is not worth much. Drop it before it becomes a commitment – but be true.

You will have to suffer through truth, but that suffering is needed. And through suffering you will mature, your inner being will become seasoned. You will attain to a sharpness and clarity that only comes through encounter, that only comes through facing facts. When you are angry, be truly angry so that you can be truly forgiving also. When you don't want to give a thing, simply say, "I don't want to give it," but don't find excuses. Don't find excuses, because you are creating a pattern every moment, and that pattern can become so ingrained that you will have to follow it. Come out of it – and every moment is a right moment.

Says Heraclitus:

*Wisdom consists in speaking and acting the truth,*
*giving heed to the nature of things.*

Look at the nature of things. Watch the natural and drop the artificial. The artificial may look beautiful, but it is not alive. Watch the natural and always move with nature. Never move with the artificial. Civilization is artificial, society is artificial – everything seems to be artificial.

I once knew a man, an old, retired professor, a neighbor. People thought that

he was a little out of his mind; a retired professor of philosophy is bound to be. But I don't make judgments, so I listened, but I never thought anything about him. But one day I had to think, because he was watering with a watering-can and I was just passing and I saw that the watering-can had no bottom. The watering-can was without a bottom! There was no water, and he was making all the gestures of watering the plants. So I asked, "Hey, what are you doing? Your watering-can has no bottom!"

He said, "That I know, but it doesn't matter because these flowers are artificial."

Your whole life has become artificial – plastic flowers. From a distance they look good, but if you come near they are plastic. Of course, they don't die so soon. They cannot die, they are plastic flowers, but a thing that cannot die is not alive.

A real flower has to pass through millions of hazards. How humble a real flower is...how fragile! In the morning it is there, how fragile! – and against this whole world. Storms come, and clouds come and the rain and animals and children and everything, and against all this a fragile flower exists – that is the beauty. And by the evening it is gone. You will not find it again, it will be there no more – but it is alive. In the morning it is there in its total beauty, and by the evening it is faded, gone, dust unto dust – but it was alive. Your plastic flower is dead, that's why it cannot die. Everything alive will die; only dead things never die.

Remember this: don't be afraid of death, don't be afraid that things may disappear. Untruth never dies. Truth dies millions of times and resurrects again and again. Remember this. Untruth is like a plastic flower, secure.

That's why marriage is secure. A marriage which has been arranged by the parents is more secure, by the society, more secure. Love is fragile like a flower in the morning; by the evening it is gone. Nobody knows how it comes, how it goes. It is mysterious. Marriage is nothing mysterious, it is a calculation. You go to the astrologer, he finds the chart, he arranges. Parents are, of course, more wise than you, worldly wise, they have known much. They arrange, they look for many things that a lover will never think about – the money, the prestige and millions of things; they think of security. But when somebody falls in love he cannot think of anything else.

But remember one thing: a dead thing never dies – that is the security in it, but it is dead. It is always possible that an alive thing may disappear any moment; that is the trouble with life – but it is alive, and worth taking all risks for.

Be true. There will be many, many troubles but each trouble will make you more mature. And being true, talking, acting true, you are getting ready for

truth to descend. When you attain to a certain maturity, suddenly the door opens. And there is no other way.

*Listening to me but not to the logos,*
*it is wise to acknowledge*
*that all things are one.*

Heraclitus says, "Listening to me" – I would also say, "Listening to me, it is wise to acknowledge that all things are one." If you listen to the logos...the logos means the law, the tao, the *rit;* the basic, the ultimate stratum of existence is the logos. You don't know anything about it. You have never penetrated to that depth. It is in you also, near the center, but you have lived on the periphery so you don't know about it. Heraclitus says, "But listening to me" – listening to a Buddha, to Heraclitus, to Lao Tzu – "it is good to acknowledge that all things are one." This is not your experience yet.

Here enters trust, *shraddha*, faith. And religion cannot exist without trust, because you don't know the ultimate stratum, what it is. And there is no way to prove it, there is no way to argue about it. If you know, you know; if you don't know, you don't know. Then what to do about it? There is only one possibility and that is that by listening to a Heraclitus – not only to what he says, but listening to his being, what he is – you will come to acknowledge one thing, that one exists in this diversity, in this "too-manyness" of the world; behind it, one exists.

You have been listening to me...you have listened to me from many, many dimensions. On the periphery sometimes you feel I am contradictory; but if you listen not only to my words but to me, to my presence, you will never feel any contradiction. And if you feel, not just think, you will start feeling, by and by, that whatsoever I say is the same. Whether I say it through Heraclitus or through Jesus or through Buddha, Lao Tzu, Chuang Tzu – whatsoever I say, I always say the same thing. The language differs, words differ, but not the logos of it.

*Listening to me...*
*it is wise to acknowledge*
*that all things are one.*

When you can listen to the logos itself, then you will know; there will be no need to acknowledge it. Then you will know; then there will be no need to trust.

Trust is needed because you don't know and you need somebody who knows. You need the hand of somebody who knows, who can take you from the known to the unknown, who can take you to the uncharted. And without trust it is not

possible; otherwise how will you come with me to the unknown? If you don't trust me, how can you come with me to the unknown? You will always stick to the boundary of the known. You will say, "Up to here I know and I am safe; beyond this is wilderness. And who are you to take me into the wilderness? And how should I trust you?"

At the boundary where known and unknown meet, there is no way except trust. You have to be in a love affair with a master, nothing less than that will do – because only love can trust. It has to be a heart to heart, depth to depth relationship; it has to be intimate.

That's why I go on insisting on sannyas and initiation. Unless you trust me, totally, you will cling to the known, you will cling to the mind, you will cling to your ego – and what is the point? You have to take at least one step with me without asking why. Love never asks why because love trusts.

A small child has to trust his father; the father takes his hand and the child follows. He is not worried; wherever the father is going, he goes on, happy. What is going to happen he is not worried about – that is trust. If the child stops and says, "Where are you going and where are you leading me? And what do you mean by trust, how can I trust you?" the child will stop growing immediately, there is no possibility of growth. The child has to trust the mother, the father.

A master is nothing but a father into the unknown. Again you are learning to walk, again you are learning to search and seek, again you are moving into something – you don't know what it is, where you are headed.

This is what Heraclitus means:

*Listening to me...*
*it is wise to acknowledge*
*that all things are one.*

*Wisdom is one –*
*to know the intelligence by which*
*all things are steered through all things.*
*Wisdom is one and unique;*
*it is unwilling and yet willing*
*to be called by the name of Zeus.*

Zeus is the supreme god. And wisdom is both willing and unwilling to be called the supreme god. It is paradoxical and very difficult for the mind to understand.

Buddha says there is no god – unwilling. Buddha says, "No need to worship me, you find your own light" – unwilling to declare his wisdom, his consciousness, to be the supreme god. And the next moment he says, "Come and surrender to me" – the next moment he contradicts himself. Why is it so? – because a man who has reached, who has arrived, has no ego, so it is difficult for him to claim anything...unwilling. The wisdom is unwilling to declare itself the supreme god, but it is. The ego is not there to claim, but it is so, it is a fact, so it cannot be denied either.

So what to do? If a Buddha says, "I am not the supreme god," he is untrue. If he says, "I am the supreme god," it gives a tinge of ego. So what is he supposed to do? Either way there is difficulty. If he says, "I am the god," you may think he is an egoist. If he says, "I am no god at all," it is untrue. So sometimes he says, "Yes, I am"; sometimes he says, "I am not." And you have to find between these two the balance. Somewhere in between he is both. He is not a god because he is no more an ego, there is nobody to claim – and he is a god precisely because there is no ego, precisely because there is nobody to claim.

*Wisdom is one and unique;*
*it is unwilling and yet willing*
*to be called by the name of Zeus.*

...Hence all the contradictions of all the enlightened ones. Whatsoever they say they have to contradict immediately, because they are saying something which is unique, one. And the unique and the one cannot be put into any language, because language depends on duality. If they say, "I am light," then who will be the darkness?...because language depends on the duality: light means not darkness. But a man who has attained is both light and darkness together. He is both – all the dualities together – that is the mystery. And because of this mystery Aristotle said, "This man Heraclitus is defective somewhere. Either his mind is defective, or his character, because he talks in absurdities."

Arthur Koestler came to the East to watch people who have attained samadhi, and he reported back to the West: "They are mad, they are absurd, because they talk absurdities. This moment they say something, next moment they contradict themselves."

Wisdom is vast, it contains all the opposites together. And you need a feeling heart to penetrate into this absurdity; that is the trust. Trust is the weapon to penetrate the absurdity of an enlightened man – and then suddenly everything fits. You can suddenly see through all the absurdity to the one, the unique.

# *Chapter* 4

GOD IS DAY AND NIGHT, WINTER AND SUMMER,
WAR AND PEACE, SATIETY AND WANT.

SEA WATER IS AT ONCE VERY PURE AND VERY FOUL:
IT IS DRINKABLE AND HEALTHFUL FOR FISHES,
BUT UNDRINKABLE AND DEADLY FOR MEN.

THE NATURE OF DAY AND NIGHT IS ONE.

THE WAY UP AND THE WAY DOWN
ARE ONE AND THE SAME.

EVEN SLEEPERS ARE WORKERS AND COLLABORATORS
IN WHAT GOES ON IN THE UNIVERSE.

IN THE CIRCLE
THE BEGINNING AND THE END ARE COMMON.

# GOD IS DAY AND NIGHT

GOD IS NOT A PERSON. Because man has always taken God as a person, a thousand and one difficulties have arisen. All the problems that theology deals with are simply futile exercises – and the base is that God is taken as a person.

God is not a person and cannot be. Let it go as deep in you as possible, because that will become a door, an opening. And particularly for those who have been raised as Jews, Christians, Mohammedans, it is very difficult to take God as anything else but a person – that becomes a closing. To think about God as a person is anthropocentric. In The Bible it is said God created man in his own image, but just the contrary seems to be the case – man has created God in his own image. And men differ, that's why there are so many gods in the world.

It happened that when for the first time Christian missionaries reached Africa, they were in trouble – because they painted God as white and the Devil as black, and the negroes felt very much offended. They wouldn't listen to them, because from the very beginning the image was in conflict. Then one missionary simply got the idea: he changed the colors. He made God black and the Devil white, and the negroes were very happy – they could accept. A negro is bound to paint his God in his own image, a Chinese in his own, an Indian in his own. We paint God as our own reflection – of course, perfect – but your image cannot be God. You are just a part, a very tiny part, one atom in existence. How can the

whole be conceived in the image of the part? The whole transcends the part, the whole is infinitely vast. If you cling to the atom, if you cling to the part, you will miss the whole.

God is not to be conceived in your image; rather, on the contrary, you have to drop your image, you have to become imageless. Then, and only then, you become a mirror and the whole reflects in you.

As man has been seeking more and more, this has become clearer and clearer – that God as a person creates troubles, because then you are always in conflict with other gods. That's why the Jewish god, the Hindu god, the Mohammedan god, the Christian god exist. This is sheer nonsense! How can God be Christian or Hindu or Mohammedan? But there are different gods because Jews have their own idea of god, Hindus have their own idea of god, and the conflict is bound to be there. Hindus think that God speaks the Sanskrit language; the English always think that he is an English gentleman.

It is said that one German and one Englishman were talking, and the German said, "We plan in every way, but why, every time, are we defeated?"

The Englishman said, "You have to be defeated, because whenever we start fighting, first we pray to God and he looks after us. You are to be defeated; you can never be victorious."

The German said, "But that we also do, we also pray."

Then the Englishman laughed. He said, "But who understands German?" To an Englishman, God is an Englishman. To Adolf Hitler he must be a Nordic, has to be because we create our own image.

I was just reading a memoir of an army priest. This priest was attached to Montgomery's wing, and one day, when they were ready to attack, it was so cloudy and there was so much mist and so much cold that it seemed impossible to move. So the priest has written in the memoir that the general, Montgomery, called him and he said, "You pray to God and tell him immediately that we, his soldiers, are on the march, and what is he doing? Is he in conspiracy with the enemy? Tell him immediately to stop all this!"

The priest was surprised: "A man like Montgomery – and what is he talking about?" He said, "But this won't look good. It doesn't look good to say to God, 'What are you doing? Stop this immediately because we are on the move and we are your soldiers.'"

The priest felt a little embarrassed, but Montgomery said, "You listen to my order! You are my priest, attached to my army, so whatsoever I say you have to do. Go and pray immediately!"

This happens. It looks absurd and foolish, but this is happening all the time, to all the people, to everybody. If you take God as a person this is bound to happen. Then you start communicating with him as a person – and he is not a person. There are millions of atheists because you have taken God as a person. The atheist is not against God, but he is against your conception of God as a person, because the whole concept is foolish. And think in what anguish you must be putting your God, because Germans are praying for their victory, the English are praying for their victory, and everybody thinks that God is with them, at their side.

I have heard: Once Junnaid, a Sufi mystic, dreamt that he saw that he was dead and the greatest sinner of the town was also dead, and both reached God's door and knocked. The sinner was received and the saint was neglected. He felt very, very hurt. He was expecting always that he should be received, welcomed, and what was happening? – just the opposite. And he knew this man who was being received with such ceremony. When the ceremony was over and the sinner was sent to his abode, the saint said, "Just one question I have to ask God: What are you doing? I have been praying continuously, twenty-four hours, day and night, calling your name, praying. Even in my sleep I have been calling your name and chanting!"

God said, "Precisely because of that – you have pestered me so much that I am really afraid of you now that you have come to heaven. What will you do here? From Earth, so far away, in twenty-four hours you have not left me a single moment of peace! This man is good, that's why we are celebrating. He never bored me, he never pestered me; he never used my name; he never created any trouble for me."

God as a person is just foolish, the whole concept is foolish. And he cannot be a person because he has to be all persons – how can he be a person himself? He cannot be somebody because he is everybody, and he cannot be anywhere because he is everywhere. You cannot define him, and personality is a definition. You cannot limit him, and as a person he becomes limited. Personality is just like a wave that comes and goes, and he is like an ocean. He is immense – he abides. Personalities come and go, they are forms; they are there and then they are no more there. Forms change; forms change into the opposites continuously, and he is the formless. He cannot be defined, it cannot be said who he is. He is all. But the moment you say, "He is all," the problem arises: how to communicate? There is no need; you cannot communicate with him like a person. You have to communicate with him in a totally different dimension – that dimension is of energy,

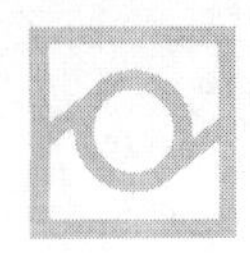



that dimension is of consciousness, not of personality.

God is energy.

God is absolute awareness.

God is bliss, ecstasy; indefinable, unlimited; no beginning, no end; always and always; eternal, timeless, beyond space – because God means the total.

The total cannot have a personality – this is the first thing to be understood, very, very deeply; not only intellectually, but as totally as possible, because if you can conceive, can feel, grope towards God as totality, then your prayer will be different. Then your prayer will not be a foolish prayer, then he cannot be on your side – he is on every side. He is also with your enemy as much as with you, and he is as much in the saint as in the sinner – because he is all! He is as much in the dark as in the light. He comprehends all. All opposites meet and mingle and become one in him. Because of the concept of God as a person we have to create a Devil against God, because all the negativities! – where will you put them? You have to create somebody to throw all the negativities onto. Then your God also becomes false, your Devil also false, because negatives and positives exist together, not separately. And all that you like you put on God's side. It is your division.

God cannot be divided – he is undivided.

First thing: God is not a person. And remember, you are also not a person. It is ignorance, it is self-ignorance: that's why you appear like a person. If you move deeper, soon personality becomes blurred; a moment comes when you don't know who you are. Sometimes it happens that if somebody wakes you suddenly, you may have observed many times, you suddenly don't know where you are – whether it is morning or evening, whether it is your house or somewhere else, what town it is; for a single moment everything is blurred, no time sense, no space sense, and you don't know who you are. Why does it happen? – because in deep sleep you move towards the center, of course unconsciously, but at the center there is no personality, an impersonal energy exists. And if somebody suddenly wakes you, you have to move from the center to the periphery in such a rush that there is no time to gather personality. In a sudden rush you simply lose identity – and this is your reality, this is who you are in fact.

Deep in meditation you will become more and more aware of the indefinable, unlimited. First it will look like a blurred phenomenon, and you may even become afraid, scared: What is happening to you? Are you losing your mind? Are you going mad? If you become afraid you will miss. Don't be worried, it is natural. You are moving to the indefinable from the defined; in between there

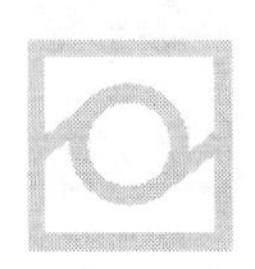

will be a ground where everything will get blurred.

That's why Zen masters have said: "Before one enters on the path, rivers are rivers, mountains are mountains. When one enters into the path, rivers are no more rivers, mountains are no more mountains. And when one has achieved the goal, again rivers are rivers, mountains are mountains." What do they mean? They mean that there comes a moment when everything becomes blurred. And that is the time a school, a master, will be needed, because when everything is blurred you are again like a small child – helpless, not knowing who you are, identity lost, not knowing where you are going, not knowing what is happening; a school is needed. This is the meaning of an ashram, of a monastery, where many people exist on many layers and they can help each other. And a master exists on the ultimate level – you need not be afraid, you can always look towards him.

When your identity is lost then the master is your only source of sanity – you will be insane. Many people work alone and many people go mad. If you move in the East, you will find many people who are hanging.... They have worked without a master; they came to the blurred territory – now they don't know where to go. They have forgotten from where they came and they don't know now where to go. They don't know who they are. They are absolutely mad. They are better than you, but mad. And now they cannot take any step, because who will take the step and where? At this moment a master is needed.

One of the greatest works Meher Baba did in his life – he lived just near Poona and he is one of the greatest masters – and never has it been done before: he traveled all over India for years, just making contact with such mad people. Not doing anything else, just doing one thing: moving from one village to another, making contact with such people who have gone mad, who are on a better ground than you but some help is needed – just a push. Just a push so that again rivers become rivers, mountains become mountains; again they achieve a new identity.

The old identity was with the form, the new identity will be with the formless. The old identity was with the name, the new identity will be with the nameless. The old identity was of this world, the new identity will be of that world. But in between the two you can hang and hang if there is no school, if there is no master to help you and bring it out. You can enter this wilderness, but coming out will be difficult on your own. Sometimes, accidentally, somebody does come out – that's not the point – but as a rule it is almost impossible for you to come out.

I have seen many mad people. And whenever somebody comes to me and he wants to do everything on his own, I feel very much, because he does not know what he is talking about. But this is the problem. I cannot force anything, because the more you force the more he will escape. I can simply say, "Okay, do whatsoever you like" – but I feel deeply because I know where he is moving unknowingly. God is energy, and if you are not prepared it can be destructive. And God is such vital, infinite energy, that if your vehicle is not ready you will simply crack. So the question is not just to know God. A deeper question is how to be ready before you can say: "Now come," before you can invite him – because you are so small and he is so vast. It is as if a drop of water is calling the ocean to come in. The ocean can come in any time, but what will happen to the drop? The drop has to attain a capacity, a receptivity so infinite that the ocean drops into the drop and disappears and the drop is not shattered. Greatest is that art, and that art is religion, Yoga, Tantra, or whatever name you want to give it.

And don't look at God according to your conceptions: Jewish, Christian, Hindu. Drop them! That is clinging to the periphery, to the knowledge. Whatsoever you have been taught, you cling to it, and God cannot be taught, nobody can teach him – indicated, of course, shown in subtle and indirect ways, of course, but he cannot be taught. Whatsoever you know about God is wrong – and I say "whatsoever" unconditionally. Whatsoever you know is wrong because that has come from teachings; somebody has taught you a conception, a theory, and God is not a conception, not a theory; God is not a hypothesis. It is nothing like that – it is absolutely different.

Drop all conceptions and only then are you ready to take the first step. Naked you go to him, with no conception, no clothes around you. Vacant you go to him, with no ideas about him in your mind. Empty you go to him, because that is the only way to go: empty you become a door, he can enter. Only receptivity is needed, not concepts, not philosophies, doctrines – this is what Heraclitus means. These words are very, very wonderful.

Listen:

*God is day and night, winter and summer,*
*war and peace, satiety and want.*

Never have such wonderful words been uttered before, and never since.

*God is day and night, winter and summer,*
*war and peace, satiety and want.*

Many have said many things about God, but no one is comparable to Heraclitus. There have been people who said: "God is light," but then where do you put the dark? Then you have to explain from where the dark comes. "God is day," many have said, "God is sun, light, the source of light," but then from where does the night come? From where does the dark come, the Devil, sin? From where? And why have people talked about God as light?

Something psychological is involved. Man is afraid of darkness; man feels very good when there is light – it is part of your fear. Why do you call God light? The Koran says God is light, the Upanishads say God is light, The Bible says God is light. There has only been a small school – in that small school Jesus was taught and brought up to be ready to receive the divine – that small school was known as the Essenes; they were the teachers and masters of Jesus. Only that school says God is dark, night. But then they never say God is light; they move to the other extreme. But they are beautiful people.

Try to understand the symbol: light-and-dark. You are not afraid in light because you can see. Nobody can attack you so easily. You can defend, you can escape, you can fight or you can take flight. You can do something, everything is known. Light is the symbol of the known – with the known you don't feel fear.

Darkness is the unknown. Fear arises in the heart; you don't know what is happening all around. Anything is possible – and you are indefensible. Light is security, darkness is insecurity. Light looks like life and darkness like death. Afraid, scared – not only psychologically, but biologically also, because man has lived for thousands of years in the dark, in the night, in the wild, forest, caves, and the night was the problem because wild animals would attack and man was indefensible. So when fire was invented, fire became the first god; it became a protection, a security. With the day everything is okay, with the night you don't know where you are – with the night everything disappears.

So man is prone to identify God with light. Light has a few beautiful things about it. It is warm, it is a source of energy – you cannot live without the sun, nothing can exist without the sun. All life, deep down, is solar energy, the energy that comes from the sun. You eat it, you drink it – you live through it. If the sun simply disappears, goes cold, within ten minutes life on this earth will disappear – within ten minutes, because it takes ten minutes for the rays to reach us. If the sun dies, then for ten minutes old rays will be coming, but by the tenth minute new rays will not be coming, and everything will simply go dead. We will not even be aware of what is happening; nobody will know that we have died. The whole planet will die – the trees, the animals, the birds, man,

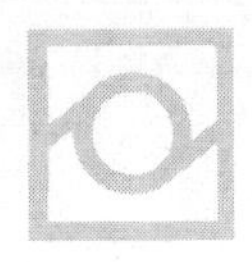



everything! Life exists through the sun – it is warm, welcoming.

Darkness also has beautiful things about it. It is infinite. Light has always a limit; darkness is limitless. And light is, deep down, an excitement, it excites you; darkness is absolutely unexciting. Light is warm, darkness is cool, cool like death, mysterious. Light comes and goes; darkness remains. That's why the Essenes called God the dark, the night, because light comes and goes, darkness remains, darkness is eternal. Light seems to be an episode, it happens. You can arrange for light, but you cannot arrange for darkness; it seems beyond you. You can put on the light, you can put off the light, but you cannot put on the dark and you cannot put off the dark. It seems beyond you – it is! Light is manageable. If it is dark you can bring light in, but you cannot bring darkness, you cannot manipulate darkness; it is simply beyond control. And you put your light on, but you know that light is momentary. When the fuel is finished the light will go – but darkness is eternal, it is always there. It exists as if without any cause, uncaused; it was always, it will be always. So the Essenes chose darkness as the symbol of God, but Heraclitus alone chooses both.

To choose one extreme is still logical, rational; reason is working. To choose both together is irrational; reason is simply bewildered. God is day and night – both together, no choice – winter and summer, war and peace. It will be difficult for people like Tolstoy, Gandhi, Bertrand Russell, if God is war *and* peace. They think God is peace; war is created by men. War is ugly, something the Devil may have invented – God is peace. Tolstoy cannot agree, a Gandhi cannot agree that God is war also. A Hitler cannot agree that God is peace also; God is war. Nietzsche cannot agree that God is peace also; God is war.

There are choosers. Heraclitus is not a chooser, he is simply a choiceless awareness. He is not to choose, he is simply to say whatsoever is the case. He doesn't bring his own morality into it, he does not bring his own mind into it, he simply reflects; he is a mirror. Gandhi, Tolstoy, Ruskin, they are choosers; they have their own idea to impose on God. They impose the idea of peace, that God is peace; then war is from the Devil. But it is not possible.

What is peace without war? Is there any possibility of peace without war? And will not that peace be simply dead if there is no war? Just think: no war in the world, just peace – what type of peace will it be? It will be cold, it will be a dark night, dead. War gives intensity, tone, sharpness, life. But if there is only war and no peace, then too death will happen. If you choose one opposite of the polarity, if you choose one polarity, everything will be dead because life exists between polarities – war and peace, both; satiety and want; contentment and

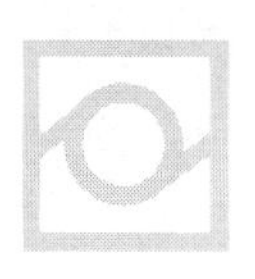

discontentment, both; hunger, want, desire, passion, peace, satiety, contentment; the way and the goal, both. Difficult to comprehend, but this is the truth.

It is God who desires in you and it is God who becomes desireless in you. This is total acceptance. It is God who is a passion in you and it is God who becomes enlightenment in you. It is God who is anger in you and it is God who becomes compassion in you. There is nothing to choose! But just look at the fact: if there is nothing to choose and everything is God, your ego simply disappears – because it exists with choosing. If there is nothing to choose and everything is just as it is, nothing can be done and God is both. With the chooser, with the choice, the ego disappears. Then you accept, then you simply accept! When you are hungry and when you are satisfied both are beautiful.

This is difficult for the mind. The mind staggers, feels bewildered, loses ground, feels dizzy – as if you are standing on the edge of an abyss. Why does it happen? – because mind wants a clearcut choice: "Either this or that." And Heraclitus says: "Neither this nor that – or both." Ask Mahavira, ask Buddha, they will say: "Desire? Leave desire! Become desireless! – choose! Become content, deeply content; leave discontent!" Heraclitus penetrates even deeper. He says: "Who is there to leave? Who will leave? God is both!" And if you can feel this, that God is both, everything is hallowed, everything becomes holy. Then in hunger also there is a contentment. Then in desire also there is a desirelessness. Then in anger also there is compassion. And if you have not known anger which is compassionate, anger which is compassion, you have not known life at all. If you have not known darkness which is light also, coolness which is warmth also – if you have not known that, you have missed the greatest climax.

Where opposites meet, there happens the ecstasy, the ultimate, the ultimate orgasm with the universe – where opposites meet. God is both man and woman, war and peace.

And man has been in difficulty because he has always been choosing. The society has always remained lopsided, all societies and civilizations have remained lopsided, because everything depends on choice. We have created a society in the world which is male-oriented, war-oriented. The woman has been cut out, she has no contribution to make – she is dark, she is peace, she is silence, she is passivity, compassion, not war; woman is satiety, not desire. Man is desire – the excitement, the adventure, war; always going somewhere, always reaching somewhere, finding something, seeking, searching. Man is the vagabond, woman is the home. But when they both meet – when the vagabond meets the home, where desire and satiety meet, where activity and passivity

meet – there arises the greatest harmony, the hidden harmony.

We created the society male-oriented, so there is war – and the peace is not true. Our peace is just a gap between two wars; it is not true, it is just a preparation for another war. Go back and look at history: the first world war and the second world war – the gap between is not peace. The gap between is just getting ready for another war. It is not real peace, it is just a preparation. And if peace is not real, the war will also be unreal.

In the past, war was beautiful; now it is ugly, because it has no opposite to it. In the past warriors were beautiful people; now warriors are just ugly. War doesn't give you anything; otherwise, it is an adventure, it brings you to a peak of existence, you put yourself totally into it. Warriors were beautiful: they encountered death, they went to meet death on the front. Now a warrior is nowhere to be seen – he is hidden behind the tanks, throwing bombs, not knowing who is going to be destroyed. Can you call this man who dropped the atom bomb on Hiroshima a warrior? What type of warrior is he? He drops the atom bomb, kills one lakh people immediately, not knowing whom he is killing, who the enemy is – small children....

I was looking at a picture somebody sent me from Japan. A small child was going upstairs to his room where he would study and go to sleep; a very small child, carrying his bag of books and thinking of his homework, and he was going to do homework and then he would go to sleep. He was just on the staircase when the bomb fell. He was totally burnt and became just a dot on the wall, with the books, with the bag, burnt, still clinging, the mind thinking about the homework, of the next day, tomorrow morning – everything burnt there. And the man who dropped the bomb, he was not aware who was going to die; and then he went back home and had a good sleep. He had done his duty, hiding himself. What type of war is this? It has become ugly. In the old days, to be a warrior was one of the greatest possibilities – bringing your potential to a peak. But now it is nothing, it is just like an ordinary mechanical duty: you push the button and the bomb falls and kills – you are not confronting anybody. War without real peace also becomes false. And when war is false, how can peace be real?

We have been choosing. We have been creating society according to a male pattern. The man has become the center, the woman has been thrown off center. It is lopsided. Now there are women who are thinking of creating a society according to the pattern of the woman, where man has to be thrown off the center. That too will be lopsided. God is both male and female; there is no choice. And male and female are opposites: dark and light, life and death. And opposites are there. A hidden harmony has to be sought. Those who come to know the hidden harmony, they have realized the truth.

*God is day and night, winter and summer,*
*war and peace, satiety and want.*

*Sea water is at once very pure and very foul:*
*it is drinkable and healthful for fishes,*
*but undrinkable and deadly for men.*

And everything is good and everything is bad – it depends. War is good sometimes, peace is bad sometimes – it depends. Sometimes peace is nothing but impotence, then it is not good; it may be peace, but it is not good. Sometimes war is nothing but madness, then it is not good. And one has to watch and see, without any prejudice. Not every war is bad and not every peace is good, and one should not become addicted. For Nietzsche, every war is good; for Gandhi, every peace is good – both are addicted. And God is both.

Says Heraclitus:

*Sea water is at once very pure and very foul....*

For fishes it is life; for you it can become death. So don't create absolute ideas, remain flexible. And remember: something may be good for you today and tomorrow may not be good, because life goes on changing and you cannot step in the same river twice. And even if you do step, you are not the same and yet you are the same. Everything is moving, a flux, so don't remain fixed. This is one of the diseases of the human mind: you become fixed, you lose flexibility – and flexibility is life.

Look at a child, he is flexible; look at an old man, he has become inflexible. The more flexible you are, the more alive and fresh and young. The more inflexible you become...already you are dead. And what is flexibility? Flexibility is to respond to the moment without any preconceived idea; to respond to the moment, not through any preconceived idea – directly, immediately. Immediacy is flexibility. You look to the situation, you become aware to the situation, you are sensitive to the situation – and then you act. The action comes through the encounter of the situation and you, not from a past mind.

*The nature of day and night is one.*

War and peace are one; and desire and desirelessness are one. The phenomenon

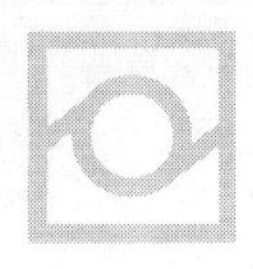



is the same: peace is war inactive; war is peace active. The nature of man and woman is one: woman is inactive, passive man; man is active woman. That's why they attract each other, because if you take them in themselves they are halves. If they become one then the whole is created; both meet and become one. That oneness is the search.

If you take them apart, as all the religions have done in the past – Catholics, Jainas, Buddhists, they have separated men and women totally. And all these religions have remained halfhearted; they cannot be total, they cannot accept the whole. Their circle is half, and half a circle is not a circle at all, because a circle, to be a circle, must be the whole – half a circle is no circle. That's why the whole of Christianity turned out to be ugly, Jainism turned out to be ugly, Buddhism turned out to be ugly. You cannot divide, you have to accept the totality.

Beauty is of the total and ugliness is of a torn part. Everything total is beautiful, fulfilled – the circle has became complete.

*The nature of day and night is one.*

The day itself becomes the night, the night itself turns into day. Can you divide where day is and where night is? Can you make a demarcation? There is no demarcation – the day, by and by, turns into night; the night, by and by, turns into day. It is one wheel. And if you can see all opposites as a wheel, you will have a transcendence. Then you will be no more a man and no more a woman, because you turn into a woman and a woman turns into a man many times. If you watch yourself for twenty-four hours, you can find at which moment you were a woman and at which moment you were a man; you can find when you are passive, when you are active. When you are passive you are a woman, when you are active you are a man – and both are hidden within you.

Now psychology accepts this, that man is bisexual: every man is woman also, and every woman is man also. The difference is only of quantity, degrees, not of quality. If you are a man that means you may be fifty-one percent man and forty-nine percent woman – that is the difference. That's why it is possible for you to change your sex; it is a difference of degrees. Just a little hormonal change and the sex will change. No need to change the hormones even: if you simply change your psyche the change will come. It happened to Ramakrishna. He tried many paths to reach the divine. Even when he had reached, still he went on trying every path just to see whether every path leads to him.

There is a path in India, a very beautiful path, and that path is to conceive of

God as the only male and you become the female, the beloved. Whether you are a man or a woman, that is not the point: God is the male and you are the female; God is Krishna and everyone is just a beloved. So those who follow this path, they start behaving like women. Clothes they cannot use like a man, they have to use feminine clothes; they sleep with a statue of Krishna. They completely forget whether they are male or female; whatsoever they are they become females. Every fourth week, for five days, they act as if their period has come. In the beginning it is just acting but, by and by, changes start happening.

To Ramakrishna it happened that he became completely a woman. It has remained a mystery. How is it possible? Menses really started! He would bleed for three or four days every month. His breasts became feminine, they grew; his voice changed, it became feminine; he started walking like a woman. For six months he was on that path – he became completely a woman. And this is a mystery, because doctors are witnesses that he started bleeding – the period would come. Just the mind changed the whole body. And after he reached through that path and left the path and started trying something else, even after that, for one year the body remained the same. It took one year to come back, to become a man again.

You are both inside; it is just a question of emphasis. And Heraclitus came to realize this:

*The nature of day and night is one.*

*The way up and the way down*
*are one and the same.*

Heaven and hell are one, God and Devil are one because it has to be so: two poles of the same phenomenon.

*Even sleepers are workers and collaborators*
*in what goes on in the universe.*

Even sleepers are responsible. What is Heraclitus wanting to say? He is saying that responsibility is not individual, karma is not individual – it is total.

This is a rare insight. I absolutely agree with him. This is a rare insight because in India they have believed that karma is individual – but that, too, is clinging to the ego. Why? When there is no ego, and you insist that there is no ego, why should karma be individual? If karma is individual, then you cannot leave the ego. In fact it will cling in a subtle way: I have to fulfill my karma and

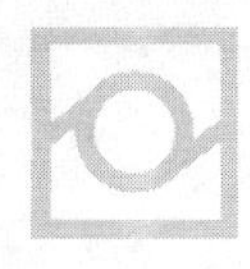



you have to fulfill your karma – where do we meet? I will become enlightened, you will remain ignorant – where do we meet?

If Heraclitus' insight is to be understood, it means there are no individuals, there are no islands; man is not an island, we are part of one whole. Then even karma is not individual. And that has many implications then; then a vast dimension opens. That means that if somebody murders somewhere, I have a part in it. Even if I am a sleeper – I was sleeping, I don't know about the man, I will never hear about him – and somebody somewhere, in the Himalayas, commits a murder, if we are not individuals I have a part in it, I am also responsible. It is not so easy to throw the responsibility: "I am not committing a murder, I am a saint."

No saint is a saint because every sinner is implied in him. And this is foolish to claim: "I am a saint because I am not committing any murder, any robbery, any sin." But there are sinners in the world, and if we are one part, one vast continent, not islands but connected, then how can you commit a sin without me? No, it is not possible. Then how can I become enlightened without you also becoming enlightened? No, that is not possible. It means that whenever there is a sin committed, the whole is involved. And whenever there is a phenomenon like enlightenment, the whole is involved.

That's why it happens that whenever a man becomes enlightened, many immediately follow in his wake, become enlightened, because he creates a possibility for the whole. It is just like this: if my head aches, it is not only the head that is ill, my whole organism becomes ill – my legs also feel it, my heart also feels it, my hand also, because I am one. It may be focused in the head, that's okay, but the whole body feels ill. A buddha becomes enlightened – it is focused there, that's all, because no individual is there. It is just a focusing, but he will vibrate all over. Existence is just like a spider's web. You touch the web from anywhere and the whole vibrates. Somewhere the touch is focused, that's right, but the whole vibrates. That's the meaning, and you have to understand it. Whenever you do something, it is not only you who is involved – the whole is involved. Your responsibility is great. It is not only that you have to be finished with your own karma; the whole history of the world is your biography.

Even while asleep I am collaborating, cooperating, so each step has to be very, very responsible and alert. If you commit sin it is the whole that you drag into sin, not only you because you are not separate. If you meditate, if you become aware, if you feel blissful, it is the whole that you are taking towards a peak. Focused you may be, but the whole is always involved.

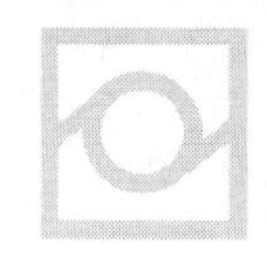

Remember this, that whatsoever you do, God is doing it; and whatsoever you are, God is that; and whatsoever you will become, God will be becoming. You are not alone, you are the destiny of the whole.

*Even sleepers are workers and collaborators*
*in what goes on in the universe.*

*In the circle*
*the beginning and the end are common.*

If you make a circle, the end and beginning meet – only then is the circle complete. If you become a circle, whole, total, in you will meet the beginning and the end. You will be the very source of the world and you will be the very climax of the world. You will be both the alpha and the omega. And unless you become that, something is incomplete; and when something is incomplete you will remain miserable. The only misery that I know is being incomplete. The whole being tends to be complete, needs to be complete, and the incomplete becomes a torture. The incompletion is the only problem. And when you become complete, the end and the beginning meet in you. God as the source and God as the ultimate flowering meet in you.

Ponder over these small fragments. Each fragment can become a vast contemplation, and each fragment can give you an insight into yourself and into the reality. And these are not philosophical statements, these are Heraclitus' insights – he knows, he has come to see. He is not theorizing; he has touched the reality, penetrated into it. And each fragment is complete in itself, it is not a system. These fragments are like gems, individually cut; every gem is complete in itself. You simply penetrate one fragment, and through that one fragment you can become totally different – that one fragment can become the door for the infinite.

Meditate, ponder over Heraclitus, what he is saying. He can have a tremendous impact on you. He can become a transformation for you.

# *Chapter* 5

LET US NOT MAKE ARBITRARY CONJECTURES
ABOUT THE GREATEST MATTERS.

MUCH LEARNING DOES NOT TEACH UNDERSTANDING.

SEEKERS AFTER GOLD
DIG UP MUCH EARTH AND FIND LITTLE.

YOU COULD NOT DISCOVER THE LIMITS OF THE SOUL
EVEN IF YOU TRAVELED EVERY ROAD TO DO SO –
SUCH IS THE DEPTH OF ITS MEANING.

# SUCH IS THE DEPTH OF ITS MEANING

THE WHOLE OF PHILOSOPHY IS nothing but arbitrary conjectures. If you want to avoid real knowledge, if you want to avoid the existential, then there is nothing like philosophy. Escape into philosophy and you can avoid all, all that creates problems. Philosophy is a cheap solution. Without entering, without encountering reality, you simply theorize – and theories are nothing but words. Arguments, rationalizations, explanations are nothing but tricks. Nothing is solved because you remain the same.

A philosopher is the most deceived person in the world because he thinks he knows without knowing anything at all. Heraclitus has laughed about Pythagoras, one of the greatest philosophers the world has ever known. Many times Heraclitus says, "If by philosophizing somebody could have become a knower, then Pythagoras would have been the first knower in the world" – because Pythagoras traveled all over the world, the known world in those days. He even came to India; he lived in Egypt, he traveled far and wide – he collected much knowledge.

Pythagoras was a contemporary of Heraclitus and he is more known than Heraclitus. In the histories of philosophy Pythagoras is a milestone. He collected much, he knew much, but without knowing anything at all. What did he do? Through scriptures, through teachers, through schools, ashrams, secret societies, he gathered knowledge. When you gather knowledge it becomes part

of your memory – you remain unaffected. Your heart is not touched, your being is not even aware of what you have collected in your memory. Unless your being is touched and transformed, knowledge is ignorance and more dangerous than ordinary ignorance – because an ordinary ignorant person knows that he is ignorant, and a philosopher thinks that he knows. And once you become addicted to knowledge you will think your knowledge is knowing. Of course, you know too much, but deep down nothing has been known, nothing has changed; you have not evolved to a higher plane of being.

Real knowledge consists in attaining higher levels of being, higher planes of being – not more knowledge, but more being. To be more, not to know more, is the real way. To know more, and not to be more, is the false way. Philosophers talk about things. They don't even have a glimpse of God, of moksha, of liberation, of other worlds, heaven and hell. Not only do they talk about it, they also talk very authoritatively – but they cannot deceive. They are deceiving nobody else except themselves.

It is said that one day, walking through a cemetery, Mulla Nasruddin found a grave, the grave of the philosopher of the town who had died just a few days before. On the grave it was written: "I am sleeping, I am not dead."

Mulla laughed loudly and said, "You are deceiving yourself and nobody else!"

But a philosopher deceives himself continuously. Instead of knowing he depends on information. Knowledge, when it is attained existentially, is authentic. For example: you can collect much knowledge about love without ever falling in love. Libraries are filled with much knowledge; you can go and collect all that has been said about love but about love is not love, about God is not God. About love means you go round and round, round and round, never penetrating the center. To love is totally different.

You can theorize about what love is, you can conclude about the nature of love, but if you have not fallen in love, what use is this knowledge? What do you gain out of it? What will you find through it? A deception is possible. Knowing about love, you may start believing that you know love, and if this happens then you have closed the door to falling in love. To fall in love is dangerous. To know about love is clever and cunning. To fall in love means to change yourself; to fall in love means to encounter millions of difficulties, because to interact with a living person is to move into the unknown. Nobody knows what is going to happen the next moment. You are thrown out of your enclosure, you are under the open sky, and every moment there will be new problems to be solved, new anxieties to be got over. It has to be so, because

problems and anxieties are the steps. If you take those steps, you grow; if you become afraid and escape, you remain juvenile.

Love is an opportunity to grow, but growth is always painful because something has to be destroyed before you can create something. The past has to be destroyed before a new future is born. Every growth is like the pain a mother goes through when she gives birth to a child. Every growth means you are continuously giving birth to yourself; every moment the child is born. And it is a continuous process, never ending; there comes no stop to it. You can rest for a while, but the journey is endless. Continuously you have to give birth to yourself, and every moment there will be pain. But if you can see that out of pain comes a new life, if you accept it, not only accept but welcome it, it is beautiful because it is through it that one grows. There is no other way to grow.

Love will give you pain, love will make you suffer, because through love one grows. There has never been any growth without suffering. That is the meaning of the cross: Jesus suffers, and suffers totally. When he suffers totally he is reborn totally, resurrected. Then he is a man no more, he becomes a god. He loved humanity so deeply that the love towards humanity became the cross.

You are afraid to love a single individual. How will you grow? And you can trick your mind – you can go to the libraries, you can collect information about love and about lovers, and you can know much without knowing anything at all. And this happens in every dimension of life. Wherever great matters are concerned, this is how you deceive. To pray is difficult; to become a priest is easy. A priest is a man who has collected all about prayer, but to pray is difficult. It is like death – because unless you die how can you invite the divine to enter in you? Unless you become empty, how can he come into you?

Søren Kierkegaard has said: "In the beginning, when I started to pray, I used to talk much to God. Then, by and by, I came to the understanding of what foolishness I was doing. I was talking – how can talking be prayer? Prayer can be only a deep listening, not a talking. You have to be silent so God can be heard. You have to be so silent that the silent and still word of God can penetrate you. In that silence the divine is revealed." Prayer is not talking, it is a listening – alert, passive, open, ready, ready like a womb. Prayer is feminine and a priest is a male phenomenon. A priest is aggressive: he is doing something. Prayer is not a doing at all – it is simply being receptive, it is simply being open. A door is open and you are waiting. It is infinite patience and waiting. A priest is aggressive. You can learn it: priesthood is an art, you can learn it. Prayer is not an art, you cannot learn it anywhere. You can learn it only in life. There exists no school,

no university, which can teach you prayer – only life.

You move in life, you suffer much, you grow and, by and by, you feel your total helplessness. By and by you feel that all egoistic claims are foolish – because who are you? Being tossed from there to here, from here to there; just drifting, a drifting wood on the sea...who are you? When you feel, "I am nobody," the first seed of prayer has entered in you. When you feel, "I am helpless, I cannot do anything, because I have been doing and doing for so long and nothing happens except misery, nothing happens through my effort," you become effortless. In that moment of helplessness the prayer takes a second step. Not that in your helplessness you start demanding from God: "Do this for me because I cannot do it" – no! If you are really helpless you cannot even demand and desire, because you come to realize: "Whatsoever I say will be wrong, whatsoever I ask will be wrong. I am wrong so all that comes through me will go wrong"; so you will say, "Thy will be done...don't listen to me, just you do whatsoever you would like to do, and I am ready to follow." This is prayer – but this is not priesthood. You can be trained as a priest; there are colleges which train priests. Every gesture of prayer is taught: how to sit, how to bow down, what words to use and what words not to use.

Leo Tolstoy has written a small parable. It happened that a man came to a priest, the greatest priest in Russia, and said, "I know three saints. They live on an island, and they have attained to God."

The priest said, "How can it happen? I am the high priest of the whole country. Without knowing me, without my knowing of the phenomenon, how is it possible that three persons have attained to God? I will go and see them."

He went in a boat. He reached the island. Those three simple people, they were sitting under a tree and doing their prayer. He listened to the prayer and laughed loudly and said, "You fools! From where have you learnt this prayer? I have never heard such nonsense even in my life, and I am the greatest priest of this country. What type of prayer is this?"

All three started trembling in fear and they said, "Forgive us! We don't know, we have never learnt. This prayer we ourselves have created." The prayer was simple. They said, "We are three" – and Christians believe in the trinity, so they said – "We have made a prayer: 'We are three, you are also three – have mercy on us!' We ourselves have made it: We are three, you are three – have mercy on us! This we continuously do, but we don't know whether this is right or wrong."

The priest said, "This is absolutely wrong and I will teach you the right, the authorized version." It was a long prayer of the church. Those three people listened, trembling. The priest was very happy. He went back thinking that he had done a virtuous deed, a really good work: he had converted three pagans to Christianity. "And these fools! – they have become famous. Many people come for their darshan, they touch their feet and worship them!"

When he was coming back, very happy that he had done something, suddenly he saw something that looked like a storm coming on the lake. He became afraid. Then he looked: those three saints were coming, running on the water. He couldn't believe his eyes. Those three saints came and they said, "Please, tell the prayer once more because we have forgotten! It is too long and we are simple folk, uneducated. Just once...?"

It is said, Leo Tolstoy writes, that the priest fell at their feet and he said, "Forgive me! I have committed a sin. You go your own way. Your prayer is right because it has come out of your heart. My prayer is useless because it has come out of my learning. Don't listen to me. Simply go and do whatsoever you were doing."

Prayer cannot be learnt. You have to pass through life with open eyes, with an understanding heart, and you will come to pray. And the prayer will be yours. It will come out of your heart, it will pour out of your heart. Words don't mean much – it is the heart that is behind them. But you can learn much through the mind; you can completely forget the heart – because heart grows through experience, and mind grows through?... thinking. And thinking is just dead. There is no growth through thinking. You can go round and round in the mind. Mind is just a computer, a biological computer; it collects information. The same can be done by a computer even better than your mind. But the heart is not a computer. The heart is totally different from the mind: it doesn't collect, it has no memory – it simply lives moment to moment; it responds to the alive moment in an alive way.

I have known a person; he was a colleague of mine in a university. He was ill and always something or other was wrong with him. So I told him, "Why don't you go to a doctor? Why don't you ask some doctor about your body? You are always complaining about this and that." So he went.

Next day he came to see me and he said, "The doctor says that I will have to give up half my sexual life."

I was surprised, so I said, "What have you decided?"

He said, "Yes, I have to follow his advice."

Then I asked him, "Which half – talking or thinking?"...because I knew the man: he had no sexual life, but he talked about it and thought about it. There are people who have no religious life. They talk about it and they think about it,

but they have no religious life; but if you listen to their talk you may feel that they are religious. Religion is not something concerned with thinking and talking – religion is something concerned with living. Either you live it or you don't live it. It is a way of life, not a philosophy; not theories about great matters, but a deep relatedness with whatsoever life means.

Just watch your mind, how it exploits opportunities when you could have become religious. You see a flower and you start thinking about it, you start talking about it – you don't live the moment. The flower is there opening its petals – a tremendously beautiful phenomenon, a miracle.

Scientists say that life is a miracle; there is no reason for it, why it should be. On millions and millions of planets and stars, only on this small tiny earth, and that, too, only for a few thousand years, life has existed. Nobody knows why, nobody knows how long it will exist, nobody knows the goal, the destiny of it, the source. Scientists, at the most, say that this is simply a miracle, seems to be just an accident. Nothing can be said. A flower is a miracle because a flower is alive. In this dead universe – millions of planets, millions of stars, just rocks and rocks and rocks, infinitely rocky – a small seed has become a plant and the plant is celebrating. A flower has come up and you simply start thinking, talking about it; you say, "How beautiful!" and you miss the beauty, because if it is really beautiful you will become silent. Whenever something tremendous is encountered you are in such a mysterious amazement, you are in such wonder, how can you talk? Talking is profane. In that moment, talking is just foolish – you are missing.

You simply remain silent, you drink, you eat the moment; you allow the flower to spread within you. In a subtle way the duality of subject and object is lost. You are no more the subject and the flower is no more the object; the boundaries meet and melt. Suddenly the flower is within you and you are in the flower – because life is one. You are also a flower; consciousness is a flowering. That's why Hindus have always symbolized it as a lotus: a flowering of a flower. And a flower is also a consciousness, alive. Meet with the flower, don't start talking and thinking. Then you know what a flower is. You may not be able to say what you know, you may not be able to create a theory about your knowing. It is difficult – when you know, it is very difficult to create a theory around it. It is so vast, experience is so vast, and theories look so narrow. You may not be able to philosophize, but that is not the point – you *know*, that is the point.

This point is the crossroads where philosophers and religious people separate from each other. Philosophers go on talking and thinking, and religious people

go on deepening their experience – and a moment comes when they are completely lost. A philosopher finally becomes just an ego, and a religious person is simply lost. You cannot find him, where he is.

If you understand this, then these fragments will become very, very meaningful – they are.

*Let us not make arbitrary conjectures*
*about the greatest matters.*

What can your mind do? Such a small and tiny thing.

It is said that one day Aristotle was walking on the beach near the sea, and he saw a man who was bringing water from the sea with a teaspoon and throwing that water in a small hole he had dug near the bank. Aristotle was worried about his own problems. He didn't bother – once, twice, he came near and saw the man, but the man was so absorbed that Aristotle became curious: "What is he doing?" He could not contain himself, and the man was absolutely absorbed. He would go to the sea, fill his teaspoon, bring the water, put it in the hole, go again.... Finally Aristotle said, "Wait! I don't want to disturb you, but what are you doing? You have made me tremendously curious."

The man said, "I am going to fill this hole with the whole ocean."

Aristotle, even Aristotle, laughed. He said, "You are foolish! This is not going to happen. You are simply mad, and you are wasting your life! Just look at the vastness of the ocean and the smallness of your hole – and with a teaspoon you are going to empty the ocean into this hole? You are simply crazy! Go home and take rest."

The man laughed even louder than Aristotle, and he said, "Yes, I will go, because my work is done."

Said Aristotle, "What do you mean?"

He said, "The same you are doing – and even more foolish. Look at your head: it is smaller than my hole. And look at the divine, the existence: it is vaster than this ocean. And look at your thoughts – are they bigger than my teaspoon?" The man went, laughing loudly. It shocked Aristotle. Nobody knows whether this happened or not because Aristotle remained the same. This story may have been invented by Heraclitus – I suspect. Or it is even possible that this man may have been Heraclitus – that too, I suspect.

What can mind do? When you think of it, it looks just absurd. How can you understand such a vastness through the head? The whole effort seems to be futile. Drop the head and then look! Don't look through the head, then you are

also vast. It is only because you are looking through the head that you also have become small. It is only because of the narrowness of the head that you are also narrow. Throw this head! – and just look at existence without the head. That means: without thinking, being fully alert but not a single thought in the mind – not theorizing, but living.

*Let us not make arbitrary conjectures....*

And our conjectures are all arbitrary. What can you say? Somebody asks, "Is there God?" What will you say? If you say yes, that too is a conjecture – have you known? If you say no, that too is a conjecture – have you known? How can you say anything? If you say yes, you are wrong. If you say no, you are wrong.

That's why buddhas have remained silent. If you ask Buddha about God he doesn't say anything. He simply remains silent, as if you have not asked anything. About God he never says a single word. He knows the stupidity of the question. And he knows that if you answer a stupid question, you also are stupid. He remains absolutely silent, neither saying yes nor no – because all are conjectures. What can you say? Christian theologians look foolish before a buddha. They even try to prove, they even give proofs, that God is. They give logical grounds that God is. But does God need logical support from you? Does the whole need any proof from you? Are you the judge? What can you prove? And whatsoever you can prove can be disproved by the same mind, because logic is a double-edged sword – you can prove, you can disprove. Logic is not a beloved. Logic is a prostitute. Whosoever pays, logic works for him.

I knew one man – he was a lawyer, a very great, famous, world famous authority on law; but he was a very forgetful man, very absent minded. Once it happened that in a privy council case in London he was fighting the case for one Indian maharaja. It was a big case. He forgot – and he argued for one hour against his own client. Even the judge became worried. The opposite party advocate couldn't believe what was happening: "Now what is he going to do?" – because all the arguments that he had prepared, this man was making. The whole thing was topsy-turvy, and the whole court couldn't believe what was happening. And the man was such an authority that nobody dared to interrupt him; even his own assistant tried many times to pull his coat and tell him what he was doing. When he finished then the assistant whispered in his ear, "What have you done? You have completely destroyed the case. We are not against this man – we are *for* him!"

This lawyer said to the judge, "My lord, these are the arguments which can

be given against my client – now I will contradict them." And he started contradicting, and he won the case.

Logic is a prostitute. You can argue for God, and the same argument can be used against God. For example, all the religions of the world, all the priests, bishops, popes, theologians, they have used as their basic proof, as the first proof in their argument for God, that everything needs a creator: "If you see furniture, you know that some carpenter has made it. If you see a painting, some painter is bound to be there. How can a painting exist without a painter? And such a vast creation, and running so systematically, following such a disciplined course, needs a creator. Creation presupposes a creator."

Then listen to the atheist. He says: "If this is true, then who created the creator? – because if nothing can be without a creator, if the painting cannot be without the painter, then who created the painter? And if you say the painter is uncreated, then you are foolish, because if the painting, such a small thing like a painting, cannot be without a creator, then how can the painter be without a creator?"

Your own logic goes against you. And if you say, "Yes, God is created by another God," then there is an infinite regress, then again, again.... A-God is created by B-God; B-God is created by C-God – and it is infinite. Finally the question will remain the same; it has not been answered. Who created the Z-God? The same question remains. Logic answers nothing. And the same argument can go for, and the same can go against.

Heraclitus says:

*Let us not make arbitrary conjectures...*

Don't make any conjectures, all theories are conjectures.

*...about the greatest matters.*

It is better not to make any conjecture.

*Much learning does not teach understanding.*

You can learn much about these conjectures, which are all arbitrary, and you can become a great pundit, you can become a great knower. In the first place all are conjectures, and in the second place you accumulate all that rubbish and you become a great scholar, and people will respect you and they will think that you know – but do you know? Talking about God, proving for or against, do you come to any conclusion? Theists, atheists, are all in the same boat.

It is said that Mulla Nasruddin used to work as a ferryman; he used to run a ferryboat. One day a priest was going to the other shore. Just in the middle, he asked Nasruddin, "Have you ever learnt anything, Nasruddin?"

He said, "I am ignorant, I don't know anything – I have never been to a school."

The priest said, "Then half your life is almost wasted, because what is a man without learning?"

Nasruddin didn't say anything. Then a storm arose and the boat was sinking He said, "Oh, great pundit, have you ever learnt swimming?"

The man said, "Never, no, I don't know."

The Mulla said, "Then your whole life is wasted, because I am going!"

Learning cannot become swimming – and existence needs experience. Learning cannot be knowing. Knowing is something that you have experienced and you have come to know. Knowing is always original, learning is always borrowed. Others may have known, may not have known; you cannot decide – you simply believe. Remember, belief won't help; it is part of learning. Trust, faith, is totally different. You have tasted something, then comes a trust. You have not tasted, trust is not there, there is only a superficially enforced belief. You believe; belief is borrowed, dead. And the more you believe, the more dead you will become. Trust is totally different. It is not belief, it is not disbelief. It has nothing to do with belief or disbelief or with the mind. People say, "We believe in God." There are people who say, "We don't believe."

One man came to Sri Aurobindo and he asked, "Do you believe in God?"

Sri Aurobindo said, "No."

He couldn't believe his own ears, because he had come from a very, very far country to ask this man, and he was thinking that he must be believing in God – and Sri Aurobindo says, "No."

The man said, "What are you saying? I cannot believe my own ears and I have come from so far just to listen to a man who knows."

Aurobindo said, "But I have not said anything about knowing. I don't believe, I *know*."

Belief is a poor substitute for knowing, really no substitute at all. You don't believe in the sun – you know. I am here: you don't believe in me, you know. You are sitting there: you don't believe that you are there, you know. You believe in God, you don't know.

Ignorance can either become belief or can become disbelief, but ignorance remains ignorance. Knowing is needed. And know one distinction, subtle: I

don't use the word knowledge, I use the word knowing because knowing is a process, knowledge is already ended. Knowledge is like a thing – finished; you can possess it, it is in your fist; you can manipulate it, it is complete. Knowing is a process, a river; it goes on and on and on. You can never possess it; you cannot say that it is finished. Existence is eternal, how can knowing be finished? How can you come to a point where you can say, "Now, I have known all"? Never does such a point come.

The more you know, the more doors open. The more you flow, the more mysteries are ready to be revealed to you. The more you know, the more you become capable of knowing – and there is no end to it. That's why I use the word knowing, not knowledge. Knowledge is a dead thing, it is past, already gone to the grave. Knowing is always in the present; it is ongoing, it is riverlike. Heraclitus will agree with me. Knowing he will agree with; knowledge, no.

Knowledge is a finished product, knowing is raw. It is always in the making, it is always in the becoming. It is always changing, flowing, taking new shapes, new forms, and you cannot finish it because you are part of it. Who can finish it? You can become knowing, but you can never become a knower.

The same is true of love, and the same is true of prayer, and the same is true of meditation, of all great matters. In fact, to use the word love is not good – loving gives the sense of process. To use the word prayer is not good, prayer is dead – praying gives the sense of a flow, of movement, of aliveness. Experience is not good – experiencing. Meditation is not good.... Language always gives the sense of dead things, and life is not dead. Even if you go to the river and you say, "The river is," even for the river you say "is" – the river is never "is." The river is always moving, becoming.

Nothing is, everything flows, and everything takes new shapes and forms and names, and everything flows one into another. Experiencing, knowing, loving, praying, meditating – remember, life is a process, it is not a thing. It is a movement from one eternity to another. It is always in the middle, always in the middle; you are always in the middle. It is a never ending, alive movement.

Learning can give you dead products, only life can give you processes. You cannot possess anything in life, you cannot even possess yourself. And if you have a possessive mind you will become a knower. Hence the insistence on nonpossessiveness, on a nonpossessive mind. Don't possess anything. Don't possess even your child, he is not a thing. Don't possess your beloved, she is not a thing. Don't possess anything – you cannot! And if you possess, you will kill, you will destroy. And the same happens with learning: we want to possess.

People come to me and they say, "We would like to know God." But why? Why would you like to know God? You want to become a knower. You would like to possess him also. You would like to put him also on display, to show that not only furniture, car and house, but God also you possess: "It is here, you can come and see. I have caught hold of him." You would like to make God also a commodity – you have already made it.

No, you cannot possess. Knowing cannot be possessed. Learning can be possessed. Knowing cannot be taught, you have to grow into it. And it is not secure, because who can be secure with a process? It is never safe; who can be safe with a process? Only with dead things is there security. It is always dangerous because you are always moving from the known to the unknown, from the light to the dark, from the day to the night. You are always moving from life to death. And if you can find the secret hidden harmony that transcends both, moves within both and yet transcends both, then you have come to know the truth.

And that is what Heraclitus means about the greatest matters:

*Much learning does not teach understanding.*

Have you seen people who know very much but act in a foolish way? It almost always happens: a man who knows too much becomes less and less aware. He acts through his knowledge, not through the real situation. He becomes foolish, he behaves in a foolish way, because to behave in a wise way needs response, and he always acts from the dead past. He always acts from a readiness, preparedness. He is never unprepared.

I have heard about a great professor of philosophy. He was studying in his room. The wife came, very, very excited, and she said, "What are you doing? Have you seen this newspaper? It says that you have died!"

The professor, without even looking at the wife or the newspaper, said, "Then remember, we should not forget to send flowers" – because whenever someone dies, flowers have to be sent – that's all. He had not listened. You cannot surprise a man of knowledge, no. He already knows. You cannot amaze him, he has lost that dimension of wonder. He is no more a child; he knows, he knows everything.

I have heard – I cannot vouch for it because I have only heard – one friend was telling me that he was sitting with Mulla Nasruddin and they were talking about many things and enjoying, and suddenly Mulla Nasruddin's dog came in and he said, "Has anybody seen today's newspaper?" So the friend was simply shocked, he couldn't believe it!

Mulla gave the dog the newspaper, and when the dog left then this friend collected his wits again and said, "It is a miracle – this dog reads?"

Mulla said, "Don't be fooled by him – he simply looks at the comics."

There are people who have no sense of wonder and mystery. They cannot be amazed, you cannot surprise them. What happens? They are always ready. They know, and when you know, how can you wonder? A child wonders – and that is the meaning of Jesus' saying: "Unless you become like children, you will not enter my kingdom of God." Why? – because wonder is the door and only an innocent heart wonders. And if you can get an innocent heart, you wonder; everything gives you a surprise. A butterfly and it is such a mystery!...

Chuang Tzu was sitting under a tree and two or three butterflies were chasing each other. He wrote a small poem and he said: "It seems to me that these butterflies are flowers – the flowers that once fell to the ground have come back, now are back on the tree." Flowers fall down to the ground, then they disappear. Says Chuang Tzu, "They have come now as butterflies back to the tree." This man will enter the kingdom of God, not you. If somebody asks anything about a butterfly, you will immediately open a book and everything that it said about butterfly you can say – but do you think all that can be said is the total? All that has been said, has all been said in it? Is there not something which has remained unsaid and which will remain always unsaid and which it will never be possible for anybody to say? If you think that nothing remains unsaid, then how can you be amazed? – then you have lost the sense of wonder.

This century knows more than any other century, and this century is further away from God than any other century ever was – piled up knowledge, libraries go on growing bigger and bigger, and everybody knows so much. Even small children, we force them to know – not towards knowing, not that their wonder should grow, that they should become more and more mysterious; inside, outside, that they should feel the mystery more; that they should be touched by flowers and butterflies and stones. No. We fill their minds with knowledge, and says Heraclitus:

*Seekers after gold*
*dig up much earth and find little.*

These knowers, pundits, they dig much earth but find little. They remove the whole mountain and a mouse comes out. What do they attain? They are like diggers after gold: too much effort, and whatsoever they achieve simply *seems* valuable. That's why he uses the word gold, because what value does gold have?

In fact, what value? The value that you give to it is just a convention. It is we who give value to gold, it is not the gold which has an intrinsic value. If man were not there, do you think there would be any value to gold? Animals don't bother, birds don't think about it. If you put gold before a dog, and a bone, he will choose the bone; he doesn't bother about your gold. What value has gold? Has it any intrinsic value? No value, just the social projection. If you think it valuable, it becomes valuable. Whatsoever you think is valuable, becomes valuable. Diggers after gold dig up much earth and find little. And this is what happens to those who are digging for knowledge, not experience; digging for truth, not for life...and life is truth! And whatsoever truth you can dig out of theories and knowledge is dead.

*You could not discover the limits of the soul*
*even if you traveled every road to do so –*
*such is the depth of its meaning.*

Try to understand three words: one word is the known, that which we already know; then there is another word, the unknown, that which we don't know yet, but there is every possibility we will know it. Science divides existence into these two words: the known and the unknown. The known we have known, and the unknown we will know; just time is needed. Religion divides this world into three words, not two: the known, the unknown and the unknowable.

You cannot exhaust the unknowable. The unknown will become known, then the known may become again unknown. It has happened many times. Many things have been known and then they became unknown because the society became uninterested in them. Many times it has happened. If you go back and ask people who work deeply into the past, they say almost all that we know has been known some time before and then it was forgotten.

Columbus was not the first man who discovered America; many people before him discovered it, and then America was lost again. In Mahabharat, one of the oldest Indian scriptures – at least five thousand years old, more is possible – there is mention of Mexico: Arjuna had many wives, one wife was a Mexican. In many other scriptures of the world America is mentioned. Columbus was not the first to discover it – he rediscovered it. There is mention of airplanes in many scriptures of the world; this is not the first time that we have discovered the airplane. We discovered it and we became uninterested in it; it was lost. I have not come to know anything that has been discovered for the first time.

Everything has been discovered and lost. It depends on the society: if the society takes an interest, it is okay; otherwise it is lost.

The known will become unknown, the unknown will become known. But there is a third dimension: the unknowable. Science doesn't believe in the unknowable. She says, "The unknowable is nothing but the unknown." And religion says it is a totally different dimension: that which will always remain unknown – because its intrinsic nature is such that the mind cannot cope with it. The vast, the infinite, the endless, the beginningless, the total – the total cannot be comprehended in any way by the part, because how can the part comprehend the total? How can the mind comprehend that from which the mind arises? How can the mind know that to which the mind goes back? It is impossible! It is simply impossible. How can we know that from which we come? We are just like waves – how can a wave comprehend the whole ocean? It can claim, because the ocean never refutes anything – it simply laughs. It is just like a child claiming something before the parents, and they laugh.

The incomprehensible is there – the unknowable is there.

Says Heraclitus:

*You could not discover the limits of the soul*
*even if you traveled every road to do so –*
*such is the depth of its meaning.*

How can you know yourself? Every religion says: "Know thyself!" But how can you really know yourself? Then who will be the knower and who will be the known? – because knowledge depends on a division. I can know you, you can know me, because I become an object and you become the knower – but how can you know yourself? And if you try to know, that which you will know will not be yourself. The knower will always recede; the knowledge will always be bracketed as an object and you will be bracketed as a subject.

For example, you can know about the body. That's why all knowers have said that you are not the body – because we can know it. You can know the mind. That is why those who know, they say you are not the mind – because the mind becomes the object and you are the knower. You recede, you go on receding; you are a subtle transcendence. Whatsoever you know, you transcend it immediately. The moment it has become known you are separate from it. If you say, "I have known myself," what do you mean? Who has known whom? Is the known you? – or the knower you? If you are the knower then you still remain unknown. Selfknowledge is impossible.

But why has it always been said, "Know thyself"? It has been said because only through the effort to know oneself will you come to the dimension of the unknowable. It has been insisted: "Know thyself" – not that you can know, don't be deceived. Nobody has ever known, nobody will ever know. And all those who have known knew this – that the great, the vast, the ultimate, remains unknowable.

Insistence is there: Know thyself! I also insist: Know thyself! – just to bring you to a point where you suddenly become aware that this is the gate for the unknowable. Just by making efforts to know yourself you will come to know the unknowable. And I don't mean when I say you will come to know the unknowable that you will know it. No! You will enter into it. It is never a knowledge, it is a jump. You take a jump into the sea and you are lost. Not that you know it – you become it. Of course, in a very, very subtle way you know, and at the same time you don't know.

That is why Heraclitus looks paradoxical, he looks defective, he looks a little mad. But such is the nature of things, such is the depth of things, such is the deeper meaning of things – nothing can be done. Hence it happens that if you move into the unknowable without getting ready to take it, you can become mad. It is such a paradox that you cannot make any head or tail of it. It is such a depth that you never come to the bottom of it. It is such an infinity that the more you enter into it the more you are lost. You can never possess it, you can only be possessed.

God cannot be possessed, you can only allow him to possess you. That's all that can be done. That's why it is a surrender. You allow him to possess, you are ready to be possessed. And for this readiness you have to be ready to lose your rationality, reason, because it is sheer madness. Nothing is clear, everything becomes confused and blurred. It looks blurred and confused because you have been trying to make a clarity out of it. It is not possible. Life comprehends all that is paradoxical.

*You could not discover the limits of the soul*
*even if you traveled every road to do so –*
*such is the depth of its meaning.*

You can travel all the paths but you will never reach the goal. All the paths combine together and you will never reach the goal. Why? – because life has no goal. It is a celebration. It has no purpose, it is not going anywhere. It is simply enjoying the going, not going anywhere. It is a play, it is a game. And don't be

serious about it, otherwise you will miss it. Be sincere, but not serious. Sincerity is something else, seriousness is something else. If you are serious you are thinking in terms of goals, means and ends, ways and achievement; you are ambitious. Seriousness is ambition and it is a disease. You may have turned your attention from this world, but your ambitious mind is now thinking about the other. Seriousness is not religious. A serious man will automatically become a philosophic man; he will start thinking. Seriousness is of the head. That's why a serious person, a thinker, becomes a long face. He cannot even laugh, he cannot smile, he cannot play, because always he is thinking: "What is to be achieved through it?" He turns life into a means – and life itself is the goal.

A sincere person is totally different. Sincerity is of the heart. He is true, but not serious. He is seeking, but not as a goal. He is seeking it just like a child seeks things: if he finds, it is okay: if he doesn't find, it is okay also. A child is running after a dog, and just in the middle he finds a butterfly; he changes. He starts running after the butterfly; and then, by the side, there comes a flower – and he has forgotten the butterfly and the flower takes his total attention. He is not serious, but very sincere. Whenever he takes anything into mind he is totally with it – that is sincerity. Now he has forgotten the butterfly and the dog, and the flower is everything. When you can pay your total attention to something, it is sincerity. And when you are paying your attention only as a means, you are cunning. You really want to reach the goal, and this is only a means. You are exploiting; you are exploiting the path to reach the goal. For the child, the path is the goal. And for the religious person also, the path is the goal.

Wherever I am, it is the goal.

Whatsoever I am, it is the goal.

At this moment, my whole life converges upon me; there is nowhere else to go. One has just to celebrate this moment in totality.

This is what a religious being is – unworried, not going anywhere, just for a morning walk. It is different. You pass by the same path when you go to your office, and then you go for the morning walk – the path is the same, the house is the same, everything is the same; you are the same, your legs are the same, but when you go for a morning walk everything is different. A religious person is just on the way for a morning walk, and a nonreligious person is going somewhere to the office, to the shop – a goal is there. The worldly man is goal oriented; whatsoever the goal, even God, a worldly man is goal oriented. A nonworldly man is not goal oriented. A nonworldly man lives here and now, everything converges here and now. And this here and now then becomes infinite. You go by all the

paths to it, but still it remains unreachable. That is the beauty also. If we could reach, everything would be lost. If we could know ourselves, then what? Then you would simply be bored by yourself. No, that boredom never comes – because it is an ongoing process, infinite, from one infinity to another infinity.

Remember these words – not in the mind, let them go deeper and settle in the heart:

*Let us not make arbitrary conjectures*
*about the greatest matters.*

*Much learning does not teach understanding.*

*Seekers after gold*
*dig up much earth and find little.*

*You could not discover the limits of the soul*
*even if you traveled every road to do so –*
*such is the depth of its meaning.*

# *Chapter* **6**

WHEN SOME VISITORS
UNEXPECTEDLY FOUND HERACLITUS
WARMING HIMSELF BY THE COOKING FIRE,
HE SAID TO THEM:
HERE, TOO, ARE THE GODS.

I HAVE SEARCHED MYSELF.

TIME IS A CHILD
MOVING COUNTERS IN A GAME;
THE ROYAL POWER IS A CHILD'S.

BIGOTRY IS THE SACRED DISEASE.

# HERE, TOO, ARE THE GODS

HERE ARE TWO WAYS TO SEEK the true: one is to borrow knowledge, the other is to seek yourself. Of course borrowing is easy, but whatsoever you borrow is never yours, and that which is not yours cannot be true. This condition must be fulfilled: truth must be yours.

I may have known truth, but I cannot transfer it to you. In the very act of transferring it becomes a lie. That is the nature of truth. So nobody can give it to you, you cannot borrow it, you cannot steal it, you cannot purchase it – you have to know it. And unless you know, your knowledge is not a knowing – it is a hiding place for your ignorance. You are deceiving yourself, you are completely misguided.

The first thing to remember is that truth is a lived phenomenon. Who can live for you? You have to live for yourself, nobody can be a substitute. Who can love for you? Servants cannot do that, friends cannot be of any help – you have to love. Jean-Paul Sartre says somewhere that sooner or later a time will come when people will engage servants to love for them. Of course, rich people are already on the way. Sooner or later those who can afford it, they will not bother themselves. Why bother when a servant can do it? You can find a beautiful, good servant, and he can love for you. You have other more important things to do – love can be left to servants.

Mulla Nasruddin once told me, "I am very much interested in my wife's happiness."

So I asked, "What are you doing?"

He said, "I have hired a private detective to search for the reasons."

But can anybody else love for you? No, there is no possibility. You cannot be alive by proxy, you cannot love by proxy – and you cannot reach truth by proxy either. That is the very nature of things. There is no way to be cunning about it and clever about it. Man has tried: "There is one who knows; we can get it from him, we can borrow it." But truth has to be lived. It is not something outside, it is an inner growth. It is not a thing, it is not an object; it is your subjectivity.

Truth is subjectivity, so how can you get it from anybody else, from scriptures, from vedas, korans and bibles? No, Jesus is not of much help, neither is Buddha. You have to go through it, there is no shortcut. You have to travel, suffer. Many times you will fall, many times you will err, many times you will go astray – that's how it is. Come back again and again; start the search again and again. Many times the path is lost. Many times you move in a circle, you come back to the same point again and again. There seems to be no progress – but go on searching. Go on searching and don't feel hopeless and dejected. Keep the hope: that is the quality of a seeker.

A seeker trusts, he hopes; he can wait, he can wait infinitely. He has patience and he goes on seeking. Not that every step leads to the goal, sometimes he is moving in just the opposite direction. But even moving in the opposite direction one learns; even erring is a part of learning. Nobody can learn if they are very much afraid of being in error. If one is very much afraid that he may go astray, then there is no possibility of traveling. This is why the mind says, "Ask the awakened, those who know – gather from them." But then it is secondhand, and there is no such thing as a secondhand truth, it is simply a lie. A secondhand truth is a lie. A truth, to be true, has to be firsthand, original. It has to be fresh, you have to reach it – it is always virgin.

Heraclitus says:

*I have searched myself.*

He is saying, "I am not saying something that I have heard – I have searched myself. It is not something that I have learnt, it is something I have grown myself. It is a growth, it is a subjectivity – it is my own experience." And when it is your experience, it transforms you.

Says Jesus: "Truth liberates." But you know many truths, and they have not liberated you. On the contrary, they have become the bondages, they are the fetters around you. Truth liberates, lies become a prison.

That's why Heraclitus says:

*Bigotry is the sacred disease.*

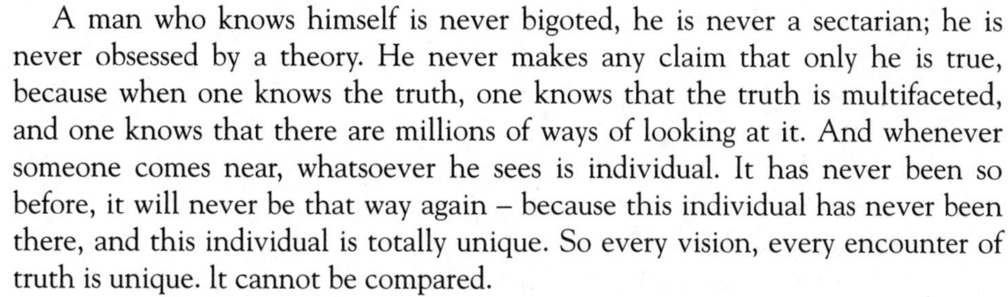

A man who knows himself is never bigoted, he is never a sectarian; he is never obsessed by a theory. He never makes any claim that only he is true, because when one knows the truth, one knows that the truth is multifaceted, and one knows that there are millions of ways of looking at it. And whenever someone comes near, whatsoever he sees is individual. It has never been so before, it will never be that way again – because this individual has never been there, and this individual is totally unique. So every vision, every encounter of truth is unique. lt cannot be compared.

A man who has known himself has also come to know that millions are the paths, millions are the faces of the truth. How can he be bigoted? How can he say, "Only my truth is true, and only my god is God; your god is a false god"? This is the language of one whose truth is borrowed. You see millions of religious people all over the world claiming truth. They have not come to know, they have not searched themselves; otherwise how can they miss? How can they miss the multifaceted experience, the phenomenon of truth? How can they say, "Only my truth," because when one comes to know that there is no "I," how can one claim? How is bigotry possible?

A really religious man has no claim. He accommodates., he does not tolerate because when you say, "I tolerate," there is intolerance. He does not say, "I am a Christian, you are a Hindu. Yes, I am a man of tolerance, I tolerate. You may also be true; I am true, you may also be true. I tolerate you." But tolerance always hides intolerance; the very word is intolerant. So whenever a person says, "I am tolerant," be aware he is intolerant, he is hiding. What do you mean by your tolerance? You think that you are somewhere higher and you are tolerating those who are lower, pitying them. Or, at the most, a Christian will say, "Yes, there are many ways, but my way is the best. Yes, people have reached by other ways also, but mine is the super highway." That, too, is intolerance. Why this claim? Why this "I"? Why this ego?

And that's why religions became so quarrelsome. They have murdered, they have killed, they have committed all sorts of sins. They are here to liberate man, and they are here to take man beyond all sins, yet they have committed all the sins. Religions have killed more than anybody else, and they have created misery and strife and struggle and conflict more than anything else on this earth. This earth is ugly because of so many churches, temples, mosques. They

have not united man, they have divided. They have not made humanity one. They talk about love, but they have created hate. They talk about peace, but they create all sorts of causes for violence to exist. They feed violence and they talk about peace. Why? The reason is not religion; the reason is bigotry.

Says Heraclitus:

*Bigotry is the sacred disease.*

Diseases are bad, and when they are sacred they are worse of course. When a disease looks as though it is sacred, you think it is the ultimate in health. Whenever someone claims, "I am the only truth," and the claim can be made in very subtle ways, then ugliness enters. These mad people have even forced their gods to say things which look absurd. Mohammedans say, "God says, 'I am the only God, and Mohammed is the only prophet.'" What do you mean? Is God exhausted in Mohammed? Then God is very poor. Then what about Mahavira? Then what about Buddha? Then what about Jesus, Krishna, Lao Tzu, Heraclitus? And what about all of you who are some day or the other going to become the prophets? What about the whole? Mohammed is beautiful, but Mohammedans claim that he is the only prophet, and then ugliness enters. Jesus is wonderful, but Christians say that he is the only begotten son. Why the only begotten son? Then what are all of you – bastards? If he is the only begotten son, then what is this whole existence? From where do you come if he comes from God? Then who is *your* father?

No, God is infinitely potential. Millions of Jesuses can come from him and he remains the same, he is not exhausted – that is the meaning of omnipotent. If he has only one son, he seems to be impotent rather than omnipotent. He goes on creating and the creativity never ends – that is the infinity. But Christians claim that Jesus is the only son. Why this claim? So that they can claim their book is the only book. The word bible means the book. They have not named it because for them this is the only book, all else is rubbish. What about the Upanishads? What about the sayings of Buddha? What about the Tao Teh Ching of Lao Tzu? Why should The Bible be the only book? It is beautiful, but when it becomes the only book it has become ill.

This is the sacred disease. When you claim for your truth that it is the whole and all, the ego has entered. Truth needs no claim. It's simply there in all its beauty; you can see it but it has no claim on you. In fact, truth never tries to convert anybody. It helps, it loves you, it would like you to be transformed, but there is no effort to convert. But Hindus try to make Christians Hindus,

Christians try to make Hindus Christians. Why this effort? – because they believe that they have the sole key and the only key and everybody else is going to hell. When people start converting they make the thing very narrow.

Infinite is the way, because to infinity it leads.

When the goal is infinite, how can the way be so narrow? In fact, whenever a man is religious he is neither a Christian, nor a Hindu, nor a Mohammedan. That's what I am trying to help you to be: neither Christians, nor Hindus, nor Mohammedans. Why can't you simply be? What need is there to carry the label of a sect? If you feel good, if you love Jesus, it is very beautiful. If you love Buddha, it is good – but why become bigoted? Why become prejudiced? Your love is beautiful, and if it helps you it is good – move accordingly. But then there are millions of people who move in different ways. Let them move, help them; wherever they are going, help them. Help them to move in their own ways, let them do their own thing. Don't force them and don't try to convert them. If they look at you and they feel something and they want to change their path, it is up to them. That's why Heraclitus is completely forgotten, because he never created a sect around him. He had followers, but he never created a sect and he never claimed anything. He never said, "This is the only truth."

Why does this appeal? When somebody says, "This is the only truth," why does this appeal? You are very uncertain and confused, so when somebody claims that his is the only truth, you think, "He must know, otherwise how can he claim?" The claim becomes a subtle influence, he looks authoritative. But remember well: a man of knowledge, a man of understanding, is always hesitant. He is not so authoritative because he sees the truth and he feels it cannot be expressed – he hesitates. You will find poetry in his words, but you will not find statements. He has a subtle aroma around him which gives you a feeling of certainty, but that certainty doesn't come from his statements. His statements are always hesitant; before he says anything he hesitates – because he knows that whatsoever is said cannot be the truth, and he knows that whatsoever he is trying to do is a dangerous thing. It is hazardous because words destroy, and when you hear the words you will give your own meaning to them.

A man of understanding hesitates. He does not know what will happen to his words. What you will do out of his words is unknown, and each single word can become very, very meaningful to you, or a meaningful effort on your part. He hesitates, he watches you, he looks all around, he tries to find your center of being, then he says something. So that it never becomes a misunderstanding, so that it doesn't misguide you, so that if his words can help it is okay and they

don't prove harmful to you – he hesitates. But a man of borrowed knowledge never hesitates. He is very, very certain. Just go and listen to Christian missionaries: they seem to be so certain that their certainty says they are stupid. Why this certainty? And they don't know anything, they have been trained – trained for everything.

I used to visit a theological college, a Christian theological college. I used to watch how they prepare priests and ministers, and I was amazed – the whole thing seems to be so stupid. Even gestures are practiced: how to stand on the pulpit, what to say, how to say it; when to raise your voice high, and when to whisper; and how to raise your hand, when to raise it exactly – everything is trained. They look like actors. And they don't know anything, but they never hesitate because they have been trained. Training cannot make you religious, discipline cannot make you religious, learning cannot make you religious. You can become an actor, you may become a very skilled actor. You may become so skilled that not only do you deceive others, but you yourself are also deceived.

If you ask psychoanalysts they have an answer: a man who feels himself hesitant within will always create a certainty outside. He is afraid of his own inner uncertainty, so he clings to certain statements. A man who is certain within doesn't bother: he can hesitate, he can afford to hesitate, there is no fear. He can say, "Perhaps"; there is no need to be certain. He can say, "God is summer and winter; God is night and day; God is satiety and hunger; God is both rest and restlessness" – he can be paradoxical. The paradox is used just to give you a feeling that the man is not claiming anything, he is simply trying to say the fact. And if the fact is complex, let it be so. If the fact is contradictory, let the statement also be contradictory – let it be a true reflection. You cannot ask a man of learning to be so paradoxical – God is summer and winter – no. He is absolutely certain of what God is: God is day, never night; God is light, never darkness; God is good, never bad; God is peace, never war. When God is both war and peace, where are you? You become uncertain, you hesitate.

Says Heraclitus:

*I have searched myself.*

That's why he is so paradoxical. Always look for the paradox. You will always find it if a man has searched himself, because then what can he do? If existence is paradoxical, what can he do? – he has to represent it as it is. But go to a missionary – he has never searched. He has learnt much, he can quote scriptures. In fact, he cannot do anything other than quote scriptures. And you know very well that

the devil is very skilled in quoting scriptures – he is the perfect missionary.

*When some visitors*
*unexpectedly found Heraclitus*
*warming himself by the cooking fire,*
*he said to them:*
*Here, too, are the gods.*

He never went to a temple, because if you are a man of perception, if your eyes are open, if you can hear and feel, then what need is there to go to a temple? Here also are gods.

God is not a person. God is all that is the case. God is existence.

Just imagine the picture: Heraclitus sitting by the fireside, warming himself. The cracking of the wood, the flames rising towards heaven, the warmth.... It must have been a cold winter night – unexpectedly some visitors come and they ask, "What are you doing?" And he says, "Here also are gods." What he is saying is that this is a prayer, this warming yourself is a prayer – if the fire becomes a divine phenomenon.

It reminds me of a Zen master, Ikkyu. He was journeying and he was staying in a temple, just overnight. The night was very, very cold, so he made a fire. But not finding wood anywhere, he took a statue of Buddha – a wooden statue that was in the temple – and burnt it. The priest was fast asleep...noise, the fire, and this Ikkyu moving here and there. He looked – he opened his eyes and looked – and he was aghast, he couldn't believe it, because this was a Buddhist monk, and not only a monk but a very famous master. The priest jumped out of his bed, he came running and he said, "What are you doing? You have burnt a Buddha!"

Ikkyu took out a small piece of wood and searched in the ashes for the Buddha – the statue was almost gone, nothing was there.

The priest said, "What are you searching for? It is no longer there."

Ikkyu said, "I am searching for the bones – Buddha must have bones."

The priest laughed and said, "Now I am completely certain you are mad. How can a wooden Buddha have bones?"

Ikkyu said, "Then bring the other two Buddhas also, because the night is still long and very cold, and the buddha within me needs a little warmth. These Buddhas are just wooden, so don't worry. Here inside are bones, and a real buddha, and this buddha needs a little warmth. These Buddhas are no good anyway, they have no bones, so don't worry."

The priest threw him out of the temple. The night was very cold, but there

are people who will worship a wooden Buddha and throw out a real buddha. In the morning he looked out to see what had happened to Ikkyu: he was sitting just outside the temple near a milestone – and worshipping it. The sun was rising, it was a beautiful morning and he had found a few flowers from somewhere. He had put those flowers on the milestone and he was worshipping. The priest came running and he said, "What are you doing? You are really completely mad! During the night you burnt a Buddha and now you are worshipping a milestone."

Said Ikkyu, "Here, also, is a god."

Heraclitus: "Here, too, are gods."

If you can feel, every moment is divine and everything is divine, and all that exists is holy. If you cannot feel, go to the temples, go to the mosques and churches, but you will not find anything there either – because it is you who need a transformation, it is not the situation that needs change. The situation remains the same: in the temple, outside the temple, everywhere God is. It is you who cannot see and so you change places: from the house you go to the temple in search of God.

You need an inner transformation.

The change in the situation won't help. You need a psychological reorientation. You need a totally new way of looking at things, then suddenly the whole world becomes the temple, then there is nothing else.

For Heraclitus, fire became the symbol – and fire is really a beautiful symbol. Heraclitus says fire is the basic substance of life. It is! Now physicists agree with Heraclitus. They agree that electricity is the base of all existence, that everything is nothing but modes of electricity. Heraclitus says it is fire. What is the difference? And fire is a more beautiful word than electricity. Fire gives a sense of more aliveness than electricity does, fire is more wild than electricity. When you say electricity is the base, it looks as if the universe is somehow mechanical because electricity has become associated with a mechanism, and then God looks like an engineer – but electricity is fire.

Hindus have called this basic element *prana*, vitality – but vitality is fire. When you are vital, alive, you are fiery, aflame. Henri Bergson has called the base of all, élan vital, just like prana. Those who have been seeking, somehow or other they come near fire. Deep down this existence is fire. Fire is life. And Zarathustra is right: he made fire the suprememost god. He must have agreed with Heraclitus – they were contemporaries, Zarathustra and Heraclitus. Fire became the supreme god for the followers of Zarathustra.

Fire has many things deep in it. You will have to understand the phenomenon of fire, the symbol, because it is a way of speaking, it is a metaphor. Something deep Heraclitus wants to indicate when he says that fire is the substratum. Watch fire some day on a winter's night; sit also by the side of a fire and just watch, just feel it, the warmth. Cold is death, warmth is life. A dead body is cold, a live body is warm – and you have to maintain a certain warmth continuously. An inner mechanism exists in man to keep the warmth always within a certain limit, because only between those certain degrees is life possible. Human life exists just between ninety-five degrees and one hundred and ten degrees, just between those fifteen degrees. There are other lives which exist at other temperatures, but human life has a span of just fifteen degrees.

Mulla Nasruddin was very, very ill, feverish, in a high fever, and the doctor took his temperature and said, "One hundred and five."

Mulla opened his eyes and asked, "What is the world record?" – because the ego always thinks in terms of world records. He was thinking, "Maybe I couldn't beat anyone in any other way, but maybe I can break the world record in fever" – but beyond one hundred and ten there is no record, because then man simply disappears, you cannot absorb so much fire. Below ninety-five you disappear: so much cold, death settles in.

That's why we say, "A warm welcome," not, "A cold welcome"; warm love, not cold love – because cold symbolizes death, warmth symbolizes life. The sun is the source, solar energy is fire. Just watch: in the evening everything becomes sad. Even trees, birds become completely silent; no song, all songs disappear. Flowers close and the whole earth waits for the morning. And in the morning, the sun has not yet risen and the earth starts becoming ready to welcome. The birds start singing even before the sun has arisen – that is a welcome sign. Flowers start flowering again; everything becomes again alive, movement enters.

Fire is a very, very meaningful symbol in other ways also. If you watch fire you will see a continuous upward movement. Water flows downwards, fire flows upwards – that's why the Hindus talk about "the fire of *kundalini*." When you rise upwards you are not like water, you are like a flame of fire. When your inner being changes, you feel a flame going upwards. Water, even water, in contact with fire starts evaporating upwards.

In a very, very old Tibetan scripture it is said that a master is like fire and the disciple is like water. If the disciple comes in deep contact with the master, the quality of the disciple changes – it becomes the quality of fire, just like water heated evaporates. Water without fire moves downwards. With fire immediately

a change comes in. Beyond one hundred degrees the fire has made the water ready to move upwards; the dimension changes.

Fire always moves upwards. Even if you hold a lamp upside down the flame will go upwards, the flame cannot go downwards. Fire is an effort to reach the highest peak, the omega point. Another thing: if you watch a flame, you can see it only for a few seconds, split seconds, then it disappears. The higher you go, the more you disappear; the lower you go, the more you become solid. Watch water: if it goes on getting lower and lower and lower and colder and colder, it becomes frozen, it becomes ice. Then it is like stone, then all movement stops – then it is dead. When water is frozen, it is dead, it is no longer alive. You will have to melt it through fire, then movement will appear again. You will have to heat it so much that it comes to a hundred degree point, then it will move upwards.

So there are three stages: no movement, that is when you are frozen; a downward movement, that is when you are like water – first stage like ice, second like water – and the third is when you evaporate: then you move upwards. In you, almost all three stages exist simultaneously. Some part of you is like fire, moving upwards, a very small part, very tiny.... That's why you have come to me, otherwise there would be no need.

Why have you come to me? You must have a tiny part which moves upwards, and that tiny part feels as though it is being pulled down by your whole being – that is the anguish. You know that something in you goes towards the divine. In some moments you feel like a bird, and you can simply fly, but only in some moments. And even in those moments the greater part of you is hanging like stone. One part hangs like stone. Almost ninety percent of you is like ice. Nine percent of you moves like water, downwards. In sex, in anger, in hatred, you move downwards – but at least it is better to move downwards than not to move at all. That's why, if I feel very much of a frozen being in you, I say fall in love, move towards sex, because at least it will melt you. Of course you will not be flying upwards, you will move downwards, but at least movement is good. And once movement is there then the direction can be changed, the dimension can be changed. But frozen...?

Just go to the monasteries and look if you want to see perfect examples of frozen ice. Go to the Catholic monasteries or Jaina monasteries. There you will find perfect frozen icecubes, no men – because they are against sex, they are against food, they are against everything. They are just negative, they have been negating. And if you negate, by and by your life loses fire, because fire is a positive force. If you negate you become cold. Negativity is a method of suicide. By and by, you die; in fragments you kill yourself, then you are frozen. But this is no achievement, in fact it is falling down.

I tell people, "If you are frozen, then move towards sex, that will help." Of course, it is not going to lead you towards the ultimate, but one thing will happen: you will start moving. When you love a person, when you feel for some other person, your bioenergy starts moving. That's why in sex you feel very much excited: fire has begun to function, and when you make love, your body temperature rises. Love is like fever, a temporary fever created by your mind. That's why after love you relax deeply, you have a flow. If you can attain to sexual orgasm, a complete flow happens, then your bioenergy is moving. Those people who cannot have deep orgasms are difficult people, for meditation also – because they cannot move, so how can they move upwards?

The first thing is movement. The second thing is to turn the movement upwards. And so many people cannot move, they are afraid, they are frozen. You can clearly see their bodies as frozen phenomena. You touch them and you will feel their bodies are cold. You shake hands with them and you will feel that you are shaking hands with the dead branch of a tree, no movement. You take their hands into your hands and you will not feel that any energy is being transmitted. The hand is there just like a dead branch. It doesn't give, it doesn't receive, it doesn't communicate. And you can watch people: just by their walking, their faces, their movements, you can see whether they are orgasmic or not.

The first thing for a master to know about you is whether you are orgasmic or not. If you are orgasmic, if your whole body vibrates when you make love, and the vibrating phenomenon is so deep that you are no more for a single second, of course then you become just a flow, from head to toe the energy moves like a flood, and there are no blocks of ice within you, everything melts. After making love you fall into sleep like a child because the energy has moved. You have played long, you are tired, but this tiredness is very nice. This tiredness is relaxation, now you can relax – and the body feels alive. Hence so much appeal of sex – because it is really your body trying to find a way to be orgasmic, to be riverlike, not frozen.

When you are frozen you cannot relate. When you are frozen you are closed within yourself, you make an imprisonment – and from this imprisonment there is no way to God. You will have to melt. And before you reach the divine, before you can relate to the divine, you will have to relate to other persons in this world, because when you relate to other persons – that is, when you love, care – then your body melts, it flows. When it flows then another step can be taken.

In a flowing energy it is very simple to heat the body in certain inner ways. All meditations are methods to give you heat, more heat than sex can give. Meditations, particularly those we are doing here, are all to create fire within you. Through breathing, fast chaotic breathing, fire is created, because breathing brings you more and more oxygen, and when there is more oxygen, more fire happens; without oxygen, there is no fire. Even if a flame burns, it burns because of oxygen. If there is no oxygen, the fire will subside automatically. More oxygen has to be brought to your body because you are too frozen. You are not alive enough, you are not warm enough.

People come to me, particularly the frozen ones, and they say, "We don't like this dynamic meditation." They don't like it because they are frozen and they have too much invested in their frozenness. They don't love, but they think they are *brahmacharins*, celibates – they are simply frozen, icecubes. In their lives there is no movement, but they think they are detached. Of course, there is a detachment that comes when you flow upwards, but that is totally different. And there is a detachment that happens when you don't flow at all. Of course a dead man is detached, a dead man is celibate – a dead man is completely dead. You can be detached like a dead man; that is what has happened in all the monasteries of the whole world. And you can be detached in a totally different way, a qualitatively, diametrically opposite way. That is when you become so much alive that the fire comes to a point where the water doesn't flow downwards, it starts flowing upwards.

More fire has to be created within you, you should become a furnace. Absorb more oxygen, make more effort, allow the body as much movement as possible, bring energy, throbbing energy. It is there – you just have to make it throbbing. Live like a flame burning from both sides together. Then only, suddenly one day, you will find that your energy is flowing upwards, that you have become a flame. Then you can see yourself up to a certain extent, and then you are no more. Then suddenly you disappear into the cosmos, then you have become one with the divine. This is the symbol of fire – that you can see it only for a few seconds and then it is disappearing.

A buddha is continuously disappearing. Look at me: if you can see, you will see that I am continuously disappearing. Just up to a certain extent you can see. That's why the aura is seen around a man who is awakened. That aura is nothing but a disappearing fire, a continuously disappearing fire. Up to a certain extent you can see it, hence the aura. Beyond that aura there is nothing, it disappears.

Heraclitus is very, very right in finding the symbol. It is not a philosophical

statement, but in Greek histories of philosophy they think Heraclitus is proposing, like others – like Thales, Anaxagoras, Anaximenes – like other Greek philosophers, that he is proposing an element... Because there are four elements: earth, water, fire, air, so there have been philosophers who proposed that earth is the basic element; somebody else proposed that water is the basic element; somebody else fire; somebody else air. Heraclitus proposes that fire is the basic element, but he should not be understood in the way Thales is understood, no. It is not a statement. It is not a statement about a philosophical theme or theory, he is not proposing any doctrine. He is a poet, he is not a philosopher at all. He is giving a symbol, and the symbol means much more than the word fire.

Watch fire outside, then watch fire inside, and become as much of a flame as possible.

That's why:

*When some visitors*
*unexpectedly found Heraclitus*
*warming himself by the cooking fire,*
*he said to them:*
*Here, too, are the gods.*

*I have searched myself.*

And I am not just saying this because others have said – I have known myself.

He says:

*Time is a child*
*moving counters in a game;*
*the royal power is a child's.*

The royal power is a child's, and time is a child moving counters in a game – the whole concept of *leela*, play, he condenses in just a few sentences. Life is like a play – don't make it a business, otherwise you will miss it. You miss it because you make a business out of it and it is a play. Play well, but don't think in terms of achieving something out of it. Just be like a child: he plays, he is not worried about what he achieves out of it. Small children, even if they are defeated in a game, jump and feel very happy. Failure is not a failure if it is a play; defeat is not a defeat if it is a play. Otherwise, if it is a business, even victory is a defeat. Ask Napoleons, Alexanders: even victory is defeat. What do you find finally? You are victorious, and nothing has been achieved. You longed for this goal so

much and now you have reached it – and you simply feel frustrated and your whole life is lost.

Remember, your life will be lost if you are after some goals, because life has no goal. It is a purposeless play. It is not going anywhere, it is simply enjoying itself.

This is the most difficult thing to understand because the mind is mathematical. It says, "Then what is the meaning of it, then what is the purpose?" There is no purpose and no meaning. Then the mind immediately says, "If there is no meaning then why live, then why not commit suicide?" But see: if there is meaning the whole thing will become ugly, then it will be like a business. If there is purpose, then all life will lose the poetry.

The poetry is there because there is no purpose. Why does the rose flower? Ask the rose; it will say, "I don't know – but flowering is so beautiful, what is the need to know? Flowering in itself, intrinsically, is so beautiful." Ask a bird, "Why do you sing?" and he will be simply puzzled at what nonsense questions you ask. Singing is so beautiful, it is such a benediction – why raise the question? But the mind looks for the goal, the mind is an achiever – it cannot simply enjoy. Something must be there in the future to be achieved, some goal must be reached, then mind feels good. If there is nothing to be achieved, it flops. But that is what the whole effort is – let it flop!

There is no purpose, there is no goal.

This moment, the whole existence is celebrating – all except you. Why not participate?

Why not be like a flower, purposelessly flowering?

And why not be like a river, meaninglessly flowing?

And why not be like the ocean, roaring, just enjoying?

This is what Heraclitus says:

*Time is a child*
*moving counters in a game;*
*the royal power is a child's.*

And every child is a king. Just watch a child – every child is simply a king, an emperor. Look at the movement: even if the child is naked, no emperor can compete with him. Why is a child so beautiful? Every child, without any exception, is beautiful. What is the beauty of a child? He is still uncontaminated by the mind, which seeks purpose, meaning, goal. He simply plays, he doesn't bother about the next day.

A small child came home. His mother was very angry and she said, "I have

heard from neighborhood children that you threw mud in a small girl's mouth, and you have been punished – you were standing outside the class the whole day!"

He said, "Yes."

His mother was horrified; she said, "Why? Why did you throw that mud?"

The small child shrugged his shoulders and said, "Well, the mouth was open." The why is meaningless. It is enough: he had mud in the hand and the mouth was open, so what to do? It simply happened.

We are asking why. Why is irrelevant for a child – it is how it happened! The mouth was open and he had the mud. He did not do it really. We punish him wrongly, he did not do it – it happened, it simply happened this way. It was a coincidence that the girl was standing with an open mouth. He didn't mean anything, he didn't mean any harm, he didn't mean any insult. He simply welcomed the opportunity, he enjoyed it. But we ask why.

Between a child and a grownup exists an abyss; they are poles apart. The child cannot understand what the adults are saying because he lives in a totally different dimension – the dimension of play. And the adults cannot understand what the child is doing because the adult is a businessman, he lives in the world of whys, reasons, causes. They never meet, they cannot meet, there is no possibility of understanding – unless the adult again becomes a child. Only a saint, a real sage, can understand a child, because he is also a child. He can understand.

I was reading a small child's diary. On the twenty-fifth of December in the diary it is written: "Got an air-gun from Uncle Joe. Uncle Joe is the greatest uncle in the world. There has never been such an uncle and never will be, etcetera, etcetera. But it is raining and I can't go out. I would like to hunt immediately."

26th December: "It is still raining, and I am feeling very, very restless."

27th December: "It is still raining, and I am frustrated and feeling very aggressive and violent."

28th December: "It is still raining – shot Uncle Joe."

This is a child's world. He moves without any purpose, playing. Playing in itself is enough.

If you can become a child again, you have achieved all. If you cannot become a child again, you have missed all. A sage is a twiceborn child. And firstborn children are not real children because they will have to grow up. The second birth is the real birth, because when somebody is twiceborn he has given birth to himself. It is a transformation, he has again become a child. He does not ask for reasons and whys, he simply lives. Whatsoever the moment presents,

he moves with it; he has no plans, he has no projections. He lives without demanding anything, and that is the only way to live; otherwise, you simply appear to be living, you are not alive. For a child there is nothing bad, nothing good, there is no God, no Devil; a child accepts everything. Again, a sage accepts everything. That's why he can say God is winter and summer, God is peace and war, God is Devil and good – both. For a sage, again all morality disappears, all distinctions fall down; everything is holy and every place is sacred.

I was staying with a family, a Christian family. The mother was talking to her child and she was saying, "This is not good, you need not pray so loudly – you almost shout. Prayers don't have to be shouted. God can hear you, you need not shout so much."

But the child said, "But it says, 'Hollered be thy name!'" A child lives somewhere else.

The mother was very, very angry. I told her, "Don't disturb him, don't disturb his childhood, it is too soon. Let him follow his own way of praying – he is enjoying it, and that enjoyment is the real thing, not the form. He jumps and hollers the name of God, and it is beautiful! Why are you teaching him?... Because this is the way it should be: if you enjoy, it becomes a prayer. If you don't enjoy, if it becomes a discipline somebody else is forcing on you, then you feel imprisoned. Let him holler, let him jump – and I can be a witness to him: God hears him. The point is not whether he hollers or not, but whether he enjoys."

A man who can be blissful need not pray – prayer is a poor substitute. A man who is blissful need not meditate. A man who is blissful can live the moment blissfully, has done all that can be done. Everything is holy and sacred. You can eat your food in such a way that it becomes prayer. You can love a man in such a way that it becomes prayer. You can dig a hole in the garden in such a way that it becomes prayer. Prayer is not a formal thing – it is the quality of prayerfulness that you bring to something.

*...the royal power is a child's.*

Why? – because the royal power means innocence. God comes to you when you are innocent. When you are cunning the door is closed. Never destroy anybody's innocence, never create doubts in somebody who is innocent, because innocence is the royal power. Never create doubt in anybody, because once trust is destroyed and innocence is broken, then it is very, very difficult – it is just like a broken mirror.

This is the problem for a master: you are all like broken mirrors, because

somewhere on the path of life your trust has been destroyed. You cannot believe, you have been raised to doubt; you have a very cultivated, sophisticated doubting mind. This is the problem. Nothing can happen to you – not God, no! – unless a trust is created again. You are like a broken mirror, and you insist on being a broken mirror. You think that to doubt is some great thing that you have – that is your poverty.

A child's heart is the royal power. With innocence the power comes to you. And when I say trust, and when all the masters of the world say trust, they mean: Become innocent. But you insist that you will doubt and you will argue and you will first rationalize. You insist that you should be convinced first about something, then you will take a step – and that is the very problem, precisely that is the problem. If you can take one step in darkness, trusting, everything becomes possible. But you cannot take that one step. And look: what have you achieved through doubting, where have you reached with this broken mirror? You have become addicted to it because it has remained with you so long.

Mulla Nasruddin was teaching his son the ways of the world – a small child, a beautiful child – and he told him to go up a ladder. The child followed. He always liked to climb, and he was surprised because Mulla was always saying, "Don't climb the tree, don't climb the ladder," so why...? But he was very happy. He climbed, he reached the top, and then Mulla said, "Now jump." The child hesitated a little, but the Mulla said, "I am your father, why are you worried? Jump!"

The child jumped...and Mulla moved away. The child fell down on the ground, started crying and weeping, and he said, "What have you done to me?"

Mulla said, "Now remember: don't believe anybody, not even your father. This is the way of the world, and I am making you ready. Don't believe anybody, not even if he is your father. You have learnt a good lesson: Don't trust!"

This is how every father, mother, teacher, schools, universities, are preparing you. Don't trust anybody because somebody may be dishonest; he may be a fraud, he may deceive you. But this is the problem: even if the whole world deceives you, you will not lose anything. But if you doubt, you will lose everything. Doubt is the real deceiver, because ultimately you will miss God. God comes through the door of innocence. Can you trust anything in your life? If you search you will find nobody, nothing you can trust.

It happened: A man came to a very great mystic, Nagarjuna. Nagarjuna said, "You love somebody, you trust somebody?"

The man said, "I don't trust anybody and I don't love – except my cow."

Nagarjuna said, "That will do. Believe completely that your cow is God – love her, trust her, feed her, care about her, and after three months you come to me."

But the man said, "How can it happen – just loving the cow and trusting the cow?"

Nagarjuna said, "Don't you worry. After three months you come to me."

The man came back completely transformed. He said, "What miracle have you done? I cannot yet believe it, and it has happened: just trusting the cow and loving and caring, I have experienced something which has made me a completely different man. I am reborn! But how could it happen – just trusting a cow?"

Nagarjuna said, "It is not a question of trusting a cow, it is a question of *trusting*." If you can trust even a small thing, from that the door widens. And when you have tasted trust, you become more capable of trust. When you taste more, you become more and more capable, and then you can take the ultimate jump.

*Time is a child*
*moving counters in a game;*
*the royal power is a child's.*

And about time, also, Heraclitus has no mathematical theory. About time, also, he says that it is just like a child moving counters in a game: the day and night, they move. Heraclitus does not believe that time is going somewhere. It is moving, it is moving in a circle. It is not linear, it is like a wheel. And this is something to be understood: all the scientists think that time is linear, that it is moving in a line; and all the knowers of the inner say it is a wheel – it is not linear, it is circular. There seems to be some reason for it. Scientists cannot see the whole, they see just a part. The scientific mind is a specific mind, specialized. The scientist can see only a part, and he also divides the part to see an even smaller part. He goes on dividing – the scientist cannot see the whole. The very discipline of science makes him capable of seeing the part more clearly. He goes on seeing more and more clearly, but less and less. His vision becomes clear and penetrating, but his object becomes smaller and smaller. He comes to the atom, the smallest; and in time also he comes to the moment, the smallest.

If you see a small sector of a circle it will look like a line, but the circle is vast – just like on the earth. We are sitting here, and if we draw a line and you think it is a straight line then you are wrong – because on a circular earth, how can you draw a straight line? If you go on drawing that line, continue it, it will become a circle, it will encompass the whole earth. So all straight lines are just parts, fragments of a vast, big circle.

Science cannot see the whole, that is why time seems to be linear. Religion sees the whole – science misses the forest, it looks at the tree; religion misses the tree, looks at the forest. And when you look at the whole, everything is circular. All movement is circular, and time is also a circular movement. It is a game, not going anywhere, moving. If you can see that time is not going anywhere, but moving in a circle, then the whole tension of the mind to reach somewhere drops. Then to reach somewhere in the future becomes useless, meaningless – then you start enjoying the moment.

Life is not an effort to attain, it is a celebration.

*Bigotry is the sacred disease.*

But even this you should not make into a theory, because the moment you make a theory and you say, "This is right," you will start converting people. The moment you say, "This is right," your ego has taken it. Now it is not a question of this being right – you are right. How can you be wrong? – then the sacred disease enters. With me also, remember this: whatsoever I say, don't make it a claim. Whatsoever I say, don't make it a belief, don't become closed by it. And whatsoever I say, the opposite of it is also true, remember – because if you say the opposite is wrong, you will become bigoted. Then, bigotry enters.

If I say God is winter, God is summer also. And there are moments when I say God is winter because that will be helpful. There are moments when I say God is summer because that will be helpful. And to some I say God is winter, and to some I say God is summer – don't create a theory around it. I am also a poet. You need not believe in what I say, you simply have to be something that I say. Let it become a transformation, not a theory in you. Don't make a sect out of it; make a life out of it, *live* it! And if you live it, you will help others also to live it.

Only through living do you help; not through talking, not through converting, not through going around and making people more enlightened, no! This is a very subtle mischief. Be enlightened and you will have a light within you and people will come and drink out of it; there is no need to go out of the way. And if somebody is following his own way, don't try to pull him out of it. Who knows? – that way may be exactly right for him. It may look wrong to you, but who are you to decide? Don't decide and don't judge, because bigotry is the sacred disease. Whenever a person becomes religious, this disease is possible. Whenever one becomes religious one becomes vulnerable to this disease, bigotry. It is very difficult to find a religious man and not bigoted.

It happened: I saw Mulla Nasruddin drinking in a bar and asked, "Nasruddin,

what are you doing? Just yesterday you told me that you have left all drinking and you have become an absolute teetotaller, so what are you doing?"

Nasruddin said, "Yes I am an absolute teetotaller – but not a bigoted one."

Whatsoever you are, remain flexible. Don't create a fixed frame around you, remain moving and flowing. Sometimes one has to go out of the discipline also. Life is bigger than your discipline and sometimes one has to go completely against one's own rules – because God is both summer and winter.

Don't be a victim of bigotry. Be religious, but don't be a Hindu, a Mohammedan, a Christian. Let the whole earth be your church, let the whole existence be your temple. And when the whole God is available, why be satisfied with a fragment? Why say Christian, why say Hindu? When you can be a human being, why choose labels? Drop all labels and drop all beliefs. Trust – and trust is totally different from beliefs. Trust life wheresoever it leads. Move with it, and help others to move on their own way. Do your thing and let others do theirs. Remain open.

If you can remain open, helping, caring, not forcing things on others, you will see that people have started drinking out of you, that people are being helped by you. Don't go directly to serve them, because service, compassion, love, care, are all indirect. Don't jump on them, don't force them towards heaven, because that violence has been the misery of the whole past. Because of that violence, Christians, Hindus, Mohammedans have been fighting, killing each other. Enough of it, no need of it now!

Now the earth has become one. The whole globe has become just like a small village. Let humanity also become one – one in the search, not in the beliefs...one, because everything is divine.

Always remember Heraclitus:

*Here, too, are the gods.*
*I have searched myself.*
*The royal power is a child's.*
*Bigotry is the sacred disease.*

# *Chapter* 7

A DRUNKEN MAN HAS TO BE LED BY A YOUNG BOY,
WHOM HE FOLLOWS STUMBLING
AND NOT KNOWING WHITHER HE GOES,
FOR HIS SOUL IS MOIST.

SOULS TAKE PLEASURE IN BECOMING MOIST.

A DRY SOUL IS WISEST AND BEST.

# A DRY SOUL IS WISEST AND BEST

JUST AS I SAID YESTERDAY, human consciousness can follow two ways. One way is that of water, flowing downwards; the other way is that of fire, moving upwards. These are symbols, water and fire, but very meaningful.

When you flow downwards you become more and more unconscious. When you flow upwards you become more and more conscious. Upwardness is consciousness; downwardness is unconsciousness.

Heraclitus calls the downward flow of consciousness the state of moisture, and the upward rise of consciousness the state of dryness. Moisture and dryness depend on fire and water. And he says the spirit, the human mind, takes pleasure in being moist.

All pleasure is downward. Wherever you are seeking pleasure, you will go downwards, because pleasure means being unconscious. Pleasure means being in a certain state where you don't know any anxiety – not that the anxieties have disappeared, but you are unconscious. The world remains the same; the anxieties are there waiting for you, increasing, not decreasing, because as time moves they will increase. Your problems remain the same, even become more complicated. While you are unconscious, everything is growing: it doesn't wait for your consciousness to be there. Your misery is growing, your anguish is growing, waiting for you. You are unconscious so you are not aware. Whenever you come to consciousness again, you will have to face all the problems you had escaped.

Pleasure is escape. That's why pleasure is not worth it. In fact it is not pleasure, it is a sort of suicide. You escape from the problems, you put your back to the problems, but this is no way to solve them. You will have to come back, because once you have become conscious, unconsciousness cannot be a permanent state of affairs. You can have a dive into unconsciousness, but how long can you remain underwater? For a second – and then you are back again to the surface. You cannot remain unconscious for long. Alcohol or drugs or sex or anything in which you become unconscious, in which you lose for a moment all your worries, forget about them – it is a forgetfulness, but forgetfulness cannot be a permanent state.

So this is not helping in any way, pleasure doesn't help. You have to come back again and again – and then it becomes a vicious circle. When you come back and you find the anguish is waiting, the anxiety, all the problems – rather, they have increased – you become afraid, you become nervous. Your whole being trembles and becomes fear; then you have to escape again and again. The more you escape, the more problems increase. The more problems you face, the more alcohol is needed. And then the quantity of the intoxicant has to be increased continuously because you become attuned to it. You take a certain quantity of a drug: the first day you feel unconscious. After a few days you are not unconscious; you are still conscious, worries are still there knocking at the door, you can hear – you need a greater quantity. The greater quantity will also become less. You can move to a point.... In India they have tried; there are a few sects which have been working through alcohol, drugs, things like marijuana, mescaline. In the West it is a new phenomenon; that's why the West is so worried about it. In the East it is one of the oldest things.

A particular sect of Tantrikas have been working through drugs, finding a way to attain consciousness through drugs, and they have found that, by and by, you become so attuned that nothing can make you unconscious. Then they have poisonous snakes – just a bite and an ordinary men will die. When no drug affects them, then they take the snake to their tongue so the tongue is bitten by the snake. Ordinarily a man will die immediately. They do it just to seek unconsciousness through the most poisonous thing – but even that doesn't affect them. A time comes when the man is completely beyond the world of drugs; you cannot make him unconscious, nothing helps. And this man, if he bites you, you will die immediately. His whole body is poisonous.

In old, ancient Indian history, there is reference to a particular detective woman. Every king had beautiful girls to be trained from their very childhood in such a way that their whole body became poisonous. They were known as *vishkanya*, as poisonous girls – very beautiful. And then the king could send those girls to the enemies, to the enemy king, and they were so beautiful that he was bound to be attracted. Once they kissed the king, the king was dead. They were absolutely poisonous. Even their kiss was enough – no need to bite.

A moment comes when no drug helps. These Tantrikas have been working through drugs towards awareness. When no drug affects you, you are already integrated, and now you can move towards the height without any fear of falling – because you cannot be made unconscious, you have crystallized your consciousness. But ordinarily one is not working through drugs for consciousness, and the path is very dangerous. Ordinarily one is seeking unconsciousness, a little forgetfulness in this world of worries, anguish, anxiety, this world which looks like a hell. One wants to forget. All your pleasures are just forgetfulness.

Heraclitus says this is a moist state of consciousness. The word is beautiful – he calls these souls, moist souls. And he says souls enjoy pleasure. Why? – because pleasure is a downward drift. No effort is needed: you don't have to do anything, you simply sink downwards. It is down the hill; you can run easily. No effort is needed, the very pull of gravity helps you come down. Moving upwards is difficult; that's why you seek pleasure, you never seek bliss.

Bliss is upward, pleasure is downward.

Pleasure is forgetfulness, bliss is remembrance.

Gurdjieff says that the only technique to become integrated is selfremembrance, and all the masters of the world have been insisting on being more and more conscious. The more conscious you become, the more a certain dryness happens inside. Literally, you become more and more dry, more and more aware, more and more conscious and alert. Because awareness is fire, that's why you become more and more dry.

Listen to these words and try to understand them. They will be a great help on the path you are following.

*A drunken man has to be led by a young boy,*
*whom he follows stumbling*
*and not knowing whither he goes,*
*for his soul is moist.*

Imagine the picture, visualize it:

*A drunken man has to be led by a young boy,*

*whom he follows stumbling*
*and not knowing whither he goes,*
*for his soul is moist.*

This is very symbolic. When you are drunk, you fall back, you regress, you become again a small boy – but this regression is not growth. You have to become like a small boy, not by regressing but by growing ahead, growing forward, growing upward. You have to become like a boy, not by falling back, but by going forward. Falling back you will become juvenile; falling back you will not gain, you will lose; falling back, the whole system inside becomes crippled. Then on the outside you look like an adult, and in the inside you are just like a small boy; not a child, but childish; not innocent, but very, very cunning. And the cunningness is so deep that you are not cunning with others – you are playing tricks with yourself, with your own consciousness, with your own future; with your own possibilities you are playing cunning tricks. You are falling back, regressing.

You carry all the stages that you have passed. Once you were in the womb. A part of you still remains of that state because you cannot throw off things. You simply grow, and all that has become past becomes your foundation. In you everything exists, not only from this life, but from other lives; not only from human lives, but from animal, vegetable lives. Everything exists, nothing is lost. You carry everything of the past – you are your past. The whole past is there and you can regress – any moment. It is just like a ladder: you can go back. And when you are drunk you go back. You will become not only like a child, you can also become like a vegetable. Just see a drunkard lying down in the gutter on the road: he does not look human at all. He has regressed, he is vegetating; you cannot even say that he is alive. How can you say this man is human? What humanity is he showing right now? What is the difference between him and a tree? The only difference is that the tree is in a better state, because at least the tree is not drunk. And this man has fallen back, he has become like a tree.

You can be so drugged.... In the West they use the word stoned. It is very good – you become like a stone. That is the last thing. You are not even a vegetable. You are rocklike, all the possibilities lost. You have come to the last step of the ladder, to the very bottom. Millions of years you have regressed – and that can be done in seconds. And then you become helpless, helpless in a negative way, an imbecile. You behave like an idiot, you don't know what you are doing. You are not, in fact; you are absent, your presence is lost. Inside now, no center exists.

This is the state of moisture: no center. You have become water, no center, and the water is overflowing everywhere – without any direction, without any inner integrity. If in this moment you die, you will not even be aware that you are dead. Whatsoever happens in this moment, you will not know. You are not. This is an absent state of mind. You have fallen down completely, you have reached to the bottom.

This is easy – and souls enjoy it because anything that is easy you enjoy. No effort is needed. You do not have to follow a path, you do not have to do anything on your part. You need not worry, you need not think – you simply drop. In fact, this is what dropping out is. You have dropped out of the whole effort of evolution. You are no more part of a growing existence, you are no more part of the constantly evolving divinity. You have lost all. This state is the worst possible. And this happens not only through intoxicants, this happens through many things. So that, too, has to be remembered. You may not be taking any intoxicant, you may not be on drugs, but there are many subtle drugs – any "trip" can become a drug.

You may just be chanting a mantra continuously; not with awareness, just chanting it. If you chant a mantra continuously without awareness, it becomes alcoholic, it gives you unconsciousness. You will feel very much pleasure, but no bliss. You are falling back. In India, that too has been used for thousands of years, and thousands of people have been chanting mantras continuously. If you go and look at them, you will find them also stoned – through mantra they have become unconscious. Of course, they don't have any worries, because to have any worries you need awareness. They are happy, but their happiness is like death – stale, stony. Their happiness is not like a flower flowering; their happiness is a stagnant pool, not like a river flowing. They are not moving at all, the whole inner movement has ceased.

I talked to you about two types of movement: one vertical, the other horizontal. They have stopped the horizontal movement, but they have not started the vertical movement. They are simply as if dead, buried alive in their own bodies; their bodies have become graves. You can go and you will find many of them near Tibet, the Himalayas. You will find many people just sitting chanting. Continuous chanting has created such a boredom within them that they have become dull, they have lost all sensitivity. They are not more alive because of it, they are less alive. They can become so dull that they can lie down on a bed of nails – because they have no sensitivity in the body they have shrunken inside. And this is a deeper intoxicant than any alcohol ever invented – because they

are the masters of their own alcohol, they can create it inside.

Chanting a word continuously without awareness, you regress. If chanting is to be done, then with awareness it has to be done; you are to remain a witness. If you are chanting Aum, Aum, Aum, you have to remain a witness to it. The chanting should be done by the body and you should remain a witness. If the witness is lost, the chanting is alcoholic – it has become an intoxicant. And there are other ways. A politician is on a drug trip. Power, prestige – they are alcoholic. So whenever somebody reaches power, he is no longer in his senses. Power corrupts and corrupts absolutely – because power is a drug. When you are powerful you are no longer in your consciousness. Then you start doing things you would never have imagined. You cannot yourself believe that you can do such things.

Read Adolf Hitler and his life, what he did. And he never smoked, he was against alcohol – he was a perfect sannyasin! Early in the morning he would get up, early in the night he would go to sleep; no smoking, no drinking...vegetarian, not a meateater. And what he did! Such a perfect Jaina you cannot find anywhere, and what he did! But he was taking the greatest drug. That's why there was no need to smoke cigarettes – they are nothing. There was no need to drink, because he was already drunk with power.

Those who watched Adolf Hitler, they say when he started to talk, soon everybody there felt that there had come a transfiguration. When he would start he was Adolf Hitler; by and by, he would become completely unconscious, as if mesmerized by his own talking: his eyes no longer showing any aliveness, as if he was not there, as if somebody else had taken possession – possessed! And then his possession and his alcoholic state, his "moisture," would immediately infect others. He could create madness very easily. He was so neurotic, and such a charismatic neurotic, that whosoever would come around him would become neurotic; he was a magnetically neurotic man. His own alcohol was overflowing, and people would become intoxicated – that's how he led the whole German race towards suicide.

Power is a drug, the greatest drug the world has ever known. And this is beautiful: politicians are always against drugs, and they are the greatest drugtakers, on the greatest drug trip! But you can make your own private drugs also. Wealth: just look when a person is achieving riches – he is no more there, absent completely! He moves, he works hard, but he doesn't know what he is doing. He is completely unconscious. And then there are private drugs. You can become a painter, you can become a poet, and that can become your trip. Anything in which you forget yourself, anything in which you lose consciousness, anything in which you become so identified – whatsoever you are doing – that the witnessing is lost, is a drug. And Heraclitus calls this the moist state. And:

*Souls take pleasure in becoming moist.*

No effort is needed, no strain, no facing of the reality. You simply hide. You hide, you escape, you close your eyes, just like an ostrich. And when you are with closed eyes, you cannot see anything – you are happy. This is all that you call happiness. But this happiness cannot last – it is momentary.

When you fall in love with a person, you feel very, very happy. This is a drug. This is a drug your body hormones create within you; it is a biological drug. Nature has to use it because nature cannot rely on you. Just think: if there is nothing like love, the world will cease – because sex is so ridiculous. If there is no love, then sex seems to be just ridiculous! Who will move into sex if there is no intoxicant around it?

Love is just like a bait. The real desire of nature is to reproduce. But you cannot be relied upon; if you don't fall in love, then you will not reproduce. You fall in love – nature is playing a trick. Nature is giving some drug, releasing some drug into your body. It has drug glands inside the body from where it releases the drug. It is a natural, biological, hormonal drug. That's why whenever someone is in love, see, he walks differently. He is no more here – absent completely, lives in the imagination and the desire and the dream, does not live in the reality. He has drugged himself unknowingly. And after a few days, when the love is gone – because no drug can last for ever – by the time the honeymoon is over, it is also over. Then you start facing reality. Then there is trouble because whatsoever you promised, you promised when you were not conscious. Now you have to fulfill promises given in a moist state, given in a state of unconsciousness. Now you have to fulfill those promises; now the burden grows. Every love affair, in the end, becomes ugly. Why? Every marriage comes to the rocks. Why? – because it is not a conscious phenomenon. If you love consciously then love can be eternal, because with consciousness everything is eternal. With unconsciousness everything is momentary.

If you can love consciously, not a victim of biological tricks, not a victim of nature, but a conscious love, then you don't fall in love, you rise in love. Then love itself becomes an integrating force, not a disintegration. Then love itself becomes an awareness. Then in relationship you become more and more aware. You care for the other, but you don't use the other. You care and share, but you

don't possess. You liberate the other, and through the other's liberation you liberate yourself. You become two partners in an ultimate journey. You help each other, because there are pitfalls; the path is long and the journey is eternal. And it is very good to be with someone who can share every anguish, who can share every pain, who can share every suffering, who can share every bliss, who can share every moment of silence; with whom you can communicate, with whom you can say what is happening to you, and on whom you can rely that he will be helpful whatsoever happens to you, on whom you can rely that he will love you in whatsoever situation you are – good or bad, angry or happy, sad or blissful. You need not hide anything with someone you love: you can remain open and vulnerable. And whatsoever the situation, the love is unconditional; it doesn't depend on conditions.

A conscious love is a totally different phenomenon. Rarely it happens, but whenever it happens it is one of the most beautiful things that is possible in this world.

But ordinarily your love is just a drug. I observe it every day: a couple comes and they say they are deeply in love, and just a week has not passed and they come again – they say everything is falling apart. Just a week! And just a week before you could not have imagined – their eyes, their faces were radiant with love, their bodies were filled with something unknown, they were intoxicated. And just a week and everything is finished! What type of love is this? It is not love at all. You have been doped by nature; nature played a trick.

Nature wants you to move into sex. It creates the dreamworld around sex, because sex in itself is ugly. It is really ridiculous! Just think: without love, you are in a sexual relationship with someone. It is simply ugly. That's why prostitutes are ugly. Howsoever beautiful the bodies they have, they cannot be beautiful because the very act, without love, makes their whole life ugly, dirty. You can tolerate sex only because of love. Because of love, the sex also looks beautiful; otherwise, the postures, the gestures of sex, are all ridiculous. But when you are drugged you are not aware of what is happening. When you are drugged you never look at yourself. The whole world looks ridiculous, not you.

It happened: Mulla Nasruddin was psychoanalyzed. And when he was brought to the psychoanalyst, the psychoanalyst asked a few questions: just a test to know what type of person this Nasruddin is. He drew a line and asked Nasruddin, "What does it remind you of?"

Nasruddin said, "Of course, a beautiful woman!" – a line! The psychiatrist was a little puzzled.

Then he drew a circle and asked, "What does *this* remind you of?"

Nasruddin said, "Of course, a beautiful woman – in the nude."

Then he drew a triangle and Nasruddin closed his eyes and said, "No, no, no, don't do this!"

The psychoanalyst said, "But what does it remind you of?"

He said, "This woman is doing something very nasty."

So the psychoanalyst said, "You seem to be very much preoccupied with sex."

Nasruddin: "What! *Me?* I am preoccupied with sex – or you? Who is drawing these nasty figures on the paper? – you or me?" You can see the whole world – but you cannot see yourself. This is the state of moisture: when one is completely unaware, oblivious of who he is, what he is doing, why he is doing it.

When you start meditating you become very, very confused in the beginning, because for the first time you become aware: What are you doing? Why are you doing it? For what? You were not aware before. You feel very much confused because for the first time the eyes are opening towards reality. And then, if you don't escape, by and by you feel that you are cracking – not only confused, you are going mad! You have always been mad but you were not aware. Now you are becoming aware and the madness has to be faced. And if you don't face it, you cannot grow. Escape is not growth, and all dimensions of intoxicants are escapes. And when you are in an unconscious state you may believe that you are doing something meaningful, but that is a sheer belief, ungrounded. When you become conscious, only then do you come to know that you have simply been doing nonsense. It has not led anywhere. And whatsoever you believed was just befooling yourself.

I have heard that Mulla Nasruddin knocked at the door of the tavern in the early morning, three o'clock. The owner of the tavern looked from an upstairs window, very angry of course, and he said, "Go away, whosoever you are! This is not the time, and you cannot get any drink."

Nasruddin said, "Who has come to get drink? I am here to take my crutches. At closing time I forgot them, and as you know, and the whole world knows, I cannot walk without my crutches. And now I have to go back to my home so give my crutches back!" He has always been walking on crutches, not knowing that he can walk without crutches – believing in them. Unconscious, he left the crutches in the tavern, and he had been wandering around the town the whole night. And now, when he is coming back to consciousness, he asks for his crutches back because he says, "The whole world knows that I cannot walk without the crutches."

Your beliefs are your crutches. You cannot walk without them, you cannot live without them. You cannot think how you will be without your beliefs – they are your crutches. When you become aware, you simply cannot think that you existed in such a state of affairs for so long.

But in a moist state of mind, things happen. You are not in control of anything. They just go on happening, and you go on reacting. A woman laughs at you, and you are in love. You start talking to her and appreciating her, and because you appreciate, she starts falling in love with you. Now the hormones have started functioning. Now you are on the drug trip. Soon you will become aware and you will have to come out of it. And when you come out of it again, it is painful. And you cannot tolerate the pain, it is too much, intolerable. Sooner or later, just to console yourself, to intoxicate yourself again, you will find another woman. And the same circle goes on being repeated…and a man who is drugged can believe anything.

I once asked Mulla Nasruddin, "Is your new relationship with the banker's daughter growing?" – because I know the banker and I know the daughter, and it seems to be a difficult thing, almost impossible. But Nasruddin beamed very happily.

He said, "Yes, recently there are signs, hints, indications. Things are falling in line."

So I asked, "What has happened? Has she started smiling at you or something?"

He said, "No, not exactly that – but last night she said, 'This is for the last time I am saying no to you!' " When one is drugged, one has his own interpretations. "The last time I am saying no to you!" When you are not in your consciousness you don't know what yes means, what no means. You don't know anything, you simply drift. This drifting state is the state of moisture.

*A drunken man has to be led by a young boy,*
*whom he follows stumbling*
*and not knowing whither he goes,*
*for his soul is moist.*

*Souls take pleasure in becoming moist.*

You all take pleasure in becoming moist because that is the easiest thing to do. That's the only pleasure in it – the easiest. You need not do anything, you simply leave yourself and you drift. You fall towards the earth and the gravitation pulls you down. And you feel very, very happy, because no strain, no effort – nothing!

People come to me: they say they cannot get up early in the morning for the meditation. Even that much effort is too much for you. And if you cannot get up early in the morning to meditate, what else can you do? What else do you think you can do? You don't want to make any effort – but your demands are very high. Even a man who cannot get up early in the morning to meditate asks how peace of mind is possible, asks, "How will I come to know God?" – asks, "Help me! I don't want to come again to this world" – but nobody comes to this world. If you live in a drifting way, if you live always falling downwards – choosing the easiest, choosing the path of least resistance, choosing the path of no challenge, no struggle, nothing, just falling, living on the gravitation – then you need not make any effort to come. There is no need to come, you *will* be coming, because this is how one comes into this world: a moist state of mind will always revolve around this world. Only a dry soul can fly towards the sky because on a dry soul there is no effect of gravitation; the downward pull doesn't exist for a dry soul. Then what is the meaning of being dry?

The meaning of being dry is: Keep alert. Whatsoever you do, do it knowingfully – whatsoever! I don't say, "Don't do this and don't do that." Simply be more alert whatsoever you do, and then, by and by, every act helps you to become more and more dry. Then a detachedness comes to you. With alertness you automatically become detached.

You love a person, but still it is not an attachment. You love a person, you care, you share your being, you give everything, but still it is not an attachment – it is very, very detached. And when there is a detached love, there is nothing like that – it is the most beautiful flowering. Love and detached: it means it comprehends both the polarities. It is paradoxical – because you can be detached without love, or you can be in love without detachment. That's easy, to choose one extreme, one polarity. To choose both the polarities together – detached and in love – what does it mean? It means you are alert. Doing whatsoever needs to be done, but remaining alert, you are detached. Then you can live in this world without being a part of this world. Then you can be in the world and the world will not be in you.

This dryness comes as more and more you close the ways of falling asleep, you close the doors of falling downwards, you close the doors of pleasures – you don't seek pleasures. Remember, happiness is not pleasure. Happiness is a different phenomenon – it is a state of being.

Pleasure is a forgetfulness, happiness is a remembrance.

And when remembrance becomes absolute, when remembrance is so absolute

that there is no possibility of falling down from it, then arises bliss. Between bliss and pleasure is happiness.

Don't ask for pleasures, because if you ask for pleasures you will become a victim of the downward drift, the gravitation. Look at a person who is too addicted to food; when he eats, just watch him. You will see that he is completely unconscious – because how many times, millions of times, has he decided not to eat too much? And again, when the food comes, he forgets or he rationalizes: "This time, once only this time again…next time I am going to follow…."

Mulla Nasruddin was dieting, and the doctor had said, "Now, it is the last time. If you don't listen to me you can be certain that you will have to leave the body. You are going to die, because so much of a burden your heart cannot carry any more" – he had had two heart attacks already.

And just the next day he was eating, eating as much as four men would find even more than enough. Then he suddenly looked at his wife and said, "What are you doing, sitting there? You don't even have that much will to stop me from going off my diet." The wife! – even for that the wife is responsible: she doesn't have that much willpower to stop him.

Nobody can stop you. Nobody's will will be of any help to you. Rather, on the contrary, it can be destructive. Somebody stops you too much; then you start going against it, you react. The upward flow cannot be forced by anybody. And this is a very subtle and delicate phenomenon to be understood: if people try too much to make you good, make efforts all around you, they will force you downwards because your ego will feel a resistance. This is very delicate, because those who want to help you towards the height cannot force you, they can only persuade you. This is all that I am doing. Even sometimes I see that this can be stopped, but I cannot stop it. I see that you are taking a step downwards and I can talk to you, I can make you aware. I can say, "Stop and this will do much," but that cannot be said because if I say too much, then *I* will help you to go downwards. You will take the step even sooner – because your ego will come in. I can only persuade you. I can divert your mind. I can give you a plaything to play with so that you forget that you were going to take a step there – your mind is diverted. But I cannot say, "No, don't take that step." If I say, "No," it is almost certain that you will take that step.

This is the problem. A master has to persuade you. And this has become more and more difficult in the modern world. In the old days it was easier because people were taught to be obedient, now they are taught to be rebellious. In the old days people were taught to be disciplined, now they are taught to be undisciplined. Now to be undisciplined is something very meaningful; now to be disciplined is just to be part of the establishment. To be disciplined is to be square, to be undisciplined is to be a revolutionary.

In the old days it was simple because the master could have said, "No," and he could have relied on it that the no would do. A simple no can save you many lives of unnecessary struggle. But now it is impossible, now it is difficult. You have to be persuaded in such an indirect way that you never feel that you are being persuaded. You have to be diverted in such a subtle way that you don't become aware that you are being led somewhere. Even if you become aware that somebody is guiding you, you resist – and then you will do just the opposite. This creates a very new phenomenon in the world, this is something new in the modern age. That's why to achieve the ultimate has become more and more difficult – unnecessary wastage of energy. I can see, I am seeing, that you are taking a step in the dark, that you will fall down, you will be crippled, but even then I cannot say, "Don't take that step," because you won't listen. And if I say no you will feel more attracted towards it.

That's how Adam fell. God said, "No, don't eat the fruit of this tree!" – and then he had to. He fell because God said no. Now, if God creates another garden of Eden, he is not going to commit that mistake again. Rather, on the contrary, it will be good to say, "Only eat the fruit of this tree, and all other trees are prohibited." Then Adam will not be tempted, then he will not go towards that tree. Particularly the modern Adam is in an absolutely chaotic state of consciousness – much too moist, falling like a dead weight, continuously falling towards the valley, the downward flow. Of course, pulling upwards will need effort.

*Souls take pleasure in becoming moist.*
*A dry soul is wisest and best.*

The whole of wisdom consists in becoming a dry soul. But try to understand: dry doesn't mean that you become insensitive; dry doesn't mean that you become uncaring; dry doesn't mean that you become aloof, indifferent – no. Dry simply means that you become aware. You care, you have a deep concern, but this concern never becomes an anxiety. You care. As much as you can do you do for others – for your wife, friend, daughter, son, your husband, father, mother – whatsoever you can do you do totally. That's all. Then whatsoever happens, you accept it. There is no frustration. You do everything that is possible, then what is the frustration? Then there is no frustration. Then you don't feel worried that you should have done this or that. No, you have done everything – then it is

finished! You come clean out of every relationship, not dirty.

But ordinarily, if the soul is moist, after every relationship you come out dirty. The relationship doesn't cleanse you, it makes you dirty. It is not really the relationship that makes you dirty, it is your moisture. It is just like when your clothes are wet and you go for a walk – when you come back you will be very, very dirty because the dirt will cling; not because the road was dirty but because your clothes were wet. And the same happens inside also: if your soul is moist, whatsoever you do you come out of it dirty – because all dirt clings to it. If you are dry then nothing clings to it. The dust is blowing there but it cannot cling to you. Buddha lives in the same world as you live in, but you feel every day you are becoming dirty. Buddha remains fresh, as if he has taken a bath just now, clean. The cleanliness depends on dryness, and dryness comes the more you become aware.

When you are aware, you become like a flame inside. The flame goes on burning; even when you are asleep, the flame burns. Ordinarily, even when you are awake, you are sleepwalkers. But when the flame is burning and you are alert, alert to every moment, alert to the whole of what is happening all around, alert – not in a concentrative way, because if you concentrate then you become alert to one point and you become unconscious of the whole thing – just alert, an opening, all doors open, all dimensions open, you are simply alert, then also when you sleep these doors remain open and the fresh air goes on flowing. Deep down a flame burns in you and that flame dries all moisture, all unconsciousness.

This is the meaning of being enlightened. It is not achieving some god – there is none – somebody waiting for you. Rather, it is becoming a god oneself, because when you are aware, you are a god; when you are perfectly aware, you are a perfect god.

God is the absolutely dry state of being.

And if you become even a little dry – *A dry soul is wisest and best* – then you start becoming wiser, because all foolishness consists in being unconscious.

There was one case against Mulla Nasruddin in the court, and the magistrate said, "What? You have come again? But I was not expecting you this time. First you came for wrong parking, then you came for fast driving, then you came because your brakes were faulty, then you came because your lights were not working in the night, then you came for drunken driving. Now for what have you come? – because last time I canceled, revoked your driving license!"

Nasruddin looked shamefacedly at the ground and then said, "Jaywalking, your honor."

A car is not needed. If all is taken from you so that then you think, "Because of this I am unconscious," that won't help – then you will be found jaywalking. You will do something else because you will remain the same. People think that because of their wives they are entangled in the world. They leave their wives and escape to the Himalayas – but this is just revoking the license. It won't help because you cannot escape from yourself. You will remain the same in the Himalayas and you will create the same situation again. The wife was there because of you. You will find another wife, you will find something else, and the same problem will arise. A dry soul is needed – that is the Himalaya: the dryness, the alertness.

Whatsoever you do, make it a point not to do it in a sleepy way. Watch every act, every thought, every feeling. Watch and move. Every moment is very precious – don't waste it in sleepiness. And if you use every moment as an opportunity to become more conscious, the consciousness grows by and by. One day, suddenly you find that the light is burning inside. If you work hard towards it, one day suddenly in the morning you rise completely a new man – dry, unattached; loving, but not in any way involved; remaining in the world and yet a watcher on the hills. This is the paradox that has to be fulfilled: remaining in the world and yet watching from the hills; at the same time, simultaneously, being in the world and not being in it. And this is the wisest and the best soul. You have the potentiality. Just as every seed can become a tree, you can become a Buddha, a Heraclitus, a Jesus. But you have to work hard for it. Lukewarm efforts won't do. You have to boil completely: one hundred degrees' heat and then evaporation happens.

Water is moist, flows downwards. Heat is dry – with heat even water flows upwards. With the flame of awareness even all that you have been thinking is wrong will become right. Love seems to be an entanglement, an imprisonment; with awareness that becomes a liberty, a freedom. Anger without consciousness is a destructive force, a suicidal force; it hurts you, it kills you by and by, it is a poison. With awareness the same energy is transfigured, becomes compassion. The same radiance comes to your face, but not in anger – in compassion. The same blood flows, the same chemistry of the body, but a new foreign element has entered into it, and the whole chemistry changes.

That is how baser metals are transformed into gold. With unconsciousness you are a base metal, with consciousness you will become gold, you are transformed. Just the fire of awareness is needed. You lack nothing else, everything is there. With the fire of awareness a new arrangement happens. You lack nothing,

remember; you have everything that a buddha needs. Just one thing is missing – and that, too, is fast asleep within you. You just have to awaken it; just a few efforts to awaken, a few efforts to become more alert.

And remember, efforts will be needed right now. Heraclitus believes in effort. Zen masters believe in no effort, Heraclitus believes in effort – but no effort is also an effort deep down because you have to attain the state of no effort.

In the West very much misunderstanding exists about Zen masters because they talk of no effort. But you see, twenty years a man has to be with the Zen master working hard to achieve no effort. With Heraclitus effort is the base, and if you make real effort, automatically the no-effort follows. When you have done all, you become skilled in it. You become so skilled that there is no need to do it – it happens then. If you try towards awareness, by and by there simply is no need to do anything about it – it is there, it is just like breathing. But as you are, Heraclitus will be more helpful than Zen masters. Zen masters came at the culmination of a school, the Buddhist school. One thousand years of hard effort and then Zen masters flowered. Zen masters are just at the end of a long effort, of a long journey. The plant is absolutely ready, then the plant flowers. There is no effort in flowering. What do you do? Nothing is needed – the tree is ready and it flowers by itself. But to make the tree ready long effort is needed. Ask the gardener how much he has been working. You just look at the flower and then you think: "No effort is needed. They come by themselves."

Zen is the culmination of a long effort that started with Buddha. Heraclitus is just the beginning. And this is a misfortune: the Greek mind completely missed Heraclitus, couldn't understand him, and there has never been a culmination – the flowering never happened. The Greek mind follows a totally different path. It never listened to Heraclitus and the flowering never happened. The seeds were lost, they never sprouted. But that's also why I have chosen Heraclitus – that will make the whole complete. I have been talking about Zen masters; that can mislead you because that is the end. I must talk about Heraclitus so that you can understand the beginning also, because in you, also, there has to be a growth from the beginning to the end. From Heraclitus to Basho you have to move, from the seed to the flower.

Become a dry soul – without becoming insensitive. If you become insensitive, you miss. Then you are simply dry without any awareness. Then the fire is not converted into awareness; then the fire has simply dried you. That won't help. Life dries many people that way automatically. Look at old people – they are dried. Look at a child – a child is moist. An old man is dried. Just the life dries all moisture out of him; just the struggle of life and he becomes insensitive; just to protect himself he becomes insulated – that is not the point. You have to be like a child – alive, elegant, graceful, agile – and yet dry like an old man.

This is what is said about Lao Tzu, a beautiful story, that Lao Tzu was born already an old man. When he was born, he was eighty-two years old; he lived in his mother's womb for eighty-two years. This is a beautiful phenomenon! It is said that he was born with gray hair – eighty-two years old, of course! A child and yet not a child...very, very old, completely dry. From his very childhood he was aware. That is the meaning – that he was perfectly aware from the very beginning.

About Buddha it is said that when he was born, the first thing he did was to walk seven steps. The first thing! – must have been very old. The first thing, just out of the womb. He was born standing and then he walked seven steps...with perfect awareness. The mother could not believe this. The whole phenomenon was so absurd that it is said she died simply out of shock. Then a story is told that whenever a buddha is born to a mother, the mother dies. It is too much, it is unbelievable; you cannot comprehend!

But these stories show something. They are not literal truths – they are symbolic, metaphorical. In the East, never ask for history. These people in the East never believed in history. They believe in myth and they say history is useless. What is history? Just a compilation of newspapers, rubbish; old newspapers, that's all. They never believed in history, they believed in myth. They say myth is the essence; history is just on the periphery, events. Myth is the very essence of all that exists at the center.

Be like a child and be like an old man – dry, all desires known, finished; all experiences known, finished; moved all over the world, reached to yourself, at home at last – sensitive like a child and dry like an old man. And this is all that wisdom is all about. This is how one becomes wise.

# *Chapter* 8

ALTHOUGH THIS LOGOS IS ETERNALLY VALID,
YET MEN ARE UNABLE TO UNDERSTAND IT –
NOT ONLY BEFORE HEARING IT,
BUT EVEN AFTER THEY HAVE HEARD IT.

WE SHOULD LET OURSELVES BE GUIDED
BY WHAT IS COMMON TO ALL.

YET, ALTHOUGH THE LOGOS IS COMMON TO ALL,
MOST MEN LIVE AS IF EACH OF THEM
HAD A PRIVATE INTELLIGENCE OF HIS OWN.

HUMAN NATURE HAS NO REAL UNDERSTANDING;
ONLY THE DIVINE NATURE HAS IT.

MAN IS NOT RATIONAL;
ONLY WHAT ENCOMPASSES HIM IS INTELLIGENT.

WHAT IS DIVINE ESCAPES MEN'S NOTICE
BECAUSE OF THEIR INCREDULITY.

ALTHOUGH INTIMATELY CONNECTED WITH THE LOGOS,
MEN KEEP SETTING THEMSELVES AGAINST IT.

HOW CAN ANYONE HIDE FROM THAT WHICH NEVER SETS?

# MAN IS NOT RATIONAL

HE LOGOS IS THE LOGIC of the whole, the logic of the existence itself. The logos is the ultimate law. It is the same as what Lao Tzu calls tao, what the Upanishads and Vedas have called the *rit:* the cosmic harmony where opposites meet and disappear, where two become one, where no polarity exists, where all paradoxes are dissolved, all contradictions disappear. What Shankara calls the brahma, Heraclitus calls the logos.

The human mind is logical, and human logic is based on the polarity. It is as if you are standing on one bank of the river and you cannot see the other bank, and whatsoever you think about the bank belongs only to this bank – but the river flows with two banks, it cannot flow with one. The other may be hiding in mist, it may be so far away that you cannot see it, but the other is there. And the other bank is not opposite to this bank, because deep down in the river they meet. They are one land and they both support the river like two hands, or like two wings. The river flows between them, the river is a harmony of the two. But you are standing on one bank; you cannot see the other, so you simply believe in this bank – and you create a system which is based on the knowledge of this bank. And when somebody talks about the other bank you think he is contradicting you, you think that he is bringing something irrational, mysterious. And the other is bound to be opposite because only the tension of the opposites can hold the river. But the oppositeness is not enmity, the oppositeness is a deep friendship; it is the peak of love.

This is the problem to be solved. If you can solve this you can understand

Heraclitus and you can understand all those who have become awakened, who have known the other shore. Whatsoever they say will be contradictory because they have to comprehend both. They have to comprehend winter and summer both, day and night both, life and death both, love and hate both, the peak and the valley both.

When someone talks about the peak, not referring at all to the valley, his statements will be very rational; you can understand them, they are easy, they are consistent. When someone talks about the valley, never referring to the peak, he will also be rational. All philosophers are rational; you can understand them very easily. To understand them you need a little learning and training, that's all, a discipline. But all the mystics are difficult to comprehend. In fact, the more you try to understand them, the more they become mysterious – because they talk about the peak and the valley together. They would like to talk about the valley and the peak simultaneously.

In the Upanishads it is said: "He is far and near." What type of statement is this? Either he is far or he is near. But immediately the seer says, "He is far," he adds, "He is near." He is the greatest and he is the smallest. He is the atom and he is the whole. He is within you and without. Heraclitus said God is summer and winter. Summer? – it is okay; you can understand. Only winter? – that too is okay, you can understand. But summer and winter both? Then you feel dizzy. Then the mind says, "This statement is contradictory."

Human logic seeks a noncontradictory statement – and the logos is contradictory. It uses contradiction just as an architect uses opposite bricks to make an arch; he puts bricks in opposition. The opposition gives the tension and the strength, and on that arch you can raise a big building. But if you do not put bricks in opposition to each other – logical, consistent, just like a peak or a valley, this bank or that, not both – then the building will fall; the arch cannot be made. It needs the tension of the opposites to create strength. Hence there is man and woman – they are the opposite bricks of life. Their very opposition creates the situation so that life can exist. They are the two banks so the river can flow. But the moment you talk about the peak and the valley together, then it becomes incomprehensible.

Human logic is consistent. The divine logos is contradictory yet consistent.

Human logic is partial. It tries to understand a part, and trying to understand a part it avoids all that contradicts it. It simply wants to forget all that is contradictory. But the divine is all. It doesn't choose, everything is involved. And it is vast; it is not partial, it is total. That's the difference between a religious approach and a philosophical approach. A philosophical approach is logical; that's why Aristotle says man is a rational being. And Heraclitus says man is irrational – because your very reason makes you irrational. The moment you choose the part you have falsified the whole thing. Now this part is only in your mind. In existence this part is always with the opposite, never alone.

Human logic says God is male; then there are some believers in God who think God is female – but the logos must comprehend both. So Hindus have a concept of *ardhanarishwar*, that God is both male and female. And that is the true concept, that comes from the logos. It looks contradictory. You must have seen statues of Shiva as half man and half woman, half with one breast, half feminine, and half male. That statue looks absurd but that is the truth. And all your statues of God as male, or God as female, are irrational; they are not true because how can God be male? Then from where does the feminine arise? Then to whom will the feminine reach? Then in what source does the feminine exist?

You talk about God as he; that is wrong. Then there are people who talk about God as she; that too is wrong. He is he plus she – but then the mind cannot understand. But mental understanding is not an understanding at all. You will be able to understand only when you try to understand from your own totality, not just from the mind, because inside you also these two opposite poles meet. You are also an ardhanarishwar; you are also he and she both. You are neither male nor female.

If you can understand your own totality, and if you bring your totality to the universe, to face the universe, you will be able to comprehend. That's a mystic vision. That is logos.

So what to do? Ordinarily you are trained to be a man or to be a woman. From the very beginning we teach children, "You are a boy – behave like a boy"; and to a girl, "You are a girl – behave like a girl." That creates the distinction more and more, and the poles are set apart.... In a better world we will teach each child, "You are both"; the difference is only of emphasis. "You are neither boy nor girl. You are both" – the difference is only of emphasis. Then the whole concept of civilization will be different. Then there will be no question of enmity between man and woman. Then there will be no problem about who dominates whom. And then you will be able to see your totality of being – and the totality is beautiful. The part is always ugly.

It is as if you have taken the tree and cut the roots. How long can the tree remain alive? You have taken the visible – the tree is visible and the roots are invisible – and you have cut the roots. And the tree goes upwards and the roots

go downwards – you have made a consistent thing. You say, "No! How can these two opposite dimensions exist simultaneously? The tree must go upwards, and if the roots go downwards then they are two separate things – cut them!" This is what has happened.

Man is a visible tree, woman is like roots. That's why all the old teachings say woman is earth and man is sky. But they are together: man is rooted in the woman, and woman is reaching higher and higher through the man – they are one. Hell and heaven are not two, just the same ladder.

Says Heraclitus: "The way up and the way down are the same." Then hell and heaven cannot be apart. This is logos: to see the whole ladder. Then God and the Devil are not two. But theologians will not agree because they will say that you are creating a confusion, that then people will be confused, then they will not know who is who. But people *are* confused, and they are confused because of the false logic of the partial human mind. In fact, everything is everything else.

It happened: In a local dogshow Mulla Nasruddin was awarding prizes, but he was very worried about a certain thing. He was worried about people's dress. So he said, "Look! What is happening in this world? Look at that man with cropped hair, pants and cigarettes, with two pups. Now I am at a loss as to how to decide whether that man is a man or a woman, a boy or a girl."

Just a bystander said, "She is a girl because she is my daughter."

Mulla Nasruddin said, "I am very, very sorry. Had I known that you were her mother, I would not have been so outspoken."

The woman said, "No, I am not her mother – I am her father."

Now a meeting of the sexes is happening. In dress, in ways of living, a meeting is happening. That is a very good sign. In dress people are becoming unisex – that's a very good sign! There is no need to make these distinctions. A nondistinct whole is the reality.

Distinctions are being made by the mind and it has created trouble, because you are both. But if you are fixed that you are a male, then what will you do with your woman inside? And the woman is there. Sometimes the woman wants to weep and cry, but you cannot weep and cry – you are a man and you have to behave like a man. You don't listen to nature; you listen to manmade theories that you are a man. But nature has made tear glands in the eyes: if nature intended that a man should never weep and cry, then there should have been no tear glands. If nature intended that a man should not feel, then there should not have been any heart. But a man feels as much as a woman. Then he suppresses his femininity; he goes on suppressing it – that creates an inner conflict. Rather than using the opposite polarities to flow, rather than using the two opposite polarities as a tension, which creates aliveness, you suppress the polarity, which deadens you, which kills your sensitivity; because a man, if he is not also a woman, is half, crippled, half his being is suppressed. And that suppressed being will take revenge. He will go mad sooner or later because a suppressed part will throw off the dominating part.

Politics is not only outside; politicians have created a politics within you. They have created a rift, they have made you to fight yourself. And then a woman is continuously suppressing the male part. It erupts. It comes up again and again because it is there! Rather than creating a harmony with these two opposite notes, you have been warring, you have been fighting, struggling. The situation would have been beautiful if you could have created a harmony; then a higher quality of being would have arisen within you.

Remember, all growth is dialectical.

This word dialectical has to be understood. It is against rational. Reason is a linear process, from one step to another step, but the plane remains the same: from A to B, but the plane remains the same. That's why reason is very, very boring. It has no qualities of the opposite; that's why it becomes boring.

You just watch: twenty persons are sitting, all male, and then suddenly a woman comes in – there is immediately a change of climate. Those twenty persons were feeling a little bored: all male, bound to feel bored – unless they are homosexuals. If they are healthy persons they are bound to feel bored. A woman enters and immediately the climate changes. You can see the change in the faces: they start smiling, they become more polite, they don't use ugly words, they behave. Just a woman entering and everything changes. A subtle phenomenon happens inside: the entry of the woman becomes a deeper entry inside of them, of their inner woman – they become whole. For a moment they are parts no more. Look at twenty women sitting, chattering, chattering, and a man comes in – immediately a difference happens.

If there is one, the same quality continues; it becomes a boring process. Dialectics means movement through the opposite. Thesis, antithesis, synthesis: that is dialectics. One thing against another, then here is a challenge, a tension, and through that tension and challenge a third reality arises: synthesis. And the synthesis is always better; it goes on a higher plane.

Reason moves horizontally, dialectics moves vertically.

If you have no enemy, and if your life is such that you are not opposed to

anything, you will lose all salt from your life. If you are not opposed to anything, you will be tasteless, you will be like a dead stone, not like a flower – because from the opposite comes movement, energy, challenge...then you grow. When a man meets a woman there is a dialectical process starting. That's why love is so very beautiful and love is such a great growth situation. To be related to the other is to be constantly in a challenging situation. To be related to oneself only is a boredom – no opposite – unless you can find the opposite in your own inner being; then one can move alone.

That is the meaning: when a man becomes total within he doesn't need a woman. When a woman becomes total within she doesn't need a man. A moment comes when a Buddha moves alone, a Mahavira moves alone – then there is no need. Not that woman is bad, but now they have found their inner feminine part, now the dialectics has entered their own being – there is no need to create it outside. Now, inside, there is a continuous thesis, antithesis, synthesis. Now they grow alone – but they also use the same dialectics.

The whole life is dialectical. Logos is dialectical – and reason is a process of the same. You can think of it in terms like this: dialectics is heterosexual; reason, rationality, is homosexual. Rationality is homosexual. That's why in the West homosexuality is growing, because the West has accepted Aristotle, reason. Heraclitus is heterosexual – he will include the opposite. If you listen to reason you will be homosexual. If you listen to reason then the whole quality that comes from the opposite, the tension, will be lost. And when it is lost life becomes a boredom. When it is lost life loses the zest, the enthusiasm, hope, possibilities. Everything is lost, because every possibility is opened by the opposite.

When for the first time you fall in love, you meet the opposite. Immediately, it is as if you have got wings, you can fly; poetry arises in your heart. What is happening? The opposite has created something in you. Silence alone is not very beautiful, sound alone is not very beautiful, but the meeting of sound and silence is very, very beautiful – that is music. The meeting of silence and sound is music.

Watch when somebody is playing a sitar or a piano, or playing on some instrument. What is happening? What is he doing? He is doing a dialectical process. He creates sound, and between two sounds he gives a valley, a silence. The greater the peak, the deeper will be the valley. He creates sound, he creates a peak, he moves higher and higher and higher, he brings a climax, and then suddenly...the gap, the silence. If you listen only to sound and miss the silence between two sounds, you don't have a musical ear. When you listen to both the sound and the silence, the peak and the valley together, then you come to encounter a new phenomenon: every peak creates the valley, every valley creates the peak. They both move like yin and yang, they move in a circle – and there is music, there is the hidden harmony.

Logos is dialectical, it is heterosexual. God creates the world because the other is needed – God alone cannot be, the world alone cannot be. And if you listen only to the world you will not come to know the inner music of the existence. And then, being fed up with the world, you can go and leave the world and only listen to God – then again you miss the harmony. When you listen to the world and when you listen to God, together, when the world becomes the opposite pole, when the world becomes one bank and God the other bank, then the river flows – then it flows tremendously, then it flows beautifully, then you hear the harmony.

And one who hears the harmony between this world and that God is a sannyasin.

One who leaves this world, he is moving to the other extreme. He is logical, rational, but not dialectical. That's why in the shops, in the markets, go and see people – just dull, because...only this world. Somehow they are working, pulling on, dragging, because they are there – so what to do? So they are doing something. But you cannot hear the music in them: the opposite is not there, the prayer is not there, the meditation is not there, the silence is not there. That's why the marketplace has become simply sound – it is a chaos.

Then go to the Himalayas and the monasteries and there also are people; the same shopkeepers who have left the world, they are sitting there. They, too, you will find, do not have any life; they will also be just dull, dirt collecting on them, dead. In the shops you will find dead people, and in the temples and monasteries also. They are the same people, just moved to the other extreme. Harmony is missing in the market and in the monastery.

A man who is harmonious is complex, his simplicity is very, very complex – because in his simplicity the opposite is involved. He has deep compassion, but he can be angry also. He is absolutely detached, but he can love also; he loves and remains detached. In him, valley and peak meet. In him, sound and silence meet. And if you have a musical ear and a heart, then you will see the harmony in such a person. And such a person is rare, because he himself has become a logos. Such are Krishna, Lao Tzu, Buddha, Heraclitus, Jesus: they live in the logos, they are miniature logoi. The working of their beings is the same as existence; in their beings the same existence mirrors. They don't reject anything, they use everything.

A man who rejects anything does not know what he is doing. And if a man rejects sound he will reject silence also, because they exist together. Have you known any silence without sound? – because silence has its own sound. If the night is completely silent, no traffic, nobody moving, everybody gone to sleep, watch and listen and you will find that the night has its own sound – very subtle, but its own sound. And when one goes deeper inside, the inner night, where all the sounds of the day have stopped, there too a sound is heard. Hindus have called it *aumkar,* the sound of the ultimate, *aum.* It is heard. It is there. When the ultimate silence descends on you, the ultimate sound also descends on you – immediately! They are together, they cannot be apart. They are two aspects of the coin – silence and sound. Yes, God is silence and sound also. This is the logos.

Now try to follow this sutra. This is very, very meaningful.

*Although this logos is eternally valid,*
*yet men are unable to understand it –*
*not only before hearing it,*
*but even after they have heard it.*

...Because this is not a question of hearing or not hearing. It is a question of inner growth.

I can talk to you about logos, I can try to explain to you, you may even have an intellectual glimpse of it – but that will not give you understanding. It is just like talking to a small child about sex. You can talk, you can bring all your Freuds and Wilhelm Reichs and talk, and the child may even listen, but can a child understand about it? If the child is very intelligent he will understand intellectually, but to understand sex a biological growth is needed, a certain maturity of the glands and hormones is needed. To understand sex the child must come to the point where he desires sex; only then can he understand, otherwise not.

I was passing through a street and two small children were walking just in front of me. One must have been seven and the other about eight. The smaller one was asking the elder one: "I go with a girl to the school. Seven times I have carried her bag and books and everything, and thrice I have gone to bring ice cream for her. What do you think? – should I now kiss her or not?"

The other pondered over it and he said, "As I see it, you have already done enough for her. No need to do anything more." For a child, this is the thing exactly! You cannot talk about sex to a child. First the sexual desire must arise;

first the child should become sexual. That is the problem about religion also. You cannot talk to anybody unless the desire arises.

Religion is just like sex. Sex is the desire to meet the opposite on the level of the body, and religion is the desire to meet the opposite on the level of being. It is a desire. It is a thirst. When it arises, only then can it be talked about. You may bring intellectual questions; that doesn't mean anything. You may ask whether God exists or not; that is not the point. Are you thirsty? Has the desire arisen to meet the opposite on the level of being – neither on the level of body nor of mind, but at the level of being, your totality? Are you ready for that jump? Then understanding is possible.

That's why Heraclitus says:

*Although this logos is eternally valid....*

The logos is everywhere present – in the trees, in the stones, in the sky, everywhere! In you, all around you the logos is present, because the whole life is working through the opposite. It is dialectical, it gets enrichment through the opposite. It moves through the antithesis, it moves higher to the synthesis, and then again the synthesis becomes the thesis. Again antithesis is created, again a higher synthesis. Life goes on moving that way. It is everywhere that way. And it is valid because it is not an argument, it is the way existence is. Remember this: Heraclitus is not arguing, he is simply making a statement. I am also not arguing, simply making a statement of fact. It is how things are! That's why he says, "I have searched..." and he has found this dialectics, a dialectical process of existence. This is the deepest insight. It is valid – no question of arguing about it. It is the way existence exists.

*...yet men are unable to understand it –*
*not only before hearing it,*
*but even after they have heard it.*

...Because hearing won't help.

Unless you change, unless you become open to the inside, unless you not only try to follow intellectually, understand intellectually, but to feel it, to exist through it, to imbibe it like food and digest it so that it flows in your bones, becomes part of your existence, only then....

These are not theories. And you need an inner growth before you can understand it.

*We should let ourselves be guided*
*by what is common to all.*

Then what is to be done? If you cannot understand before hearing it, and you cannot understand after hearing it, then what is to be done? A very beautiful suggestion he makes. It can become really helpful to you. He says:

*We should let ourselves be guided*
*by what is common to all.*

*Yet, although the logos is common to all,*
*most men live as if each of them*
*had a private intelligence of his own.*

Logos is common to all, logos is the common ground, logos is the common continent. And you think of yourselves as islands, separate from everybody, and then you follow your own intelligence. That is the only foolishness that is possible: private intelligence is the foolishness, the greatest stupidity. Existence is total; intelligence is also total, it is of the whole, so you should look to the common.

That is what Zen masters say: "Become ordinary, become common. Don't try to become extraordinary." The more common you become, the more ordinary you become, the more capable you become of understanding the logos. Don't try to be very extraordinary, exceptional, because the more you try the more you will become like an island, closed, caved in upon yourself. Then you are losing your moorings in the existence. Then you are cutting your roots, you are getting uprooted. That has happened in the West: a feeling of uprootedness. Nobody knows where the roots are. And when you feel uprooted, then you become an egoist, then you exist as a selfsufficient entity – and that is not possible!

Existence is interrelated, we move into each other. When I am talking to you, what am I doing? I am moving continuously in you. When you are listening to me, you are allowing, you are giving a door to me. You breathe and existence enters you; you open the eyes and the sun enters you – every moment, twenty-four hours, you are a crossroad. Millions of points meet, millions of lines meet in you. You are not separate! Just think: can you exist separately? Can you exist totally insulated? You will die within seconds. You are a porous being; existence comes and moves through you. You are just like a room: air comes, the sun comes and goes continuously; that is why the room remains clean and fresh. If you are closed you will be dead.

The more open you are, the more existence will flow through you. And the

more existence flows, the more you will be able to understand what logos is.

You are not. The whole is. You are a false entity. Hence the insistence of all the awakened ones on surrender. Don't fight with existence, because you don't know what you are doing, with whom you are fighting. How can you fight with existence? It is as if a wave is fighting with the ocean, a leaf is fighting the tree – it is foolish! And don't try to move upstream; that will simply exhaust you. You will be tired and you will feel frustrated because you cannot succeed.

Against existence there is no success. That's why you and everybody are such failures. Ask your successful people and they are all failures; deep down, they have missed. Your Napoleons, your Hitlers, your Rothschilds, ask them – they are failures, they have failed. What have they attained? They fought, they tried to move upstream, they wanted to become extraordinary in some way or other – they simply destroyed themselves. To try to become extraordinary is suicidal; it is a gradual suicide, a slow poisoning of the whole system. Surrender to existence, flow with it, wheresoever it goes – willy-nilly, wheresoever it goes.

This word willy-nilly is good. Willy means whether it goes according to your will or not; nilly means whether it negates you or not. Willy means will, and nilly means against the will. Willy-nilly, wherever it goes, you surrender, you float with it. Swimming, even swimming, is not needed.

Why have a private goal of your own? Why not move with the destiny of the whole? Why are you so much worried to achieve something on your own? And how can you achieve it? You cannot achieve – this is simply not possible. Only the whole has a destiny, not you. Only the whole is going somewhere, not you. If you can surrender to the whole, everything is achieved – because you become the whole, and the whole's destiny becomes your destiny, and the goal of the whole is your goal. And the goal is not somewhere else – the whole is happy right now, the whole is blissful right now. Only you are worried. Only you are worried because you are not flowing with the river. You are trying to cut small corners for yourself. And who are you? And how do you think it can be possible? You will simply fail.

Man always fails, only God succeeds.

Listen:

*We should let ourselves be guided*
*by what is common to all.*

Look to the commonness of things, and find the common: the more common, the truer; the more exceptional, the more false. Be ordinary – then you are nearer

the ground, then you are nearer the truth. If you can be absolutely ordinary, what else is needed? – because every moment becomes such a benediction. What is the problem when you are absolutely ordinary? You eat and eating is a sacrament. You sleep and sleep is a sacrament. You walk in the sun, and what more do you need? You breathe – what else is needed to be happy? You love – what more are you asking? Everything is already given; you are just trying to be exceptional. Follow the rule, the common, and don't try to be the exception, otherwise you will be in misery.

Hell is for all extraordinary people. They may be in politics, in art, literature – wherever they are, hell is for all geniuses, for all extraordinary people, all egoists. Ego is the hell, it gives you suffering – because unnecessarily you start conflicting with everything. You are never at ease, unease becomes your style of life; with the ego you will always be at unease. Ego is a discomfort; it is a nail in the shoe, it continuously pinches, but you want to be extraordinary. Then....

I was sitting with Mulla Nasruddin and his wife came through and went out of the door. He said, "Look! There goes a great woman."

I said, "What do you mean by 'great'?"

He said, "She is trying to have a size four shoe on size six feet – there goes an extraordinary woman!" And she is suffering, but she is trying to be exceptional.

In China it happened for millions of women: just to make the feet small, so that it looks extraordinary, iron shoes were used. Chinese women suffered long, for their whole life, because they were almost crippled. But long feet belonged to laborers, poor people, not rich people. It seems life belongs to the poor, not to rich people. So the higher the status of the woman, the queen...the queens in China, for thousands of years, were not even able to walk because they had such small feet. It was impossible...because the feet exist in the right proportion to the body. You cannot have small feet because nature knows better than you. But they were trying, they were trying to improve nature, improve upon nature. They suffered long. And the whole misery of man is this, it can be reduced to a single law: if you try to be exceptional you will suffer. Then nothing will satisfy you; everywhere you will find discontent.

Mulla Nasruddin was admitted to hospital – he was ill. And he created a hell around him there, because you cannot find a greater complaint-maker than Mulla Nasruddin; he is simply a continuous complaint. The whole hospital was in trouble – the nurses, the doctors. Just to get rid of him, they treated him as carefully as possible so he would be okay and go away. Then he was okay and the day came when he was to be released, but he was again complaining. The doctor heard his noise so he asked the nurse, "Now what is he complaining about? Now there is nothing to complain about – he is going to leave today."

The nurse said, "Now he is saying, 'Before the medicines are finished, how can I be cured? Before all the medicines are finished, how can I be cured? There must be something wrong.'"

This type of mind automatically comes to an egoist. He is in search of finding something wrong. And when you are in search you will find – more than you ask you will find. This is the trouble in the world: whatsoever you try to find you will find. If you are trying to find wrongs...and the ego always tries to find wrongs because an ego needs continuous discomfort, it exists in discomfort. When everything is okay the ego disappears. Says Chuang Tzu: "When the shoe fits, the body is forgotten, the feet are forgotten." And when everything is forgotten, how can you cling to the ego? Ego needs that shoes should continue pinching so that you can remember who you are. That's why an egoist cannot love, cannot meditate, cannot pray, because if he really prays, then everything fits – then the ego disappears. Ego means a selfconsciousness. When something is wrong, only then is selfconsciousness there. When everything is right, there is no selfconsciousness.

Look to the common, watch for the common – don't try to be exceptional.

But we want to be exceptional. People come to me. If I tell them, "You just sit silently, don't be too much bothered about meditation and prayer, and by and by it will grow," they say, "But just sitting?..." They need something exceptional. If I tell them, "Stand on your head," then it is okay. That's why there are so many teachers flourishing all over the world who teach people to stand on their heads – something difficult, uncomfortable, appeals. Ridiculous postures people try in the name of Yoga. Simply ridiculous! The more ridiculous, the better; the more difficult...if you cannot do them, then ego gets a challenge. So do them! Make postures, absurd, and you think you are doing something great.

Life is simply great – there is no need to improve upon it.

If nature wanted you to sit on the head or stand on the head, you would have been created that way. Listen to nature and follow nature and don't create any conflict with nature; just follow it and soon you will attain to a deep silence which comes when one becomes ordinary.

Just a few days ago – and in India it is a constant problem – a young man came and he asked, "Should I marry or not?"

I told him, "Just be ordinary. Why not marry?"

But he was not willing – not marrying is something exceptional. Marrying is

ordinary, having children is so ordinary, becoming a householder is so ordinary. He said, "But all great men have remained unmarried."

So I said to him, "If you want to be great, then go somewhere else. To me that is a disease. If you want to be ordinary, then only come to me." Whatsoever your nature and whatsoever your inner feeling.... Then I asked him, "Just look inside. Close your eyes and tell me what you would like."

He said, "Of course I would like to marry but that looks so ordinary: wasting your life in ordinary things." But the whole life consists of ordinary things. And greatness is not in things – greatness is in the quality that you bring to your life, to ordinary things.

Just look at Jesus having supper with his friends: he looks more ordinary than a Buddha sitting under the bodhi tree. But the gesture of being ordinary is so beautiful; drinking, eating with the friends is so beautiful that nobody can be so beautiful just sitting under a bodhi tree. Jesus has a quality of being just ordinary.

Buddha remained a king even under the bodhi tree. He was born exceptional, extraordinary; he lived like a prince, he was brought up like a prince. That became his structure – even under the bodhi tree he is not a beggar. If you go near him you can feel it. You can miss a Jesus if you meet him on the road – you cannot miss Buddha. But I tell you: Jesus is nearer logos. It happened that way to Buddha because he was brought up that way; all his past just was that way. But how many people can be born as princes, and how many people can be taught that way? Jesus is more human, but in all his humanity he is divine, because this ordinariness is to follow the common.

Jainas and Buddhists come to me and they say, "But this Jesus – he also drinks, eats, like ordinary people; stays with ordinary people. How can you tell that he is just of the same stature as Buddha and Mahavira?" But I tell you that he is exactly how one should be. Mahavira and Buddha may be exceptional, but not everybody can be exceptional, and there is no need. It may have been natural to them, so it is okay if they followed their nature. But millions of people, millions and millions, they cannot sit under bodhi trees just doing nothing. They will have to move in the world and work and do things, ordinary things.

And if there is no way to reach the logos ordinarily, then it will remain only for a chosen few. And that doesn't look just: then the whole existence seems to favor only a few. But remember, if the existence favors only a few, if it is partial, then what need is there to give you birth? No, nature never favors anybody – it is for all, for all those who are ready to partake. The bliss is for all, if you are ready to participate. Jesus is a carpenter's son, a poor man. And that's how, for millions of people, it should be. Somebody is a carpenter's son, somebody is a goldsmith's son, and somebody is a shoemaker's son – this is how life is! And we have lived too much according to the exceptional people, and because of that much misery has been unnecessarily created.

Live ordinarily, find the common and don't try to be uncommon; otherwise, the very effort will cut your roots from the logos. The logos is common to all yet most men live as if each of them had a private intelligence of his own. And if you live according to the common, if you follow the common and you don't try to become an individual, you will be nearer logos and you will be able to understand it.

This is the paradox: those who try to be exceptional individuals miss, miss all individuality and miss all extraordinariness; and those who remain with the ordinary, with such an ordinariness that there is nothing to claim about it, those who never strive to be individuals, attain to the greatest individuality this existence can offer to you. Those who remain ordinary become most extraordinary. But that extraordinariness comes as a gift; it is nothing on your part, you have not been striving for it. Human nature has no real understanding; only the divine nature has it. Yes, it is as it should be.

We come from the whole, we go back to the whole. Unknown we come, unknown we go...not knowing from where we are coming, not knowing to what we are going. The whole process is mysterious. How can you have a private intelligence?

This is a little difficult; has to be understood very deeply. And it is one of the most important points Heraclitus has given. Consciousness is also common. Just as fishes exist in the ocean, in the common ocean, we exist in a common consciousness. Your consciousness and my consciousness are not two, but just two centers of the same. All around you is consciousness. We are all forms, but within the forms flows the same, the one. That's why sometimes you also feel a common ground.

Somebody is sad. He has not said a single thing to you. You are sitting by his side, and suddenly you feel a sadness spreading in you. Somebody is happy, just happy, not saying anything to you – but suddenly you feel a happiness entering you. If twenty persons are sitting happy and you bring a sad man there, within minutes he will feel a change; his climate is changing. With sad people you become sad. With long faces you become long faces. With happy people you become happy. That's why if you enjoy playing with children you become children again. Playing with a child you suddenly forget the whole worry and the

world – you become like a child. It is very refreshing. How does it happen? It happens because consciousness is a common phenomenon. When you play with a child you have to become a child because the child and you meet on the common ground.

Because of this, in the East they have insisted that just being near the master, just being near an awakened one, is very, very valuable – just being near, in the presence. In the West they cannot understand: "What do you mean, 'in the presence'?" In the East they say: "We are going for a *darshan*." Darshan means just to see the master; nothing to ask, just being in the presence. They have a certain word for this being in the presence – they call it *satsang,* being near the truth. If you sit silently with a master, sooner or later you dissolve into each other. The consciousnesses meet. The master enters into you, you enter into the master. If you don't do anything, just simply being near the master, one day you can attain – not even making a single effort. That too is possible, but then you have to be very, very open. Just sitting silently, not doing, not creating any barriers, relaxing, you can attain. Many have attained – because consciousness is the ocean and we are the fishes in it. And everything affects everybody else.

Whatsoever happens in this existence affects everybody else. Not only now – whatsoever has happened in the past is affecting. And not only that – whatsoever is going to happen in the future is also affecting, because at this moment the whole existence culminates. Past, future, present – they culminate, they converge.

There is no possibility of a private intelligence. And those people we call very, very talented, geniuses, they also feel it. Ask Einstein or Madame Curie; they also feel it. Einstein says that whatsoever he discovered, he discovered in moments when he was not, when suddenly something possessed him – the total consciousness. Ask the poets; they say whenever something happens, they are not. They become a vehicle – the common consciousness possesses them.

Madame Curie got the Nobel prize. The Nobel prize should have been given to the common ground. She was making all efforts to find a solution to a particular mathematical problem, and she could not find the way. For two years she struggled and struggled, and then one night, tired, she fell asleep. And in sleep something happened – because in sleep you are more open. In sleep you are not an egoist, in sleep you are a nobody, in sleep you don't cling to the identity.

That's why in the morning you also feel fresh, younger, rejuvenated, because you have been into the common ground. You moved into consciousness, the ocean. You were not clinging to the private intelligence. For a few seconds you

dropped into the whole and the whole revived you, refreshed you.

In the night something happened. She got up, she went to her table and she wrote the solution that she had been working for years to find. Then she slept and in the morning she completely forgot what had happened in the night. She took her bath, her breakfast, everything, and then she went to the table...she was simply amazed – the solution was there! "But who has done it? – because there is nobody else." Only she was in the room; only the servant had come, and the servant could not have done it. She had been working hard – "What is happening?" Then she looked minutely – it was her own handwriting! a little different, because in the night, in the sleep.... Then she closed her eyes and tried to remember what had happened. Then she saw the whole thing like a dream: that she got up, she had something, she wrote it down....

Common consciousness – you unnecessarily claim that it is yours. It has never been yours. It is always floating. It is all around you. Become more porous, become more allowing, a deep letgo – because only the whole can understand the whole. How can the part understand the whole? How can an atomic part understand the whole? But the whole can flow through the part, and if the part allows it.... And that's what meditation is all about: allowing the whole to flow; you disappear completely from the scene...and then suddenly you have become the whole.

*Human nature has no real understanding;*
*only the divine nature has it.*

*Man is not rational;*
*only what encompasses him is intelligent.*

Not you, but the ocean around you, what encompasses, what surrounds you – not you; what is within you and without you, but not you because "you" is just a fallacy.

*Man is not rational;*
*only what encompasses him is intelligent.*

*What is divine escapes men's notice*
*because of their incredulity.*

Because you doubt, because you cannot believe, because you cannot trust, that's why what is divine escapes men's notice – because of their incredulity.

Only one barrier is there and that is doubt. And only one gate is there and

that is trust. If you trust nature everything falls into its right place. If you distrust nature everything is disturbed.

But why is it so difficult to be natural? Only one difficulty: if you are natural you cannot be somebody – there is no other difficulty. Sex arises, you follow it; *brahmacharya*, celibacy, becomes a fight against nature. You are hungry, you eat; fasting becomes a conflict with nature. When you don't feel hungry, then you go on forcing eating; that, too, is a fighting with nature. When you don't feel like making love and you go on making love – because the wife needs, because the society…and this and that – then you go against nature. Nature means just follow the inner being, whatsoever it feels, without any imposition from your ego on it. It will destroy and shatter your ego.

Live like an animal – with only one difference: alert. That's all. Live like an animal – with only one difference: aware.

Don't fight with nature; just be a witness to it and allow it. And wherever it leads, it is good. All your mind-projected goals are false. And whatsoever you do, you will not be able to succeed. Finally nature succeeds because finally, only the whole can succeed. So why in the beginning unnecessarily move into a fight? But I see people fighting in millions of ways – they change extremes, but they fight.

In the East – in the past, in the West also – people were fighting against sex. They said something is wrong, in sex something is wrong – because in sex you become natural like an animal, and all the preachers have been saying that you should not be like an animal. What is wrong in being animal? Look at the birds, look at the animals, go to the forest and see! Don't go to the zoo because there you will not see real animals; they are corrupted by human beings. Go to the wild.

What is wrong with animals? They look so beautiful, nothing is ugly around them, but all the moralists, all the so-called religious people, they have been teaching you: "Don't be an animal!" And your ego feels this is a good goal. How can you be an animal? And sex brings you to animality totally. In sex you feel so absolutely animal. You don't feel like that in anything else because everything you have changed, polished. Everything you have painted, cultured, cultivated – everything! You eat, but you have made such a ritual of eating, around it, that it doesn't seem to be at all related with hunger – does not seem to be related at all with hunger. What you eat is not nutritious; it is a show, a façade. Everything is false, plastic flowers all around. But when you move in love, you make love to a woman or to a man, you become absolutely animal.

You have tried to hide that too. That's why man makes love in the night. Only

man makes love in the night; otherwise, animals make love in the day. And if you make love in the day it will be deeper, because with the sun in the atmosphere you are more vital. The night is for rest, but man makes love in the night because animals make love in the day and he has to make a distinction. What type of egoist effort is this? And then in the dark, not even with the light on, so that in the dark you don't face the reality that you are behaving like animals. Then you don't make any sound while making love. In fact you make love as if something has to be done and finished as soon as possible; within seconds it is finished. You have been taught to be against it – and your ego feels good.

Now, in the West, the wheel has turned a complete circle. Since Freud and Wilhelm Reich they have been teaching sex more and more. Now a new thing is happening in the West: if you don't make love one day, you feel guilty. It seems you have to feel guilty whatsoever you do. Before you were making love and you were feeling guilty: Why do you make love? Why this animality? When will you transcend this? When will that day come when you will not need it? Now in the West, if one day you don't feel like making love, you are tired, then you feel guilty that you are doing something wrong – you have to make it.

You have to do something, you cannot allow nature to have its own course. Both are the same to me, there is no difference.

In the past women were not allowed to have orgasm, because how can a woman, so pure, have orgasm? A woman is a goddess; she should behave like a goddess. So in the past women were simply tolerating sex, just lying like dead bodies, corpses. Even if you make love to a corpse, the corpse will move a little, but not women – goddesses! So pure in nature, innocent, they don't know what is happening; it is just the man who is dragging them into it. So they would just lie down, with closed eyes – because even if a woman looks with open eyes, that seems that she is curious, interested – with closed eyes. Now, in the West, they have created the opposite. Now if a woman cannot achieve orgasm then it is a problem, then something is wrong. Now it is a sin not to achieve orgasm. Before, it was a sin to achieve orgasm.

So in the East, and in the past in the West also, women completely forgot that they can achieve orgasm. They completely forgot that a beautiful ecstasy is possible through sex, because if you don't move...and if nature is allowed, then while making love the lovers will go completely wild: they will scream, they will make noises, they will go mad – and that is so animal-like. They will be so ecstatic. And if you can be ecstatic in love, soon that ecstasy opens a door for a

higher ecstasy. Then you transcend, and then only does the real *brahmacharya* happen. And that is not anything you can force on yourself, that happens through nature itself.

If one follows nature, one reaches.

There is no need for you to make any arrangements for the ultimate goal to happen – nature has already made everything. You are a seed, and the whole blueprint exists in you if you allow nature. It is just like a seed: we sow the seed in the ground and the seed has the whole blueprint – the whole architecture of the tree, every leaf of the tree that will happen in the future, every flower that will happen in the future. The seed has every blueprint – only nature has to be allowed.

You have to water, you have to take care, good soil, fertilizers – finished! You need not do anything. You need not teach the seed: "Behave! Do this and that. And never do this, otherwise you will never be a tree." If you teach seeds, trees will not exist in the world because the seeds will go completely mad not knowing what to do. Seeds depend on the universal consciousness, not on a private intelligence.

Man has the blueprint to be a god, nothing less, just to be a god. Man is the seed of God – because human consciousness is just the beginning. It has to grow and grow and grow, and come to a point where it becomes universal. Nothing is needed on your part to do it – no discipline in fact, no creed, no dogma, no religion in fact. Nature is enough! You simply have to allow it. You have to be receptive to it and move in trust, because only in trust can you move.

If the seed asks, "What is the guarantee that if I leave my shell, which covers me and protects me, I will grow into a tree? What is the guarantee? And if there is no guarantee I will cling to my shell," then what will happen?

If the bird in the egg says, "How can I come out? Who is there to give me a guarantee that it will be a better world than I am already in?" then what will happen? The shell is a security, it protects. The bird is beautifully protected in the egg – but this is not life. It is like death; protected completely, of course, but protected in a grave. And who can give the guarantee? There is nobody to give you a guarantee – you have to trust.

The seed trusts and dissolves into the earth, sprouts into a beautiful tree, flowers, enjoys existence, becomes ecstatic.

The bird comes out of the egg, leaves the known for the unknown, takes wing and moves into the vast sky. Nobody knows what is going to happen. With no goal in view, with no purpose, plan, it just takes wing, feels ecstatic on the winds, moves, goes to the farthest corner of the sky – moves into the unknown.

That is how it is going to happen to you also. You are a seed, you are an egg, you are a possibility. And Heraclitus hits exactly right, comes to the exact point where you miss:

*What is divine escapes men's notice*
*because of their incredulity.*

Because you doubt, you miss. Trust and you can reach. Nothing else is needed – just trust, so that nature can unfold.

*Although intimately connected with the logos,*
*men keep setting themselves against it.*

*How can anyone hide from that which never sets?*

Existence is always, always and always. It never sets. How can you hide yourself from it? It ever, ever lasts. How can you fight with it? What you are doing is simply ridiculous, absurd. It is stupid to fight! The only wisdom consists in a letgo, a surrender. And then all that is beautiful starts happening. It is a happening, it is not a doing.

You can create barriers, but you cannot bring it. You can escape from it, you can close your eyes to it, but you cannot create it – it is already there, it is already the case! Only you are missing because you are sitting with closed eyes…doubt closing your eyes, doubt closing your heart, doubt – as if you are asleep, intoxicated in doubt.

Karl Marx has said: "Religion is the opium for the masses." Exactly the opposite is the case: doubt is the opium, not religion.

Through doubt you miss the truth. Through trust you allow it to reach you, and you allow yourself to reach it.

Meditate more and more on trust. Imbibe the feeling of trust. Vibrate with a trusting heart. Sing, dance, pray, with a trusting heart, and soon you will see that only trust pays finally.

Doubt can kill. It is negative, it cannot give you life. Doubt is death.

Trust is life. And as the trust grows more and more, more abundant life becomes available to you.

# *Chapter* 9

THIS UNIVERSE,
WHICH IS THE SAME FOR ALL,
HAS NOT BEEN MADE BY ANY GOD OR MAN,
BUT IT HAS ALWAYS BEEN, IS, AND WILL BE –
AN EVERLIVING FIRE,
KINDLING ITSELF BY REGULAR MEASURES
AND GOING OUT BY REGULAR MEASURES.

THE PHASES OF FIRE ARE CRAVING AND SATIETY.

THE SUN IS NEW EACH DAY.

# THE SUN IS NEW EACH DAY

HERE IS NO GOD AS a separate creator of the world, and cannot be because the creation, the creator and the creativity are the same, they are not separate. Existence is one – then how can the creator and the created be separate? Existence itself is divine. There is no creator who is creating it. It itself is the creator. It itself is the creativity.

Heraclitus is a nondualist. All those who have known are bound to know that duality exists because of the mind, because the mind cannot see the one, it can only see the two. The moment it perceives anything, it divides. With the mind, the other is necessary. If it sees creation immediately it thinks of the creator because "How is creation possible without a creator?" But if with this mind you encounter the creator, then again the mind will see that there must be some other creator – "Otherwise how can this creator be?"

Mind is an infinite regress. It goes on and on dividing. That's why mind never reaches any conclusive state. Philosophy believes in the mind; that's why philosophy also never reaches any conclusion. One has to see the totality without bringing mind in, because mind is the factor of duality: it divides. Division is the nature of mind. If you say "day" then the mind immediately brings night, because "How can the day be without night?" If you say "love" then the mind brings hate: "How can love be without hate?" If you bring life, the mind brings death: "How can life be without death?" But life and death are one – one

phenomenon, one energy. Life is the manifestation of that energy, and death is again relaxation. Life is coming to a form, and death is moving again into the formless. The end and the beginning meet. Life is not separate from death, death is not separate from life – they meet and mingle. Even to say they meet is not right because the mind immediately brings: "If there is a meeting then there must be two." It is not a meeting, it is one phenomenon.

Heraclitus says desire and satiety – these are two. You feel hunger and then you eat, and then you feel satisfied. Have you ever observed that the hunger and the satiety are one? They have to be one because the same thing, food, changes both. Food becomes a bridge between hunger and satiety, desire and desirelessness. If they are really separate then they cannot be bridged. If they are really different then there is no possibility of any bridge. Then hunger will remain hunger and satiety will remain satiety. Where will they meet? And how will they meet? But they meet. Mind thinks hunger is against satiety. Just try to understand it. Move a little deeper into it. Mind says hunger is different from satiety, but when you are satisfied again a circle has started which will bring hunger; and when you are hungry a circle has started which will bring satiety. Are they two or just a single phenomenon? When you eat, hunger disappears, but the moment hunger disappears a new circle starts.

A new morning is a beginning of the evening. A new birth is a beginning of death.

But you cannot see so far away. Every morning you become hungry and you eat and you become satisfied. In the evening you are again hungry and then you eat and you achieve satiety – but you never see that they both are one. One helps to bring the other. If you are never hungry, can you be satisfied? Is there any possibility of satiety if you are never hungry? If you are never hungry, don't think that you will be in a state of satiety – the satiety cannot come without hunger. If there is no morning, don't think that there will be evening always and always – there will be no evening at all. And if there is no death, don't think that there will be life eternal – there will be no life at all...because death creates the situation, sets an energy phenomenon. Every life brings death, every death brings life again.

These two appear two to the mind because the mind cannot see through opposites. When you don't see from the mind, from the logical standpoint, when you simply look into the phenomenon itself, the totality of it, the two disappears and only one remains.

That is the thing with God as creator and universe as creation. Not only are

ordinary persons deceived by the mind – great theologians, they are also deceived by it. They also say, "God created the world." This statement is juvenile, it is childish. Nobody has created existence – it is, it is simply there – because if you bring in creation then millions of problems arise. And that is why theology brings more problems and no solution. And they create a theory, a hypothesis, to solve many problems. Nothing is solved. On the contrary, around the hypothesis new questions arise. They tried to solve the problem of existence by bringing God in, that God created it. Then they created millions of problems – and they have not been able to solve them. Once you start on a wrong line you will go on missing, because one thing leads to another. And there is a relatedness: if one thing is wrong, then it will lead to another wrong proposition. Unless you start from the very beginning towards the truth, you will never reach – because the beginning is the end.

Theology brings in God to solve a few problems, because there *are* problems: "Who created the world?..." The curiosity arises: "Such a beautiful phenomenon! – who created it?" And then the mind has an itching sensation – it should be answered: "Who created?" But the first thing is to ask whether the question is right. Never raise a question without asking first: "Is the question relevant?" And what is the criterion of a question being relevant? The criterion is that if a question is such that whatever answer is given, the same question can be raised again – then the question is irrelevant, it is not right. You ask, "Who created the world?" Somebody says, "God!" You can ask the same question again: "Who created God?" The question has not changed, not a bit. The same question is still relevant. So somebody says, "God A created the world," and then you ask, "Who created God A?" He says, "God B created the God A," then you ask, "Who created God B?" And he says, "God C created the God B" – but the question remains the same so all answers are false.

If the question is not changing a little bit, then you are not progressing towards truth at all. And if all the answers to a question are false, then please meditate upon the question again. In the very base the question itself must be wrong; otherwise how can all the answers be wrong? At least one answer must be true – but no answer has proved to be true. Hindus, Mohammedans, Christians, they have all provided answers, but the question remains. Thousands of years working on the question "Who created the world?" and not a single answer has been given which satisfied. This means that in the very base, from the very beginning, you have taken a wrong line of research, a wrong attitude from the very beginning.

So the first thing about a question is to question the question itself, whether it is relevant.

This question is irrelevant: "Who created the existence?" – for many reasons ...because then the question is possible: "Why did he create it? What was the need? Why couldn't he live without creating it? What desire possessed him? And if God created this universe, then why is there so much misery, suffering, suffering which cannot be accounted for?"

A child is born crippled, blind, ill – why? If God is the creator, can't he correct the pattern of the world? Or is your God a little neurotic, enjoys suffering? A sadist, enjoys this torture? Millions of people dying in a war, being killed, thrown into fire and gas chambers – he is the creator, and he is simply not worried! He cannot even stop a Hitler killing millions of Jews – unnecessarily, for no reason at all. What type of creator is this? If God creates the world then he must be a Devil, because the world doesn't seem so good. It cannot come out of good, seems to be inconsistent with good. God means "the good," and this world doesn't show any sign of goodness – exploitation, violence, war, killing, misery, anguish, tension, madness.... For what has this creation been created? And if God is responsible, then he is the greatest criminal.

These problems arise, and theologians cannot solve them. Then they have to create more false theories. Then they say there is a Devil also, and it is the work of the Devil. But they get into their own trap. First they create God, that God created the world; then they have to create a Devil because they cannot explain the world through goodness. The world looks so evil that they have to create a Devil. Then the question arises: "Who created the Devil?" Then they go on and on. And they get into such a desertlike effort which leads nowhere. Nobody reads their big volumes on theology – nobody! – because if you start you reach nowhere, and they go on and on and on. It seems like a broken gramophone record: the same they go on repeating, and you go on asking the same question and they go on round about. Beating around the bush is all that theology is. Not a single problem has been solved. The most useless effort that man has made ever is theology. And it starts with: "God created the world."

Men like Heraclitus, Gautam Buddha, Lao Tzu, Zarathustra, they don't talk about these things. They simply say: "Existence is God. Nobody has created it. There is no creator who is responsible for it, so don't raise unnecessary questions. And don't waste your time in unnecessary answering." Existence is, and God is not separate from it. God is existence, the totality, not a separate being, a person – the totality. It comes out of its own...and dissolves. Says Heraclitus, it

is fire. Fire is a beautiful symbol. It gives you a very dynamic energy, indicates that existence is a dynamic, dialectical energy – it moves on its own. When you say "energy" it means something. When you say "God" you have moved into something which will not lead anywhere.

Energy is truth.

You can feel it here and now: you are energy, the birds singing in the trees are energy, the trees going toward the sky are energy; the stars moving, the sun rising every day – everything is energy. And energy is neither good nor bad. Energy is always neutral. So there is no need to create a Devil, no need to explain anything – energy is neutral.

If you are miserable it is because of you, not because of a God or because of a Devil. If you are miserable, you are behaving with the energy in a wrong way. You will be happy and blissful if you move with the energy. If you move against it, it is you who are responsible. Remember, if there is no God then you are responsible for whatsoever happens. And if you are responsible then there is a possibility to transform oneself. If God is responsible, then how is one going to transform oneself? God seems to be a trick of the mind to throw responsibility on somebody else, because the mind is always throwing responsibility on somebody else. Whatsoever happens, you always throw responsibility on somebody else. If you are angry, then somebody has insulted you – he has created anger. If you are sad, somebody is making you sad and unhappy. If you are frustrated, somebody is blocking your way. Always somebody else is responsible, never you. This is the attitude of the mind: to make somebody else responsible. Then you are freed of the responsibility. But…this is why you are miserable.

Responsibility is yours. And if you take it as yours, you can do something about it. If it is somebody else's, what can you do? If others create sadness, you will always remain sad because what can you do about it? Millions of others are all around: if others make you frustrated then nothing can be done. You will remain frustrated, then this is your destiny – because how can you change others? If you are responsible, immediately you become a master. Now you can do something. You can change yourself, you can change your attitudes. You can look through different attitudes towards the world, and you can feel that if you feel miserable, somewhere you are a misfit in the total energy system. That's all that sin means: you are a misfit, not knowing how to move in this total energy system. And the energy system is neutral. If you follow it you will be happy. If you don't follow it, you will be miserable. This is the logos, the rit, the tao.

For example: if you are feeling thirsty and you don't drink water you will be

miserable, because in this energy system water gives you satiety, the thirst disappears. If you are feeling cold you move near fire, because in this energy system fire is the source of all warmth, heat. But if when you feel cold you move away from fire, then you will be miserable. Nobody is responsible. If when you are feeling thirsty, hot, you move near fire, you will be in hell!

I have heard that a man, a great sinner, died. Everybody knew that he was going to hell. It was so certain, it was obvious; there was no question about it. And when the procession – because he was a great sinner but a very great leader also, a very rich man, because sin has many successes, it pays in this world, so thousands were following, everybody fully aware that this man was going to hell, but still this man was very powerful – when the procession was going towards the cemetery, a truck loaded with coal, by accident, came on the road and started following the procession. The truck was going its own way, but it coincided.... Mulla Nasruddin, who was in the procession, exclaimed: "I was absolutely certain that this man is going to hell – but I could never have imagined that he has to provide his own coal!"

Hell is hot, fire. But I tell you, you are providing your own coal.

This is how things are: If you move against nature you will be in misery. Misery means moving against nature, and misery is a good indication – if you understand. It shows that somewhere you are going wrong, that's all. Put things right! Misery is a help. Anguish, anxiety, tension, are indications that somewhere something is going wrong. You are not with the total. Somewhere you have started your own private movement – and then you will be in misery. Says Heraclitus: "Private intelligence is false." Intelligence is with the whole. Don't be too clever. You cannot be intelligent on your own. If you move with the existence you will be intelligent, you will have a clarity of perception, you will be wise. If you move on your own you will be a fool.

An idiot is a person who is completely closed within himself, caved in. He has no contact with the total energy system. That is his idiocy. And a wise man is one who is not closed at all – the air flows through him, the cosmos flows through him. He has no barriers, no doors closed. He has no privacy of his being. He is porous. And whenever he feels miserable, immediately he puts himself right; immediately he takes the indication. It is a symptom! It is just like illness: when you are not behaving with your body naturally, some illness erupts. That illness is a friend. It shows: "Behave, change your ways! Somewhere you are going against nature." If you don't take food for three or four days, you feel dizzy, you feel hungry, you feel sad. The whole body is saying to you, "Take

food!" because the body needs energy.

Always remember: The energy is neutral, so the whole quality of your being depends on you. You can be happy, you can be unhappy – it is up to you. Nobody else is responsible.

When you feel hungry, eat. When you feel thirsty, drink. When you feel sleepy, go to sleep. Don't force nature. For a little while you can force it, because that much freedom is there. If you want to fast, you can fast for a few days, but every day you will become weaker and weaker and weaker, and every day you will be in more and more misery. If you don't want to breathe, for a few seconds you can stop breathing, but only for a few seconds – that much freedom is possible. But that is not very much, and soon you will feel a choking, dying sensation if you don't breathe well.

All misery exists to indicate to you that somewhere you have gone wrong, you have gone off the track. Come back immediately! If you start listening to the body, listening to nature, listening to your inner being, you will be more and more happy. Become a good listener to nature. Listen to the logos. Listen to those who have been awakened to the logos, and you will find them always, always natural. They don't force anything, they don't push the river, they simply flow with it – and that is their blissfulness.

There is no God who is responsible.

We create God out of our own fear and necessity and need. We feel so helpless in our misery, so powerless, so impotent in our pain, that out of this fear we create a God to whom we can pray, to whom we can say, "Don't give me so much trouble"; who we can praise and feel that if we praise him, he will become more and more favorable towards us. Do you think God can become prejudiced? If you pray, do you think he will be on your side? If you don't pray, then he will not be on your side?

One small child was being told by his parents: "If you don't behave well, God will punish you." The child had always been put right in the past. Whenever he was not behaving well, or doing something which the parents thought was not good, they had used this trick: "God will punish you; he will be angry," and this had always helped. But this time the child laughed. He said, "I am not worried about God because he does not know me at all."

They said, "This is something new! You never said this before. How did you come to know that he doesn't know you?"

The child said, "For two weeks I have not prayed and nothing has happened. So either he thinks I am dead, or he has completely forgotten me. So now,

no need to be worried about it. Now I am free! Otherwise, two weeks and no indication.... "

We have created God out of our need. God has not created you, you have created God. It is your need because you are helpless. And then you project everything that you miss on him. If you are powerless, you say he is omnipotent. If you are ignorant, you say he is all knowing. If you are blind and move and grope in darkness, you say he is omniscient. This is a trick of the mind. Whatsoever you miss in yourself you project on him, and then you think the balance is recovered: "Now I can pray to this omnipotent, omniscient, omnipresent being and he will be helping me."

These are tricks. You can be helped only by yourself. Of course, nature will be with you if you are with nature. No other prayer will do. This is the only prayer. To me, prayer is a feeling, a flowing with nature. If you want to talk, talk, but remember, your talk is not going to affect the existence. It will affect you, and that may be good, but prayer is not going to change God's mind. It may change you, but if it is not changing you then it is a trick. You can go on praying for years, but if it doesn't change you, drop it, throw it, it is rubbish; don't carry it any more. Prayer is not going to change God. You always think that if you pray, God's mind will change; he will be more favorable, he will be tipped a little towards your side. There is nobody who is listening to you. This vast sky cannot listen. This vast sky can be with you if you are with it – there is no other way to pray.

I also suggest to pray, but praying should be just an energy phenomenon; not a devotee and God phenomenon, but an energy phenomenon. You simply become silent, you simply open yourself. You raise both your hands towards the sky, palms uppermost, head up, just feeling existence flowing in you. As the energy, or *prana*, flows down your arms, you will feel a gentle tremor. Be like a leaf in a breeze, trembling. Allow it, help it. Then let your whole body vibrate with energy, and just let whatever happens happen. You feel again a flowing with the earth. Earth and heaven, above and below, yin and yang, male and female – you float, you mix, you drop yourself completely. You are not. You become one...merge. After two to three minutes, or whenever you feel completely filled, lean down to the earth and kiss the earth. You simply become a vehicle to allow the divine energy to unite with that of the earth.

These two stages should be repeated six more times so that each of the chakras can become unblocked. More times can be done, but if you do less you will feel restless and unable to sleep. It is best to do this prayer at night, in a darkened room, going to sleep immediately afterwards; or it can be done in the morning, but it must be followed by fifteen minutes' rest. This rest is necessary, otherwise you will feel as if you are drunk, in a stupor.

This merging with energy is prayer. It changes you. And when you change, the whole existence changes – because with your attitude the whole existence changes for you. Not that the existence is changing – the existence remains the same – but now you are flowing with it, there is no antagonism. There is no fight, no struggle – you are surrendered to it. Otherwise, all things are tricks. And man goes on inventing....

I have heard, once it happened: A rabbi came to a village on his horse. He was going to some other town. He was very tired, he wanted a little rest, so he went into the inn and left his horse under a tree outside with some hay for the horse to eat and rest also. Mulla Nasruddin was sitting under another tree, drunk. The horse was beautiful. He came near just to watch. When he was standing near the horse a man passed, a man who was a businessman dealing in horses. The horse was a rare thing, really beautiful. He asked Nasruddin, "Is it your horse?"

Drunk, and then feeling very good that "such a beautiful horse belongs to me," he said, "Yes."

But, one thing leads to another. That man asked, "I would like to purchase it. How much would you like to take for this horse?"

Now Nasruddin was caught. He simply asked an impossible price so there would be no problem. He said, "Two thousand rupees."

The horse was not worth more than five hundred rupees, so nobody was going to pay two thousand rupees, so, simply, the matter would be settled. But as it happened the man said, "Okay, take these two thousand rupees."

Then he was in trouble. But two thousand rupees.... And then he thought: "The rabbi is inside and he doesn't know – why not take these two thousand rupees? And there is nobody looking, and there is no problem at all involved." So he said, "Okay." He took the two thousand rupees; the businessman took the horse.

The moment the horse was gone the rabbi came out. Nasruddin was in a puzzle as to what to do now – with two thousand rupees, and he was so drunk he could not even run away. Then he started working it out inside his mind; he found a solution. He leaned down on all fours as if he was a horse and put some hay in his mouth. The rabbi couldn't believe what had happened. He said, "What are you doing? Are you mad?"

Nasruddin said, "First listen to my story." Now his mind was working fast –

he had become a theologian: now he was working out one answer, then another question, then he had got into his own trap. He said, "Twenty years ago, I was a young man and I committed a sin with a woman. And what did God do? He was so angry that he punished me and made me into a horse – your horse, rabbi. And for twenty years I served you, but it seems now the punishment is over and I am again restored to being a man."

The rabbi himself started trembling, seeing that a sinner had been punished – and who is not a sinner? The rabbi himself had sinned, with many women, so he started trembling seeing this phenomenon. He fell on his knees, started praying. But then there was a practical problem to be solved. He said, "It is okay. But I have to go to the other town, so what to do?"

Nasruddin suggested: "The market is not very far: you can go and find a horse."

So the rabbi went to the market – and there was his own horse standing at the horsedealer's! He started trembling again. He went near the horse, near its ear, and said, "What, Nasruddin! So soon again?"

Mind goes on and on playing tricks, creating a god, then praying, then being punished, then being sent into hell and heaven – and the whole thing is just imagination. There is no god, no hell, no heaven; only you are there and existence, energy, infinite energy. If you are with it, it is with you. This is the state of a Buddha, a Heraclitus: totally with the total. Then there is no problem. Then one is not there, really, to create problems. Then there is bliss – when you are not, then there is bliss. Otherwise, if you are fighting against it, moving away from it, doing things on your own, your private intelligence, behaving like an island, then you will be in trouble. Then whatever explanations and rationalizations you create are futile, just imagination.

All your churches, temples and mosques stand on man's fertile imagination. All your gods and statues and all your prayers, they are creations of your imagination. And you have created them because you are miserable. And this won't help. Your temples, mosques, churches – no! Your popes and priests and rabbis – no! They can't help. They are exploiting your imagination. And it is a good business. You have to drop imagining. You have to feel that misery comes when you are out of step with nature, and happiness comes when you are not out of step.

Hell is being out of step with the logos. Heaven is being in step with the logos. And that is the hidden harmony. If you can find it, you become blissful. If you cannot find it, you are miserable – nobody else is responsible.

You have to find and seek. There is no God, but everybody is divine. The whole existence is divine, godly, but there is no God. So don't waste your time

and don't look upwards for somebody who is to help you. The help will come, but there is nobody to give it to you – you have to take it. But this seems to be arduous, difficult, because then you have to change yourself. To be in step with nature you will need a radical transformation. To avoid that radical transformation you create every type of explanation.

Now try to enter these beautiful lines.

*This universe,*
*which is the same for all,*
*has not been made by any god or man,*
*but it has always been, is, and will be –*
*an everliving fire,*
*kindling itself by regular measures*
*and going out by regular measures.*

Evolution and involution; things coming to a peak, then disappearing in a valley; the waves rising to touch the sky, and then moving back to the depth of the ocean – in regular measures.

Says Heraclitus: the world is energy, existence is fire. In regular measures it manifests itself and then unmanifests itself. Just like day and night: in the day you work, awake, and in the night you rest. So there are periods when existence is in the day, and there are periods when existence moves into night...creation and uncreation, evolution and involution, day and night, summer and winter, life and death.

This is a creation period. Soon there will be a decreation period. Hindus call that *pralaya*, when everything disappears. Hindus have a beautiful theory for it – Heraclitus would have nodded assent. Hindus say that the brahma, the creator, has his own day, a twenty-four hour day, a twenty-four hour circle: a twelve-hour day and a twelve-hour night. His twelve-hour day is our creation – millions and millions of years, aeons and aeons of time. Then comes the night of brahma, then everything disappears, sleeps, rests – tired, of course. To rejuvenate itself, to come back, it goes into nonexistence. Existence is the day, nonexistence is the night. In a regular measure, for the same time, existence disappears, energy rests. When it has rested, again the day comes, the sun rises; things appear again, everything starts again. It is a circle. Half the circle is of manifestation and half is unmanifestation.

...Just like a tree grows and grows and grows, and then it dies – but it does not die completely. It collects itself into seeds, becomes unmanifest, moves into the subtle. Seeds fall down on the ground, the tree disappears, but in the right

season the seeds will sprout again and the whole tree will be there again. And it happens – not because there is some controller, a god or a man or somebody – there is nobody. Energy itself is enough. It needs no control, it needs nobody to be there. Energy has its own intrinsic discipline. And this seems to be exactly right, because if you watch you will feel this is how it happens. You feel hungry, you take food; hunger disappears. Where has the hunger gone? It has become unmanifest, moved to the seeds, to the subtle. It is not on the periphery; it has gone to the center again. Then after a few hours you feel hungry again, the hunger has come back. You take food, hunger disappears. Where does it go? If it disappears completely then it cannot come back. It comes again and again and again. It goes again and again and again – in the same measure.

In the day you are awake. Where has the sleep gone? It has moved to the seeds, become subtle; it is there inside you watching for the right time to become manifest; then by the night it again becomes manifest. Then where does your day disappear to? Have you ever observed? While asleep, where has the whole world of the day gone? The market, the politics, the identity, everything disappears – you have gone to the seeds. But in the morning the sun rises and you rise again. From where do you come? From the unmanifest to the manifest again – it is a centrifugal and centripetal movement. The lotus closes and the lotus opens...in a regular measure.

And this is an energy phenomenon – no personality in it, it is impersonal. Impersonal it is beautiful; if it is personal then it will become ugly. And all religions have become ugly because they make it personal, they create a person in it. That person is just an imaginary phenomenon you have created. That's why thousands of gods exist and everybody has his own notion about God. And when you have a notion about God, others' notions look wrong, then there is conflict, argument. And your notion of God cannot be right, because *you* are not right. A person who is right needs no god.

Look at Buddha, Heraclitus – they don't need any God. H.G. Wells has written about Buddha that he is the most godless man and yet the most godly. Can you find a man more godly than Buddha? – and more godless? He never talks about God – because he doesn't project. He has no fear inside to create a projection; he is fearless. Then God disappears – your fear is the cause. And when God disappears, then this whole existence is for you to enjoy and celebrate.

Energy is delight. Blake has said energy is delight.

When there is no God, you are free, totally free. With a God up there manipulating, you can never be free – you can only be puppets, and all the

threads are in his hand. All religious people become puppets because for everything someone else is responsible.

A really religious person is totally free.

Religiousness is freedom.

And with God, there can be no freedom. How can there be freedom if there is a creator? – because any moment he can change his mind – and he seems to be a little crazy; any moment he can change his mind and say, "Okay, disappear!" Just as it is said in The Bible that he said, "Let there be light," and light was born, any moment he can say, "Let there be no light." Then what? – light disappears. Then you must simply be puppets. Then it seems that he is playing chess and you are just on the chessboard, so whatsoever he wants to make of you he makes. The whole thing looks ugly.

If there is no freedom there cannot be any consciousness, because consciousness grows with more freedom.

And the total freedom is possible only if there is no person controlling, manipulating, no boss in existence; only then is there freedom. But freedom makes you afraid. You don't want to be free. You want to be slaves – that's why you create God. And if there is no God...for example, the communists tried a religion without a god. But man is so afraid, he cannot live without gods; so communism has created its own gods. Lenin has become a god; now they worship him. Now Lenin is no ordinary mortal – he is a god. You cannot escape because you are afraid.

Only a man who is totally unafraid, fearless, one who has come to terms with existence, one who has understood that to be with existence and to flow with it is to be blissful, can live without God, can live without any person being projected on existence, can live without imagination – can live with truth. It is hard to live with truth. It is very easy to live with lies. That's why you create lies around you. Ninety-nine percent of the things around you are lies. But you feel cozy with them, in comfort; they are comfortable lies. Truth is uncomfortable because it requires a radical change. And this is the most radical change that can happen to a man – that he lives without God. And if you can live without God, you become a god, you become godly. If you go on imagining a god, you remain a slave. With a boss overhead you will be a slave. When the boss is no more there you yourself have become a god.

I tell you, there is no God – but everybody is God, everything is godly. There is no person controlling, because then the whole existence would be ugly, a slavery, a great concentration camp; it would be a prison. No God: life is a freedom.

Then you can choose! If you want to be miserable, be miserable, that's your choice. If you want to be happy, be happy, that is your choice. If you feel happy with being miserable, it's okay. There are people who feel very, very happy with being miserable, because through their misery they attract compassion. Through their misery they ask for sympathy; through their misery, they are begging for love. But who can love a miserable person? Unless one is a buddha it is impossible to love any miserable person. You are on a suicidal path. If you are asking for love through being miserable, you can get a little sympathy, but not love. And that little sympathy will be given to you very grudgingly, because who is ready to give love to a miserable person? And he himself is in need, he himself is miserable. That's why people talk too much about their miseries. Listen to their talk: ninety-nine percent they talk about miseries, and they magnify their miseries, they make them look as great as possible. It is not possible, because you are so tiny that you cannot carry such big miseries – but you are asking for sympathy.

And man is afraid of freedom. There is a deeprooted fear of freedom because with freedom comes insecurity, with freedom comes the unknown, with freedom you don't know beforehand what is going to happen. With a God and a destiny everything is certain. You can ask the astrologer and you can go to the palmist and they can tell you about your future. With no God there, there is no destiny. And the astrologers are useless. Nothing can be said about the future. The future remains an open situation – nothing fixed, everything flexible and fluid. With freedom you become a fluidity. With God there bossing you, you are secure; somebody is looking after you and he knows better what to do and what not to do.

In this sense, Heraclitus' insight is deeper than Jesus'. In this sense, Heraclitus comes through better than Jesus or Mohammed – his insight is exactly as deep as Zarathustra, Buddha, Mahavira – because Jesus goes on speaking and talking in terms of God, creation, father, son. Maybe because of the juvenile attitude of the Jews, maybe because of the people around him, he has to talk in those terms. But Heraclitus doesn't bother about you, he says exactly what is true. He doesn't bother whether you will be able to understand or not: he simply states the truth. If you want to understand, you have to grow. He will not come down to you, you will have to go to him.

And this is exactly my attitude also. I will say exactly what I feel. If you want to understand me you have to grow towards me.

I am not going to come down to talk to you on your terms, because that never helps. Because of that, Jesus missed the whole thing and Christianity was born – which is nothing but a new edition of the Jewish religion, nothing new:

Jews modified a little here and there, nothing new – because Jesus used the whole Jewish terminology. How can you create a new world out of the old? He compromised – because Jesus never thought that there was going to be a new religion. He remained a Jew, he died a Jew; he was never a Christian. And he never imagined that there was going to be something new; he lived in the fold. And he used past, rotten words – hence the ugly face of Christianity.

Heraclitus is absolutely fresh. That's why the Greek mind couldn't understand him at all – because he has no roots in the past.

When I am dead, where will you put me? In India you will not find any roots for me. I was born a Jaina, but you will not find any roots in Jainism for me; simply, you cannot find any roots. If you say exactly what you have understood, what you have realized, then there are no roots, because truth has no roots in society – it has roots in existence, but not in society.

That's why a man like Heraclitus becomes puzzling, and even a genius like Aristotle says, "This Heraclitus is absurd. He creates puzzles, and philosophy is to solve something, not to create puzzles." He is not creating any puzzle. He looks puzzling because he is stating a fresh phenomenon that he has come to encounter. He is not using old, used, secondhand terms for it.

Says he:

*This universe,*
*which is the same for all,*
*has not been made by any god or man,*
*but it has always been, is, and will be –*
*an everliving fire,*
*kindling itself by regular measures*
*and going out by regular measures.*

This energy has its own intrinsic system. It is a cosmos, not a chaos – and without a boss. Energy plus freedom, and yet there is a discipline, and that discipline is the inner harmony, the hidden harmony. No boss and yet there is no chaos; nobody managing, and yet everything is managed so beautifully – you cannot improve upon it. This is the hidden harmony. If there is a manager and he manages, you can be certain that things will go wrong here and there. It is so beautiful a cosmos because there is no manager in it.

This will be difficult to understand. Religious people say, "How can this world become a cosmos if there is nobody who controls? Without a controller everything will fall apart!" But Heraclitus will say, "Exactly, precisely because

there is no controller, things cannot fall apart." When you control, you mismanage. You cannot find greater mismanagers than managers – they mismanage. That's what Lao Tzu says. He says: When there were no rulers everything was beautiful; when there was no law there was no crime, and when there was no wise man there were no fools. Things moved in their cosmic beauty. Then entered the rulers; they said rules are needed. With rules entered misrule, because the opposite is always there. Then came wise men and they said man must be disciplined. And then man became rebellious and everything went wrong. Then laws came, laws and more laws, and man became more and more criminal.

This is what Heraclitus says. He says that precisely because there is nobody to control, how can things go out of control? Energy itself has an intrinsic, an inner guide.

And listen to this for your life also. If you are guided by your inner insight, if you can listen to your heart, there will be no need for any discipline. You can move completely in trust, everything will be good. But because you cannot listen to your own heart you have to listen to many manipulators who go on manipulating. They say, "Do this!" and they say so much, "Do this! Don't do this!" that you are confused, you don't know what to do. One religion teaches one thing, another another thing. One morality says this is moral, another morality says this is immoral. You are simply confused. And you cannot find your own heart from where the intrinsic, the natural, the spontaneous guide comes. The more you have been taught, the more confused you have become.

Heraclitus says everything moves by an inner harmony. Who is controlling these trees? Who teaches them, "Now it is the right time to bring your flowers"? Who says to the clouds, "Now the time is coming near and you have to shower and you have to bring rains"? Nobody. Remember, if there is somebody then things will go wrong, because how can such a vast thing be managed? Even if there were a God, either he would have cracked up.... Just think of the immensity of things, the tremendousness of things, the vastness of things! Even God would have already cracked up long ago, gone mad, simply disappeared from the world, or the world would have fallen down. It can remain a cosmos only because the harmony is not being forced from above, the harmony grows from within.

There are two types of discipline: one discipline that is forced from without – somebody says "Do this!" – and the other discipline that comes from within. You feel what will be natural, you feel where your being is flowing, and you move with your feeling; then an inner discipline comes in. Outer discipline is a deception and that creates confusion and a rift in you. But then the inner and outer are opposed, they become antagonistic.

Just a few days ago, a man came to me and he said – as all religious people will agree, he said, "I again and again become a victim of outer things, and again and again I forget the inner."

So I asked him, "You please give me a concrete example – what do you mean?"

He said, "For example, my inner knows that I should remain faithful to my wife, but again and again I fall in love with other women."

So I had to tell him, "You seem to be confused. You don't know which is inner and which is outer. The wife is the outer and you think that is the inner. Do you love your wife?"

He said, "Of course not. If I had been in love with her, why should I fall for others?"

Then the wife is the outer, forced by the society, forced by your own ego, pretensions that you would like to keep of an image in the society, that you are a good husband. This is outer and he is saying this is inner. And when you fall in love with another woman – which nobody is forcing you to do, rather, on the contrary, everybody is preventing you – that is inner! But the society has confused you completely, it has made you disoriented. The outer, it says, is the inner – it has deceived you completely. The inner, it says, is the outer.

You go on a fast and you think this is the inner voice – this is your religion, your scriptures, your priests. And then your inner says, "You are hungry, eat!" And you think this is outer, the Devil is tempting you. What foolishness! The priest has tempted you to fast. The Devil is not there! The priests are the only devilish forces in the world. Hunger comes, this is inner. The whole body, every cell of it says, "Eat!" and you say, "This is outer. Somebody is tempting me, some evil forces." Or, "This is desire, this is the body, and the body is the enemy – and my soul is on a fast." Soul on a fast? The soul never needs any food so how can it go on a fast? You are forcing the poor body. But there is a natural fast also; it happens in animals. No preacher is there, no priest teaching them, but it happens. If you observe a dog: if he is not feeling well he will not eat – this is the inner. A dog's fast is inner. What absurdity! And a man's fast is almost always outer. Only a dog can fast inwardly because he is still in contact with nature, you are not.

When the body is ill, no animal can be forced to eat. If you force him to eat he will vomit. This is beautiful. The body doesn't need it; it is ill. The whole energy is needed for the body to cure itself, and that energy will be diverted if

you take food, because then the energy will be needed to digest food: it will be a burden. The body is not in a good condition; the whole energy is needed for the body to cure itself, and if food is thrown in the body, that will be a division. Now the whole of the energy will move towards curing; it will be prevented – first the food has to be digested. If in your illness you simply listen inwards and don't eat, that's beautiful. Sometimes you don't feel hungry, then don't eat. But don't take a vow, "I will fast for a few days," because who knows? – in the evening you may feel hungry. Move with nature. When nature wants you to fast, fast. When nature wants you to eat, eat.

The inner has to be found because the society has completely confused you. What is inner and what is outer: there is a vast confusion. And almost always, whatsoever you think is the outer is likely to be the inner, and whatsoever you think is the inner is bound to be the outer, because priests have done that – priests are the destructive forces.

To me, there is only one religion and that religion is to find the inner voice, the inner guide. And the person who helps you to find your inner guide is the master. He helps you – not to give yourself an outer discipline, he simply helps you to find the inner harmony which gives discipline. That discipline has a grace because it is not forced. And that discipline has a beauty of its own because it is always fresh. And with that discipline you cannot go astray because you cannot revolt with that discipline. It is you, your very innermost core. And the same is happening on a vaster scale in the whole cosmos.

*The phases of fire are craving and satiety.*

And the fire has two phases: craving, when you are hungry...Hindus call it *jatharagni,* the fire of hunger. Your stomach really feels fiery when you are hungry – if you are really hungry. Because you are in such bad shape, you don't know when you are hungry and when you are not. Every day you take your food at one o'clock, then at one o'clock every day hunger comes. That hunger is psychological. Then you will not feel fire in the stomach; that is just because of the clock. The clock says it is one o'clock, then the mind says, "Now the time has come to be hungry." Immediately you feel a hunger. This is a projection. This is a false hunger. And if you wait for half an hour, it will disappear automatically. How can a real hunger disappear so easily? The real hunger will grow more and more. The fire will become more and more fiery in the stomach. You will start feeling pain in the stomach, a burning sensation all over the body. You will feel feverish. The body needs satiety, the body is demanding; energy is

needed. But if it is a false hunger, it will disappear. When the clock has moved to two o'clock, the hunger disappears.

Watch! Feel really hungry, and then eat. Watch! Feel really sleepy, and then sleep. It will take a few months to settle because the whole civilization, culture, society, education, they have all helped to push you from the right path. The right path is always natural – the logos.

*The phases of fire are craving and satiety.*

These are the two phases of fire, the inner biofire, the bioenergy. You feel hungry, you eat, you feel satisfied. That satisfaction is also a phase of fire. The fire has subsided, now there are no flames, it has disappeared. It is a *pralaya*, a de-creation, an involution. Then again comes the other phase. The circle moves, the wheel moves: again comes the phase of hunger, again satiety. You feel sexual, lust, then satiety. You feel love and satiety.

You cannot love twenty-four hours because the fire has two phases. And husbands and wives try to do the impossible: they want to love each other twenty-four hours, then everything goes astray. You cannot because you cannot eat twenty-four hours. Love is food. Can you eat twenty-four hours? You have to give gaps so that the food is absorbed, the energy used, the body becomes hungry again. How can you love twenty-four hours? And if you try the impossible, you will be in bad shape. The more you force, the more everything will become false.

That's why husbands and wives lose the whole beauty of love. Everything becomes false and forced. When they were lovers everything was beautiful, because sometimes they would meet and there would be hunger and it would need satiety. And sometimes they would have to wait for the day to pass, then the lover would be coming – and there would be hunger. And when there is deep hunger, love satisfies deeply. When husbands and wives cling together twenty-four hours, around each other like shadows, then there is no hunger. Of course, then there is no satiety. Then the whole beauty disappears. Remember this: if you love a person, leave the person to be alone also so that the hunger arises. One has to, otherwise the love will be according to the clock.

One day Mulla Nasruddin came home and found his greatest friend kissing his wife. He said, "What! I cannot believe my eyes. I *have* to, but why you?"

A husband cannot believe it because love becomes a duty. When love becomes a duty it is already dead – then it is an outer enforcement, then the inner thing is lost. Love is a hunger, not a duty. Then it has a satiety phase. When love is satisfied you feel absolutely blissful; everything is okay; you can bless the

whole existence and be blessed by it. Everything is simply wonderful...but it has to be through hunger.

Heraclitus is saying that man is a miniature of the whole cosmos. And the same is true of the whole: the whole passes also through two phases. When the whole is in hunger, then there is much activity and creation. Things grow, manifestation comes in, trees flower, people love, children are born – everything is a dynamic activity. Then, satisfied, the existence moves into a satiety phase – everything disappears. No trees, no earth, no stars, no sun – the fire is resting.

*The sun is new each day.*

And this is one of the most penetrating maxims of Heraclitus.

*The sun is new each day.*

The hunger is new each day. The love is new each day. The life is new each day. To say "each day" is not good – each movement, each gesture, each moment, everything is new. From where does the old come then? Then why do you get bored? If everything is so new, and you cannot step in the same river twice, and you cannot see the same sunrise again; if everything is so new and fresh, then why do you become dead and bored? – because you don't live out of the inner harmony. You live out of the mind. Mind is old.

Each sun is new, each morning is new, each hunger is new, each satiety – but the mind is old. Mind is past, mind is the accumulated memory. And if you look through the mind it gives a deadness and oldness to everything, then everything looks dusty, dirty – it is because of the mind. Put aside the mind, put aside memories! If you can put aside memories, your wife is new every day, because it is only because of memories that you think you have lived with this woman thirty years and you know her well. Who knows? Nobody ever knows. We remain strangers, strangers eternally. How can you know a person? A thing can be known, not a person, because a thing can be exhausted. And now scientists say that even things cannot be known because they cannot be exhausted either.

How can you know a person? A person is freedom. Each moment he changes. If you cannot step twice in a river, how can you encounter the same person again? If even rivers are so changing, the consciousness, the stream of consciousness, cannot be old. If you put aside the mind, if you don't look from the old eyes, then your wife is new, every gesture is new. Then there is a constant, a continuous excitement in your life, a continuous aliveness. This day you will feel hungry – that hunger is new. And this day again, when you eat

food, that food is new – because nothing can be old in existence. Existence has no past. Past is part of the mind. Existence is always in the present, new, fresh, always moving, a dynamic force, a dialectical movement; riverlike it flows.

If this insight happens to you, then you will never be bored. And boredom is the greatest disease. It kills deeply, it is a slow poisoning. By and by, you are so bored that you become a dead weight on yourself. Then the whole poetry of life disappears. Then no flowers flower and no birds sing. Then you are already entombed, you have entered your grave. It is said that people die nearabout thirty and are buried nearabout seventy. Even thirty seems too long; this proverb must be from the very ancient days; now that's not true – nearabout twenty. Or even that seems to be too late. Young people come to me, young, just eighteen, twenty, and they say, "We feel bored." They have become old already. You have taught them, you have conditioned their minds already. Already they are dying. Before being young they are dying.

Remember, youth is a quality of being.

If you can look at the world without the mind you will remain young for ever and ever.

Even in your death you will be young, excited that death is approaching; excited very much – a great adventure, a culmination, a door opens now to the infinity. Hunger has passed, now comes satiety. Now you are moving into rest. Now you will be a seed, and the seed will rest and sleep for many, many years. And then again you will sprout, again you will open your eyes – but it is never the same.

Nothing is ever the same. Everything goes on changing. Only mind is old and dead. To be capable of looking at life without mind is meditation.

# *Chapter* 10

IT WOULD NOT BE BETTER
IF THINGS HAPPENED TO MEN
JUST AS THEY WISH.

UNLESS YOU EXPECT THE UNEXPECTED
YOU WILL NEVER FIND THE TRUTH,
FOR IT IS HARD TO DISCOVER
AND HARD TO ATTAIN.

NATURE LOVES TO HIDE.

THE LORD WHOSE ORACLE IS AT DELPHI
NEITHER SPEAKS NOR CONCEALS –
BUT GIVES SIGNS.

# NATURE LOVES TO HIDE

XISTENCE HAS NO LANGUAGE...and if you depend on language there can be no communication with existence. Existence is a mystery, you cannot interpret it. If you interpret, you miss. Existence can be lived, but not thought about. It is more like poetry, less like philosophy. It is a sign, it is a door. It shows, but it says nothing.

That's why, through mind, there is no approach to existence. If you think about it, you can go on thinking and thinking, about and about, but you will never reach it – because it is precisely thinking that is the barrier.

Look! See! Feel! Touch! – you will be nearer. But don't think. The moment thinking enters, you are thrown off the track – then you live in a private world. Thinking is a private world; it belongs to you. Then you are enclosed, encapsulated, imprisoned within yourself. Nonthinking, you are no more, you are enclosed no more. Nonthinking, you open, you become porous; existence flows in you and you flow into existence.

But the tendency of the mind is to interpret. Before you see something you have already interpreted it. You hear me: even before I have said anything you are already thinking about it. That's how listening becomes impossible. You will have to learn to listen. Listening means you are open, vulnerable, receptive, but you are not in any way thinking. Thinking is a positive action. Listening is passivity: you become like a valley and receive; you become like a womb and you receive. If you can listen, then nature speaks – but it is not a language. Nature doesn't use words.

Then what does nature use? Says Heraclitus, it uses signs. A flower is there: what is the sign in it? It is not saying anything, but can you say it is not saying anything really? It is saying much, but it is not using any words – a wordless message.

To hear the wordless you will have to become wordless, because only the same can hear the same, only the same can relate to the same.

Sitting by a flower, don't be a man, be a flower. Sitting by the tree, don't be a man, be a tree. Taking a bath in a river, don't be a man, be a river. And then millions of signs are given to you. And it is not a communication – it is a communion. Then nature speaks, speaks in thousands of tongues, but not in language. It speaks through millions of directions, but you cannot consult a dictionary about it and you cannot ask a philosopher what it means. The moment you start thinking what it means you are already on the path of going astray.

Somebody who had come to visit Picasso, a very learned man, a critic, he looked at Picasso's paintings and then he said, "They look beautiful, but what do they mean? For example this painting" – the painting just before which they were standing – "what does it mean?"

Picasso shrugged his shoulders and said, "Look outside the window – what does this tree mean? And that bird who is singing? And what is the meaning of the sun rising? And if this whole exists without meaning anything, why can't my painting exist without any meaning?"

Why do you ask what it means? You want to interpret it. You want to give it a linguistic pattern. You want to communicate, not commune. No, it doesn't mean anything. It is there in its total glory. It is a meaning but it doesn't mean anything. The meaning is existential. Look, watch, feel, move into it; allow it to move into you – but don't ask questions. If you ask questions, enter a university – you cannot enter the universe. If you want to enter the universe, don't ask... there is nobody to reply to you. You will have a totally different quality of being; only then will you be in contact with it.

It is reported of a Zen master – a very rare phenomenon, unbelievable because the mind boggles – that he had done a painting in the king's palace, and the king was asking again and again, "Is it complete?"

And he would say, "Wait a little more, wait a little more."

Years passed and the king said, "It is taking too much time. You don't allow me even to enter the room" – because he would lock the room and then paint – "and I am getting old. And I am getting more and more excited as to what you are doing inside the room. Is not the painting ready yet?"

The master said, "The painting is ready, but I am watching for you – you are not ready. The painting was ready long ago, but that is not the point. Unless *you* are ready, to whom will I show it?"

Existence is there, always waiting, ready. At every moment, at every turn of the road, just by the corner, it is always and always waiting. It is an infinite patience, waiting – but you are not ready.

Then it is said that the king became ready and the painter said, "Okay, the time has come."

They entered the room – nobody else was allowed in the room. The painting was really wonderful. It was difficult to say that it was a painting – it looked real. The painter had done a painting of hills, valleys, and they looked almost three-dimensional, as if they existed. And by the hills there was a small path going somewhere inside. Now comes the most difficult part of the story. The king asked, "Where does this road lead?"

The painter said, "I have not myself traveled yet on this road, but you wait, I will go and see." And he entered the path, and disappeared beyond the hills, and never came back.

This is what a mystery means.

It says many things without saying anything.

If you move into nature to find where it leads, don't stand outside it and ask because then nothing can be done; you have to move into it. If you move you will never come back, because the very movement into existence...and you are losing your ego, you are disappearing. You will reach to the goal, but you will never come back to relate the story about it. The painter never came back. Nobody comes back. Nobody can come back, because the more existential you become, the more you are lost.

Existence opens millions of doors for you, but you stand outside and you would like to know something about it from the outside. There is no outside in nature. I would like to repeat these words: there is no outside to nature, everything is inside...because how can anything exist outside nature? The whole is the inner. And the mind is trying the impossible; it is trying to stand outside, to watch, to see what it means. No, you have to participate. You have to move into it and become one, and disperse like a cloud – whereabouts unknown.

Now listen to these words of Heraclitus:

*It would not be better*
*if things happened to men*
*just as they wish.*

Why? Why would it not be better? – because whatsoever you wish will be wrong because *you* are wrong! How can you wish, desire, something right? To desire something right, you have to be right in the first place. Out of ignorance, whatsoever is desired will lead you to a deeper and deeper hell – because a desire is part of you, it comes out of you. How can anything else come? All that will come will be you. That's why your desires create problems, more and more. The more you desire, the more problems you create. The more you achieve your desires, the more you are in difficulty. But there is no going back, you have to go on and on and on. Hence the insistence of all the knowers that to meet the existence, the first point is to become desireless.

Nothing is wrong in desiring; desiring in itself is beautiful…if a buddha desires. But you desiring, how can you desire something which will lead you towards bliss? No – because desire comes out of you, it is part of you, it is a continuity. And if you are wrong, the desire is going to be wrong. It will repeat you again and again; in different situations, of course, in different worlds, on different planets, in different lives, but your desire will repeat you. Your desire cannot transform you. That's why I say to people, "If you want to take sannyas, if you want to take a jump into the unknown, don't think about it – leave it to me!" Why the emphasis on leaving it to me? Just so that you don't desire it. Let it be something which has not come from you, because whatsoever comes out of you will be you – modified, colored in different ways, but it will be you.

If you are a businessman and desire *moksha*, it will be a business; it cannot be otherwise. You will be looking for profit – in the other world, of course, but whatsoever comes out of your mind will be out of your past. And a break is needed, a complete rift is needed, a rift which is unbridgeable.

That is the meaning of going to a master and surrendering. What do you surrender? You surrender your desiring – what else can you surrender? Nothing else have you got. You say, "Now I will not desire. Now you say something and I will do it." You are allowing something else to enter in your past. If you say, "Yes, I'm convinced. I'm ready to take sannyas," the sannyas will be futile. If out of your conviction a sannyas happens, it is meaningless. But this is the trouble: you would like to be convinced first; you would like to argue about it first. Your mind would like to settle for it.

People come to me and they say, "Unless the desire comes to us, how can we take the jump?" But precisely this is the problem. You have been desiring out of yourself continuously for many lives. It leads nowhere – it cannot. Can you see the point? You are wrong, you desire, the desire goes wrong. You are wrong, you

believe, the belief goes wrong. You have heard about King Midas? Whatsoever he touches becomes gold. Whatsoever you touch, even if it is gold, it is immediately turned into dust. The question is not of a right desire or a wrong desire, the question is of a right being or a wrong being. The question is not of a right act or a wrong act. There are no right acts and no wrong acts, there are no right desires or wrong desires. There is only a desiring being. If it is ignorant, whatsoever comes out of it is going to be wrong. And if the desiring being is not ignorant, then something totally different is born out of him.

Remember: Being matters and only being matters – nothing else.

*It would not be better*
*if things happened to men*
*just as they wish.*

Stop wishing! You have been living in hells because you have been wishing. Stop desiring! Stop desiring and the doors are open. Desiring is bringing your mind into existence. Try to understand the nature of desire. Desiring means projecting your past into the future, and the future is unknown, and whatsoever you ask will be from the past. All desiring will repeat the past again and again. How can you desire the unknown? That which is in the future, how can you desire it? You don't know it. The future is the unknown, the past is the known. If you desire, it will be from the past.

Mulla Nasruddin was on his deathbed. Somebody asked him, "If you were born again, would you like to make any change or would you like to live the same life again?"

Mulla brooded long. Then he opened his eyes; he said, "One thing: I always wanted to part my hair in the middle – and that would be the only change. I have been parting my hair on the right and I always wanted to part it in the middle. Otherwise, everything would be repeated as it is." It looks stupid but this is how it is. If you think, if another chance is given to you, what will you do? All the changes that you will want to make will not be more than Mulla is asking: they will be just a parting of the hair in the middle. You would like to have another woman, but what difference does it make? You would like another profession. What difference does it make? It will not be more than parting the hair in the middle.

You cannot ask from the past, and the future is unknown. Because you go on asking from the past, you move in a vicious circle. That circle is the world, the *sansar*, the coming and going, being born again and dying again. Again and

again you do the same. Not a single basic change! There cannot be because whatsoever you think, you think out of the known. The known is your past. Then what to do? Don't desire. Let the future come without you desiring it. The future *will* come – it need not be desired. It is already coming. You need not force your projections on it. Be passive, don't be active about it. Let it come! Don't ask anything about it – that's what the meaning of desirelessness is. It is not moving from the world, renouncing the world and going to the Himalayas – all those things are immature.

Leaving, renouncing, means not desiring, and waiting without any desire. Just waiting: "Whatsoever happens we will be a witness to it." If you can wait without desiring, everything will happen to you – and then it happens from the totality, from the whole, from God itself. If you ask, desire, it will happen, but it will happen out of you. And then you move within yourself, never allowing existence to happen to you – enclosed.

*It would not be better*
*if things happened to men*
*just as they wish.*

Says Heraclitus, "It is good that things don't happen as you wish them." That is the only possibility of your awakening. That's why he says it is good – because if every desire is fulfilled you will be completely in a coma because there will be no disturbance. You wanted riches, and riches are there. You wanted beautiful women, and beautiful women are there. You wanted success and success is there. You wanted a ladder to reach to heaven and the ladder is there. You will be in a coma, you will be in a dream. If everything is fulfilled you will never try to seek the truth, there will be no gap for you...because only misery, *dukkha*, unhappiness, the hell that you create around you, helps you to wake. It shocks you towards waking.

In Hindu mythology they say that in heaven, where gods exist, every wish is fulfilled immediately, with no time gap. In the Hindu conception of heaven, there are wishfulfilling trees, *kalptarus*. You just sit under them and wish anything, and without a time gap – here you wish and there it is. Not even a single moment is lost: you ask for a beautiful woman and she is there. But these gods must be living in a dream, they must be living in a drugged, stoned state.

Hindus say that from heaven there is no way towards truth. This is very beautiful. They say if a god wishes to be liberated completely, he will have to come to the earth. Why? – because in heaven there is no unhappiness, there is

no misery to wake anyone. It is a long peaceful sleep where dreams are continuously fulfilled. When every dream is fulfilled, why should one open the eyes? Even gods have to come to earth; only then can they be liberated. This is a rare conception. Christians don't have that type of conception; their heaven is the last thing. But Hindus say it is not the last thing – it is just a beautiful, good dreamstate. Good, beautiful, long, very long, for thousands of years it can last, but it is a dreamstate. If gods are to be liberated they have to fall back to earth. Why to earth? – because on the earth there is misery, pain, anguish...and only anguish is needed. Only that can shock you out of your slumber.

Heraclitus is right:

*It would not be better*
*if things happened to men*
*just as they wish.*

Something or other always goes wrong. That's beautiful! If nothing goes wrong, if everything as it is, is as you would like it to be, then who wants truth? Then who seeks existence? Then who wants freedom, total freedom, moksha? Nobody!

Through drugs, man is trying to be like gods in the Hindu heaven. You take marijuana, or hashish, or LSD, and you are in a dreamstate, a beautiful dreamstate; you are under a wishfulfilling tree. Drugs are against truth because truth needs an awakening: awakening from the past, awakening from the dreams, awakening from your desires – to see the whole fallacy that you have created around you and to drop it. And to drop it without any effort – just to see that it is wrong and to drop it.

Remember, if you make much effort to drop it, the very effort makes you ugly. Understanding needs, really, no effort. You understand a thing, you see the reality, and you drop it! Can't you see that you are miserable because of your desires? Is it something to be argued? Something to be convinced of? Can't you see it – it is so clear that out of desires you have created a hell; then why make an effort? In a sheer, intense moment of understanding, why not drop it immediately? And if you can drop it immediately, then you have a beauty, a grace. This grace you will not find in so-called monks. All over the world, in Catholic, Hindu, Jaina monks, you will not find this grace because they are *trying* to drop it. The very effort to drop it shows that they are still clinging; otherwise, why make any effort? They would like to stop desiring, but this is again a desiring. That's why there is effort. They cling and they would like to drop it. They have

not come to a moment of understanding, a moment of truth.

My whole effort with you is to bring you to a moment of understanding where effort is useless. The understanding is so intense, so fiery, that, simply, everything burns. You see and your very seeing becomes the dropping.

This is possible – this has happened to me, this can happen to you. I am in no way exceptional, just an ordinary man. If it happens to me, just an ordinary man, why not to you? Just make an intense search towards understanding. Understanding is transformation, mutation, a revelation. Understanding liberates.

Listen to these words:

*It would not be better*
*if things happened to men*
*just as they wish.*

*Unless you expect the unexpected*
*you will never find the truth,*
*for it is hard to discover*
*and hard to attain.*

Let these words enter your heart:

*Unless you expect the unexpected,*
*you will never find the truth...*

...Because the truth cannot be your expectation.

Whatsoever you expect will be a lie. Whatsoever you expect will be a projection. Whatsoever you expect will be a part of your mind. No, truth cannot be expected. It takes you unawares. In fact, it comes when you were not even waiting for it. It is a sudden enlightenment.

Expectation means your known projecting itself into the future, into the unknown. That's why I say if you are a Christian, or a Hindu, or a Buddhist, or a Jaina, you will miss – because what does to be a Christian mean? It means a Christian expectation. It means a god seen through Christian eyes. It means a conception, a philosophy. What does it mean to be a Hindu? It means a system of belief. It gives an expectation: you expect a god, you expect the truth; the truth will be like this, the god will be like this – the face, the figure, the form, the name you expect.

Your expectation is the barrier because God is the unexpected, the truth is the unexpected. It has never been theorized about, it has never been brought into language, it cannot be forced into words; nobody has ever been able to and nobody ever will. It remains the unexpected! It is a stranger. Whenever God knocks at your door you will not find a familiar face, no. It is the unfamiliar, the stranger. You never thought about it, you never heard about it, you never read about it. Just the stranger.... And if you cannot accept the stranger, if you ask for the familiar, truth is not for you.

Truth is a stranger.

It comes without giving any intimation that it is coming. It comes when you are not expecting, not waiting.

Remember this, that people meditate and meditate and meditate – that's a must – but truth never happens in meditation. It happens outside. But meditation helps: it makes you alert, it makes you watchful, it makes you more aware and conscious. And then suddenly somewhere – it happens in such unexpected moments, you cannot believe why God chooses such unexpected moments.

A nun is carrying water, and the bamboo breaks, and the earthen pot falls on the ground, and the water flows...and suddenly she is awakened. What happened? For forty, fifty years she was meditating and it never knocked – because meditation means you are expecting, you are watching for something that is going to happen. Your mind is there, working – very subtly, very, very subtly; you may not even be able to detect where it is. You may think that now everything is silent, no thought, but this is also a thought. You feel absolute silence, but even this feeling that now there is absolute silence, now soon the door is going to open – this is a thought. When you become absolutely silent, even this thought is not there, that "I am silent," but that means you must not be meditating. And this is the paradox: meditate as much as you can to bring a moment of a nonmeditative meditation.

That happened to that nun. Carrying water, she was not worried about God; the bamboo was old, and she was worried about the bamboo. She was holding it this way and that, worried that it may break any moment. And the pot was earthen, and it would break! She was not at all at the door, and the door was open because she had meditated for forty years. So the door was open and she was not there at all...suddenly the bamboo breaks, the pot falls, breaks, and the water flows. It is a shock! For a moment even this worry dissolves. Now whatsoever was to happen has happened. Now she is in a nonmeditative moment – and God is there. And it happened.

It has been happening that way always – in such moments one never expected. When you expect, you miss, because you are there in your expectation.

When you don't expect, it happens, because you are not there, nobody is there. When your house is totally empty, so empty that you are not even aware that "I am empty" – because that much will be enough disturbance, when even emptiness is thrown, he comes.

*Unless you expect the unexpected....*

Drop all your notions about God. All notions are false. You may have heard Hindus say Christian notions are false, Christians say Hindu notions are false, Jainas say Christians and Hindus are false, Buddhists say Jainas, Hindus, Christians are false – I say all notions are false. Not that my notion is right – no! Notion as such is false, because it makes a theory out of the unknown, which is not possible. All theories are false – without any exception. All theories are false – absolutely, categorically, mine included – because the unexpected remains the unexpected.

*Unless you expect the unexpected*
*you will never find the truth,*
*for it is hard to discover*
*and hard to attain.*

In fact, it is not hard to attain and not hard to discover. It is because of you that it is hard to attain and hard to discover – because how to put this mind aside? Mind is subtle: even in putting it aside it remains. The mind says, "Okay, I will not be here," but this is also mind. The mind says, "Now, let God knock at the door. I am not," but this is also the mind. The mind says, "I will meditate." The mind says, "I will drop all thoughts." The mind says, "Look! I have dropped all thoughts. Look! I am empty." But this is also mind. This is the problem: whatsoever you do the mind stands there.

See the point – no effort will help. Just seeing the point – mind exists through claims.... See the point! Why do I say see the point? – because if you see the point then there is no claim. If you don't see the point, then the mind can claim, "I am here without any claim." See the point! Emptiness is needed, not the claim, "I am empty." Awareness is needed, not the claim, "I am awareness" – because wherever comes the "I" you have entered the dark night of the mind. When the "I" is not there, it is light, everything is clear – a clarity, a perception, infinite. You can see far and wide, you can see the whole.

So the only thing that can be done is to watch the trickiness of the mind – and don't try to do the opposite. For example: your mind is filled with thoughts.

Don't try to fight with the thoughts, because this fighter is the mind. And if you fight, the mind will claim the opposite. "Look!" he will say, "I have dropped all the thoughts. Now, where is your God? Where is enlightenment?" Don't do the opposite, don't create a fight, because with fight comes the claim. You simply watch and relax. You simply watch and enjoy the trickiness of the mind. Just enjoy it. So beautiful! How deceptive! How elusive! How it comes and comes and comes, again and again! Hindus have always been saying it is just like the tail of the dog. For even twelve years you keep it straight, but the moment you stop the effort it is crooked again.

One small child was talking to me one day and he was saying, "We are making many efforts to straighten out a friend – because he doesn't believe in Santa Claus." Then one day he said, "After seven days' effort, now he has yielded and he has said, 'Okay, I believe.' But next day again the boy said, "Now more efforts have to be made."

So I asked, "What is the matter? – because just the other day you said you had straightened him out. Now what is the need?"

He said, "But he is crooked again – we straighten him out, he becomes crooked again and again."

This is the nature of the mind. You cannot do anything about it – this is the nature of the mind. Understand it, that's all. Understanding is enough. Otherwise it is a hard thing to attain. You can go on and on and the mind will go with you like a shadow, and whatsoever you claim will be the mind's claim. That's why all the knowers have said: "Those who claim that they have known, they have not known. Those who say that they have achieved, they have not achieved." Why? – because the very claim is dangerous.

*Unless you expect the unexpected*
*you will never find the truth,*
*for it is hard to discover*
*and hard to attain.*

*Nature loves to hide.*

It is a hide-and-seek game. It is beautiful as it is! Nature is not on the surface, it is hidden in the center. Nature is like the roots of the trees, deep underground – the most essential is hidden. Never think that the tree is the most essential. The tree is just the periphery where flowers and leaves and fruits come; it is the periphery. The real tree exists underground in the dark. In the dark womb of the

earth it is hidden. You can cut the tree; a new tree will come out. But cut the roots and everything disappears.

You are not on the surface of your skin; that is the periphery. You are deep, hidden underground. And God is not on the surface. Science goes on learning more and more about the surface, learning more and more about the skin. Howsoever deep science goes, it never really goes deep because it learns from the outside. From the outside you can learn only about the skin. The real is hidden in the inside, in the innermost shrine. In you also it is hidden in the innermost shrine. You live on the periphery, you miss it. And existence has a center – that center is hidden.

*Nature loves to hide.*

Why? Why does nature love to hide? – because it is a game. In your childhood you must have played the game of hide-and-seek. For Heraclitus, existence is a game; it is a *leela*, a play. It hides, and it is beautiful! – and you have to discover. And in the very effort to discover, you grow.

There are two types of people. One I call nondiscoverers: they remain on the periphery; and discoverers: they move towards the center. People who live on the periphery are the worldly people. The market is the periphery; politics is the periphery; success, achievement is the periphery. They are nondiscoverers, non-adventurers. Even if they go to the moon it is not an adventure because they remain on the periphery. The real adventure is religious. It is to move to the very center of being. First you have to move in yourself, because you are a miniature world. You move to your center, and from that center you have the first glimpse of how things are.

The real is hidden.

On the periphery are waves, on the periphery are dreams, on the periphery is just a show. Deep inside, in the innermost core of existence, is the hidden one. That Heraclitus calls the hidden harmony.

Move towards the being, the center, the very ground. Always seek the roots. Don't be befooled by the foliage. But you *are* befooled by the foliage. If a woman is beautiful on the surface, you fall in love; you have fallen in love with the foliage. But the woman may not be beautiful inside; she may be absolutely ugly – then you are trapped. There is an inner grace when the light burns inside, when the light comes to the periphery also; you cannot see from where it is coming. You can see a beautiful woman and yet ugly. And you can see just the opposite also happening: an ugly woman and yet beautiful. When an ugly

woman is beautiful, you cannot find the source, where the source is, because the skin on the surface, the structure, the physiology, is not attractive, but something inner attracts you. When it happens that the woman is beautiful on the surface and in the inner being also, then it is very mysterious. Then what happens is charisma. Sometimes you feel a charisma around a person. Charisma means now there is some hidden harmony between the surface and the center, and then the personality has a magnetism, something of the divine.

This meeting of the periphery with the center is a hidden harmony.

*Nature loves to hide.*

Why? – because only through hiding can the play go on and on; otherwise, the play will stop. The game continues, it is an eternal game.

And remember this also: even if you have found, the game continues, but the game then has a different quality. Never think at any moment that when you have found the innermost core, the game stops. No, the game continues. Now, knowingly, many times you move away from the hidden center, knowingly you give a chance to nature to hide again – but now it is knowingly. It is just like two children playing, and the one knows where the other is hiding. Except that place he seeks everywhere, runs around and around to give the game a quality. He knows where you are hiding, he can simply go and catch you, but he will go around and around.

Buddhas continue to play, but the game changes. Now they know, now there is no anxiety. Now there is no desire, now nothing to be achieved. Now it is a simple game. There is no goal to it…it continues.

So there are two possibilities: an ignorant game, that is what is happening to you…. And because you are ignorant you take the game very seriously. Seriousness becomes a disease. You become sad about it. People come to me: if they meditate and they are not attaining, they are very serious, they feel frustrated. I say: Don't be frustrated, because that is the whole point to be understood – it is a game! There is no hurry to finish it. It is not a business. Let it go on as long as possible. Why be in such a hurry? Why be so tense? Infinity is there, eternal time is there, there is no hurry. You will always be there, and the game will always be there – it has always been there, and will always be there.

Take it easily! Take it easy!

It is always by the corner, any moment it can be discovered. But why be in such a hurry? Relax – if you can relax, you reach to the center sooner. If you are in a hurry you remain on the surface, because a hurried, a tense state of mind,

cannot move to the deeper realms of being. Only patience helps you to settle to the bottom, to the very bottom.

*Nature loves to hide.*

It is beautiful that nature loves to hide. Nature is *not* an exhibitionist. Nature is not an exhibitionist. The expression that is all the foliage is just a way to hide. In a flower God is hiding in a subtle way. If you simply see the flower you will miss.

One English poet, Tennyson, has said, and said absolutely rightly, "If I can understand a flower in its totality, I will understand God." He is right! If you can understand a pebble on the shore in its totality you will understand God, because these are all hiding-places. A flower is a hiding-place. A pebble is also a hiding-place. He is hiding everywhere – millions of forms. Wherever you are, he is there in all the forms around you. Any form can become a door. Once you have the readiness to enter, once you are not expecting, once you are not desiring, once you are not asking for something, projecting something, suddenly the door is open.

*The lord whose oracle is at Delphi*
*neither speaks nor conceals –*
*but gives signs.*

At Delphi there is an old Greek shrine, and people used to go to the oracle of Delphi to ask. But the oracle of Delphi never said anything, it simply gave signs. Heraclitus is using that as a parable. He says that God, the total, the whole, never speaks in terms of yes or no – he simply gives signs. He is poetic. He gives you symbols. Don't try to interpret them. If you interpret, you will miss. Just watch, and let the sign go deeper in you and be imprinted on the heart. Don't try to find the meaning immediately, because who will find the meaning? If you find the meaning, it will be your meaning. Just let the sign, the symbol, be imprinted on your heart and some day life will reveal the meaning. You simply live with it, you simply let it be there.

For example, you come to me and you ask, "How is my meditation going on?" You ask me, I smile; I have given you a sign. Now what will you do about it? You can interpret. That is the first tendency of the mind. You will think, "Okay, so he smiles; that means I am achieving; he says yes, so everything is okay. I am going on the right path." Your ego feels fulfilled. If you are in a positive mood, this will be the interpretation. If you are in a negative mood, you will think, "He smiles – he doesn't say yes, was polite, but I am going nowhere."

You missed either way, because if there was a yes to be said, I would have said it. I would not have put you to such trouble to find the interpretation. If there was a yes to be said, I would have said it. If there was a no to be said, I would have said it. But I have simply smiled. I have neither said yes nor no. In fact, I have not said anything – I have given you a sign. Don't interpret it. Let this smile move deeper into your heart. Let this smile be there. Remember it sometimes, put it back into the heart. Let it dissolve into you, don't try to find the meaning – and this will help your meditation. Suddenly, one day, in a deep meditative state, you will start smiling the same way I smiled, because that moment will be the moment of understanding. Then you can laugh, because you will know what the meaning was .

Life is subtle. Yes and no cannot be used. Life is so subtle that if you say yes you falsify it, if you say no you falsify it. Language is very poor. It knows only two things: yes or no. And life is very rich: it knows infinite postures, positions, between yes and no – infinite gradations. It is a spectrum of many, many millions of colors. Yes and no are very poor – you say nothing. Yes and no means you have divided life into black and white; but life has millions of colors, it is a rainbow.

Black and white, in fact, are not colors. Except for black and white, all colors exist. You must understand this. Black is the absence of all colors; it is not a color. When no color is present, the emptiness is blackness. It is not a color in itself. That's why in nature you don't find black. It is not much. It is an absence. And white is not a color either, it is a mixture of all colors. If you mix all the colors it becomes white. It is not a color. White is one pole, black is the other. The presence of all colors is white, the absence of all colors is black. Between these two polarities real colors exist – green and red and yellow and all the shades of them, millions of shades.

When I smile, I am not saying black or white, yes or no – I am giving you a color in the spectrum, a real color. Don't try to interpret, because if you interpret you will either say it is black or white, and it is neither. It is somewhere in between and it is so subtle that words cannot express it. If words could express it I would have given you a word. I would not put you in trouble unnecessarily.

You come to me and you say something and I don't answer. Sometimes it happens that you come to see me and I don't even ask; I simply forget about you. I ask others and simply drop you out of the count. You will interpret it. Why? Don't interpret. Just let this gesture be deep in you. Some day, in a very,

very meditative mood, the meaning will flower. I am sowing seeds in you, not giving you words and theories.

When I am gone, please remember me as a poet, not as a philosopher.

Poetry has to be understood in a different way – you have to love poetry, not interpret. You have to repeat the poetry many times so it mixes with your blood, with your bones, with your very marrow. You have to chant poetry many times so that you can feel all the nuances, subtle shades of it. You have to simply sit and let the poetry move within you so it becomes a live force. You digest it, and then you forget about it; it moves deeper and deeper and deeper and changes you.

Let me be remembered as a poet. Of course, I am not writing poetry in words. I am writing poetry in a more alive medium – in you. And that's what the whole existence is doing.

Says Heraclitus:

*The lord whose oracle is at Delphi*
*neither speaks nor conceals –*
*but gives signs.*

A sign is not to be interpreted. A sign is to be lived through. Your mind will have the temptation to interpret. Don't be tempted by the mind. Just say to the mind, "This is not your field, this is not for you. You play with other things. Let this go deeper in my being." And that's what I am doing while I am talking to you.

I am not talking to your minds – I am talking to you as beings, as luminous beings, as gods incarnate, as possibilities, as infinite potentialities. I am talking to your future, not to your past. Your past is rubbish, throw it! Don't carry it! I am talking to your future – the unexpected, the unknown. By and by you will become capable of listening to this music, the music of the unknown, the music in which all the opposites disappear and a hidden harmony arises.

Yes, nature loves to hide, because nature is a mystery. It is not a question, it is not a puzzle to be solved. It is a mystery to be lived, enjoyed, celebrated.

# *Chapter* 11

INTO THE SAME RIVERS WE STEP AND DO NOT STEP.

YOU CANNOT STEP TWICE IN THE SAME RIVER.

EVERYTHING FLOWS AND NOTHING ABIDES.
EVERYTHING GIVES WAY AND NOTHING STAYS FIXED.

COOL THINGS BECOME WARM, THE WARM GROWS COOL.
THE MOIST DRIES, THE PARCHED BECOMES MOIST.

IT IS BY DISEASE THAT HEALTH IS PLEASANT;
BY EVIL THAT GOOD IS PLEASANT,
BY HUNGER, SATIETY; BY WEARINESS, REST.

IT IS ONE AND THE SAME THING TO BE LIVING OR DEAD,
AWAKE OR ASLEEP, YOUNG OR OLD.
THE FORMER ASPECT IN EACH CASE BECOMES THE LATTER,
AND THE LATTER AGAIN THE FORMER,
BY SUDDEN UNEXPECTED REVERSAL.

IT THROWS APART
AND THEN BRINGS TOGETHER AGAIN.

ALL THINGS COME IN THEIR DUE SEASONS.

# YOU CANNOT STEP TWICE INTO THE SAME RIVER

I*NTO THE SAME RIVERS WE STEP AND DO NOT STEP...*

...because the appearance, and remember, only the appearance, remains the same. Otherwise, everything changes and flows.

Here is the basic difference between the ordinary religious conception and the really religious. Hindus say that that which changes is the appearance, the maya; and that which never changes, is permanent, is brahma. Heraclitus says just the opposite: that which appears permanent is the appearance, the maya, and that which changes is the brahma. And the same is the understanding of Buddha, that change is the only permanence, change is the only eternal phenomenon. Only change abides, nothing else. My feeling is also the same.

In search of a permanent truth you are searching for nothing but your own ego. In search of a permanent God, what are you seeking? You are seeking permanence in some way or other. You would like to abide so that if this world changes there is nothing to worry about. Your mind says, "Seek the divine and there will be no change, and you will live for ever and ever."

The ordinary religious conception – Hindu, Jewish or Christian – is basically an ego-trip. Why do you say that change is appearance? – because with change you are afraid. Change looks like death. You would like something absolutely permanent to stand upon. You would like a house that will be always and always. In this world you cannot find that house that abides. In this world you cannot find any relationship that abides. Then you project a relationship with God, because God abides, and with God you will abide. But this search, this

desire, this seeking to abide forever – this is the problem! Why do you want to be? Why not *not* be? Why are you so afraid of not being? If you are afraid of nonbeing, nothingness, emptiness, death, you cannot know the truth. One knows the true when one is ready to drop oneself totally, utterly.

That's why Buddha says, "There is no soul. You are not a self, not an *atma*. You are an *anatta*, a no-self. There is nothing permanent in you, nothing substantial – you are a flow, a river." Why does Buddha insist on a no-self? He insists because if you accept nonbeing, if you accept nothingness, then there is no fear of death, then you can drop yourself completely. And when you drop yourself completely, the vision arises. Then you are capable of knowing. With your ego you cannot know. Only in an egolessness, in a deep abyss, in the absence of the ego, does the perception happen – then you become a mirror. With the ego you will always interpret, you cannot know the truth. With the ego you will always be there interpreting in subtle ways, and your interpretation is not the truth. You are the medium of all falsification. Through you everything becomes false. When you are not there, the true reflects.

Somehow you have to come to an understanding: the understanding of the no-self, of a changeless flux, no substance as such – just a river flowing and flowing. Then you are a mirror, a clarity. Then there is nobody to disturb and nobody to interpret and nobody to distract. Then existence mirrors in you as it is. That mirroring of existence as it is, is the truth.

Second thing: if you want to abide always and always, you have not lived the moment. One who has lived his life truly, authentically, one who has enjoyed it, is always ready to die, is always ready to leave. One who has not enjoyed and celebrated, one who has not lived the moment, the life, is always afraid to leave because "the time has come to leave and I am yet unfulfilled." The fear of death is not the fear of death, it is a fear of remaining unfulfilled. You are going to die, and nothing, nothing at all could you experience through life – no maturity, no growth, no flowering. Emptyhanded you came, emptyhanded you are going. This is the fear!

One who has lived is always ready to die. His readiness is not a forced attitude. His readiness is just like a flower. When the flower has flowered, has sent its perfume to the infinite corners of existence, enjoyed the moment, lived it, danced through the breeze, risen against the wind, looked at the sky, watched the sunrise, lived it, a fulfillment comes by the evening and the flower is ready to drop to the earth, to go back, to rest. And it is always beautiful – when you have lived, rest is beautiful. It is the thing! The flower simply drops to the earth

and goes to sleep. There is no tension, no anguish, no cry, no effort to cling.

You cling to life because your life is unfulfilled. You have not risen against a strong wind. You have not known the morning, and the evening has come. You have never been young, and old age is knocking at the door. You never loved, and death is coming. This unfulfilled state and the coming of death creates the fear. Buddha says that if you have lived you will always be ready to die. And that readiness will not be something forced upon you. It will be the thing, it will be a natural thing! As you are born, you die. As you come, you go. This is the wheel of existence. You lived the being part, now you will live the nonbeing part. You existed, now you will not exist. You rose, you manifested, now you will move into the unmanifested. You were visible, embodied, now you will move without the body to the invisible. You had your day; now you will take rest in the night. What is wrong in it?

The search for the permanent shows that you remain unfulfilled. The search to have a permanent self is a clinging. You know that death is going to be there, so what to do? The body will disintegrate, disappear; now you have your hopes that some permanent self must be there which will go on and on and on. Remember: those who are afraid, they always believe in the eternal soul.

Look in this country: the whole country believes that the soul is eternal, but you cannot find a more cowardly country in the world. It is not accidental. Why are Indians so cowardly? In fact, if they know that the soul is never going to die they should be the bravest – because death doesn't exist! They go on talking about the deathless, and if you watch their life they are more afraid of death than anybody else. Otherwise, how can you explain the one thousand years of slavery of this country? Very small races – England is no bigger than a small province of India. Three crore people only were able to dominate a country of fifty crore. It seems simply impossible! How did it happen? – because the country is cowardly. They cannot fight, they are afraid of death. They talk about the deathless – and this is not accidental, there is a reasoning behind it.

Whenever somebody talks too much about the deathless it means he is afraid of death, he is a coward. And India has not lived because of the priests. India has not lived life because of the priests. They have been teaching people to renounce, so everybody is ready, before he has lived, to renounce. Then the fear comes in. If you have lived, lived to your total capacity, to the optimum, the fear of death disappears. Only then does the fear of death disappear, never before it. If you renounce life, if you don't love, if you don't eat, if you don't enjoy and dance; if you simply renounce and condemn and you say, "This is all materialistic. I am

against it"...who is this "I" who says "I am against it"? This is the ego.

You cannot find greater egoists than so called spiritualists. They are always condemning the materialist. They are always saying: "What! You are wasting your life. Eat, drink, and be merry – this is your religion. You are a burden on the earth. You have to be thrown into hell." Who is condemning? What is wrong in "Eat, drink, and be merry"? What is wrong in it? That is the first part of life. It should be so. You should eat, drink, and be merry. You should celebrate. Only then, when you have celebrated to the optimum, are you ready to go, are you ready to leave and with no grudge, with no complaint. You lived the day, now the night has come. And when the day was so beautiful – you rose with the waves in the sky, and you did whatsoever the moment demanded – then the rest, then going back to the earth is beautiful.

India has been renouncing, and a religion that renounces is false. A religion that makes you capable of celebrating to the optimum is the true religion. And this is the beauty of it: if you live life, a renunciation comes automatically. It happens – that is the nature. If you eat well, satiety comes. If you drink well, the thirst disappears. If you lived well, the clinging to life disappears. It has to be so. This is the law, the logos. If you have not lived well, then you always remain clinging, then you always dream about how to live. And if you have renounced this life you have to project another life. You need a permanent self, otherwise what will you do? You missed this life, and there is no other life? You need a permanent self. You have to believe and console yourself: "Okay, the body dies but the self never dies."

If you listen to Buddha and Heraclitus and to me, the self dies even before the body dies – because the self is of a more dreamy stuff than the body. The body is more substantial – at least it takes seventy years to die, and the self dies every moment. Watch: in the morning you have one self, by the afternoon another. In the morning you were happy and it was a different self; by the afternoon it has gone, already gone. Yes, Heraclitus is right:

*Into the same rivers we step and do not step.*

It simply appears that in the afternoon you are the same self. It simply appears. Where is the self of the morning when you were so happy, and you could sing with the birds, and you could dance with the rising sun? Where is that self? By the afternoon you are already sad; the evening has already descended on you. In the middle of the afternoon it has already become night – you are sad. Is this the same self? When you hate and when you love, do you think it is the same self? When you are depressed and when you reach a peak of joy, is this the same self? It is not, it simply appears to be. It appears the same, just like if you go the Ganges: in the morning, in the afternoon, in the evening, it appears the same Ganges – but it is not. It is constantly flowing.

Heraclitus loves the symbol of the river, Buddha loves the symbol of the flame. That symbol of the flame is even more subtle. The flame appears to be the same but it is not. Every moment it is disappearing; the old is going and the new is coming. Buddha says that in the evening you light a candle, and in the morning you blow it out – but never think that it is the same candle. It cannot be. The whole night it burnt and burnt and burnt. The whole night the flame disappeared and disappeared and disappeared, and a new flame was constantly being supplied. But the difference between the two flames – the old going out and the new coming in, the gap – is so subtle that you cannot see it.

Buddha says, "The self that is born will not die – it has died already. The man you were born as and the man you will be when you die are not the same." Buddha says, "It is the same continuum, but not the same thing." The flame in the evening and the flame in the morning constitute the same continuum, the same series of flames, but not the same self. The Ganges looks the same; it is not the same. And everything is changing....

The nature of the reality is change.

Permanence is illusion.

And this is a deeper insight than the Hindus'. This is the deepest ever attained...because the mind would like to have a permanent home, to have a permanent standing ground, to have permanent roots. Permanence is false; it appears because of the sameness of things. Your face remains the same in the evening and the morning, so we think you are the same person. You were here yesterday, the day before yesterday; your face appears to be the same, but are you the same? When you came to see me this morning you were different, you have already changed. And when you leave you will not be the same person – because you listened to me and something else has entered into you. Your self has already changed. New rivers falling into the Ganges, new rivulets, new streams. I have fallen into you. How can you be the same again? You will never be the same. There is no way. Every moment millions of streams are falling into your consciousness. You pass by the road and a flower smiles – the flower is changing you. And a cold breeze comes and gives you a cool bath – the breeze is changing you. And then the sun rises, and you feel a warmth – the sun is changing you.

Every moment, everything is changing. And there is no permanent thing.

What will happen if you can understand this? If you can understand this, this becomes the greatest situation to drop the ego. When everything is changing, why cling? And even by your clinging you cannot make change stop. You cannot stop the river. It flows! Stopping is not possible. And because we like to stop things, to make them permanent, we create a hell around us. Nothing can be stopped. I love you this morning – who knows what will happen tomorrow morning? But you would like to stop the love: as it is this morning, tomorrow also. If you cling and stop, you are dead. Tomorrow morning nobody knows – the unknown, the unexpected.

You can only expect if things are permanent. If nothing is permanent expectation drops. When there is no expectation because things are moving and moving and moving, how can you be frustrated? If you expect, there is frustration. If you don't expect, there is no frustration. You expect because you think that things are permanent. Nothing is permanent.

*Into the same rivers we step and do not step.*

Just the appearance is the same – of the river, and of you also.

*You cannot step twice in the same river…*

…because the river will never be the same again. And you also will never be the same again. That's why each moment is unique, incomparable. It has been never before and will never be again. This is beautiful! It is not a repetition, it is absolutely fresh. You will miss this freshness if you have a clinging and possessive mind and are seeking something permanent. And just try to think: if you have a permanent self, that self will be like a rock. Even rocks change. But the self cannot be like a flower. If you have a permanent self, and if things have a permanent self, a substratum, then the whole existence will be a boredom, it cannot be a celebration.

Celebration is possible if each moment brings you something new.

If each moment brings you something from the unknown, if each moment is a penetration of the unknown into the known, then life is an excitement – without expectation. Then life is a constant movement into the unknown. Nothing can frustrate you because in the first place you never expected that anything was going to be the same for ever.

Why is there so much frustration in the world? – because everybody is expecting permanence. And permanence is not the nature of things. Nothing can be done about it. You have to grow and drop the idea of permanence. You have to grow and become a flow. Don't be like solid rocks; be like fragile flowers. Your brahma is just a solid rock. The absolute of Hegel and Shankara is a solid rock. But the nirvana of Buddha, the understanding of Heraclitus, is like a fragile flower, changing. Enjoy it while it lasts, and don't ask for more.

You are in love – celebrate while it is there! Don't start making arrangements so that it is always there; otherwise you will miss the moment in making arrangements. And by the time arrangements are ready, the flower is dead. By the time you are ready to enjoy, the moment has already gone. And nobody can bring it back, there is no going back. The river is onward and onward flowing, and you are being thrown to new shores every moment.

This is the problem, the anxiety of man, the anguish, that the mind thinks of the shores that are no more. The mind wants to project the shores that are no more into the future, and every moment the river is reaching to new shores – unknown, unexpected. But this is beautiful. If your wish is fulfilled you will make the whole life ugly.

Just think: Hindus, Jainas, have a conception of a *moksha*, of a state of consciousness where nothing changes. Just think for a moment – nothing changes, and people who have become enlightened, according to Jainas and Hindus, they will remain in that absolutely permanent moksha, nothing changing, not at all – that will be absolute boredom. You cannot improve on it. That will be absolute. You cannot think of a more boring situation: God sitting there and you sitting there and nothing changing, nothing to say even. Even one moment will look like eternity – so boring. No, for Heraclitus and Buddha and Lao Tzu, the soul of existence is change. And change beautifies everything.

A young woman – you would like her to remain always young and the same. But if it really happens you will be bored. If it really happens that a young woman, by some biological device, some trick of science...and it is possible! Sooner or later, man is so foolish, it is possible that you may find some biological trick, inject some hormones in the body, and a person remains at the same age. A girl of twenty remains twenty and twenty and twenty – can you love this girl? It will be a plastic girl. It will remain the same but there will be no changing seasons, no summer, no winter, no spring, no fall. The woman will be dead! You cannot love such a woman; it will be a nightmare. You will want to escape to the other corner of the world to escape from this woman.

Seasons are beautiful, and through seasons every moment you become new – every moment a new mood, every moment a new nuance of being; every moment new eyes and a new face.

And who has told you that an old woman is ugly? The old woman will be ugly if she is still trying to look young; then she will be ugly. Then her face will be painted...and lipstick and this and that, and then she will be ugly. But if an old woman accepts old age as natural, as it should be, then you cannot find a more beautiful face than an old face – wrinkled; wrinkled through many seasons, seasoned; many experiences, mature, grownup.

An old person becomes beautiful if he has lived life. If he has not lived, then he wants to cling to some past moment which is there no more. And this is the ugly man: when youth has passed and you are trying to show that you are young; when sex has passed – should have passed if you have lived – and you are still seeking things which are good in their season, which are beautiful in certain moments of life. But an old man is ridiculous falling in love...ridiculous! He is as ridiculous as a young man *not* falling in love – out of season, out of step with life.

That's why they say "dirty old man." The saying is good. Whenever an old man thinks about sex, it *is* dirty; it shows that he has not grown. Sex was good at its own stage, but an old man now should be getting ready to leave, now should be ready to die, now should make arrangements – because soon his ship will be ready and he will be leaving for the unknown shore. He should make arrangements for it now, and he is behaving like a young man or a child. Nothing is more ugly than that: pretending something which has passed, living in the past. He is mad!

Everything is beautiful at its moment, and everything has a moment for it. Never be out of step. That's what I call being religious – never to be out of step. Be true to the moment: when young, be young; when old, be old. And don't get mixed, otherwise you will be a mess, and a mess is ugly. There is no need to do anything on your part really; you simply have to follow nature. Whatsoever you do goes wrong. Doing itself is wrong...simply flowing.

*Into the same rivers we step and do not step.*
*You cannot step twice in the same river.*

You cannot be young again if you are old. You cannot be a child again if you are young. If you are young and trying to be a child, you are retarded. And that shows only one thing: that when you were a child you missed it; hence the hanging feeling. Even old people desire their childhood. They miss their whole life because they missed the first step. When they were children they must have been thinking of becoming young, becoming big, being powerful; being like daddy, being like the big people around. When they were children they must

have thought about it; they missed childhood, then in the end they are asking for childhood again. And they talk and they write poetry saying that childhood was beautiful, it was a paradise.

These are the people who have missed. When you miss a paradise you talk about it. When you have lived it there is no talk about it. And if you lived your childhood paradise then your youth will be a beautiful phenomenon. It will be based on the paradise that you lived in childhood. It will have a grace, a beauty. And when you lived your youth, your old age becomes the peak, the Gourishankar, the Everest. And white hair on an old head is just like snow on a great peak. And with everything gone and everything changed, all rivers tasted, all shores known, you can rest. For the first time there is no restlessness. You can be yourself. There is nowhere to go, nothing to do – you can relax!

If an old man cannot relax, that means he has not lived life. And if you cannot relax, how can you die? And those who cannot die, they create desire for a permanent self, for a permanent God. Know well: The only change is the God. Change is the only permanence in the world, only change is eternal. Everything else is changing except change, only change is the exception; otherwise, everything is changing.

*Everything flows and nothing abides.*
*Everything gives way and nothing stays fixed.*

You should be ready! This is what I call meditation: you should be ready. When something goes, you should be ready. You should let it go. You should not complain, you should not create a scene – when something goes, it goes.

You loved a woman, you loved a man, and then the moment comes to part. Then, this moment shows the real man. If you complain, are reluctant, not willing, angry, violent, destructive, you have not loved that person at all. If you have loved that person, parting will be a beautiful phenomenon. You will be grateful. Now the time has come to part you can say goodbye with your total heart – if you loved the person. You will be grateful! But you never loved – you were thinking about love, you were doing everything but never loving. Now the parting moment has come you cannot give a beautiful goodbye, because now you realize you missed the point, you missed the time; you never loved, and this man, this woman, is leaving. You become angry, you become violent, you become aggressive. The parting moment shows everything because it is the culmination. And then for your whole life you will complain against this woman: she destroyed your life. And you will go on complaining. Then you will always be

carrying a wound. A love should make you flower. But as it happens, as I see it happening all around, all over the world, it always gives you a wound.

While someone is with you, love, because nobody knows the next step, and the parting comes. If you love a person really, you will part beautifully. If you loved life, you will part with life also beautifully. You will be thankful. Your last words, leaving this shore to the other, will be of gratitude – that life gave you so much, and life gave you so many experiences. Life made you whatsoever you are. There were miseries, but there were blessings also. There was suffering, but there was happiness also. And if you have lived both you will know that the suffering exists to make you blissful. The night exists to give you a new day. It is a gestalt – because bliss cannot exist without suffering, hence suffering exists. You will be grateful, not only to the blissful moments but to the suffering moments also, because without them the blissful moments cannot exist. You will be grateful to life in its totality. There will be no choice, because a man who has passed through life and grown and has known what life is, in its suffering, in its bliss, will come to know what Heraclitus says: God is winter and summer, God is life and death, God is day and night. God is suffering and bliss...both!

Then you don't say that suffering was wrong. If somebody says suffering was wrong, he has not grown. Then you don't say, "I would like only the blissful moments. I would not like the suffering, that was wrong." If you do, then you are childish, you are juvenile. You are asking for the impossible. You are asking for the hills, the peaks, without the valleys. You are simply stupid. It is not possible, it is not in the nature of things. The valley has to exist with the peak. The greater the peak, the deeper will be the valley. And one who understands this is happy with both. There are moments when you would like to come down to the valley from the peak, because the valley gives rest. The peak is good – it is excitement, it is a climax. But after excitement and climax one feels tired – and then the valley is there. To move into the darkness of the valley and to rest and be forgotten, completely, as if you don't exist.... Both are beautiful: suffering and bliss both. If somebody says, "I choose only bliss, and I don't choose suffering," he is juvenile, he has still not known what reality is.

*Everything flows and nothing abides.*
*Everything gives way and nothing stays fixed.*

*Cool things become warm, the warm grows cool.*
*The moist dries, the parched becomes moist.*

*It is by disease that health is pleasant;*
*by evil that good is pleasant;*
*by hunger, satiety; by weariness, rest.*

Don't choose! You choose, and you fall in the trap. Remain choiceless and let life flow in its totality. Half is not possible. That is the absurdity – that mind clings. It wants the half. You would like to be loved, you would not like to be hated – but lovers hate also. With love enters hate. And if the lover cannot hate, the lover cannot love. Love means coming together, hate means going away. It is a rhythm. You come together – a peak; then you go apart, then you move to your own individualities. This is what the hate moment means. This creates you again, it makes you ready again to come together.

Life is a rhythm. It is just a centrifugal and centripetal rhythm. Everything falls apart and comes together, falls apart and comes together.

It happened in a Mohammedan country: The king was in love with a woman. The woman was in love with somebody else; a slave she was in love with, a slave of the king himself. And this was very difficult for the king to understand, that the woman doesn't pay any attention to him and he is the king – and she is after a slave who is nothing! The king can kill that man immediately, he is just like dirt! But this is how it happened. Life is mysterious. You cannot be mathematical about it. Nobody knows. You may be a king, but you cannot force love. He may be a slave, but love will make a king out of him. Nobody knows! Life is mysterious. It is not arithmetical, it is not economics.

The king tried and tried, but the more he tried the more he was a failure. Then he was very, very angry. But he was really in love with the woman so he was afraid to kill that slave. He could have killed him; just a word was enough. But then he was afraid the woman might be hurt. And he really loved the woman, so this became more problematic – what to do? She may be hurt, she may commit suicide, she was so mad. So he asked a wise man. The wise man must have been like a Heraclitus. All wise men are like Heraclitus; Heraclitus is the superb wise man. The wise man said, "What you have been doing is wrong" – because the king had been trying in every way to keep them separate. He said, "This is wrong. The more you keep them separate, the more they would like to be together. Keep them together, and soon it will be finished. And keep them together in such a way that they cannot go apart."

The king said, "How to do that?"

He said, "Bring them both, force them to make love, and chain them, bind

them together. And don't allow them to separate." So this was done. They were chained to a pillar, making love to each other naked. But if you are chained to a woman or with a man, how long can you love that woman or that man? That's why in marriage love disappears. You are chained, in a bondage; you cannot escape. But that was the experiment.

After a few minutes they started hating each other. After a few hours they dirtied each other's bodies – because you cannot wait, the bowels have to move, the urine has to be thrown out of the bladder. What to do? For a few hours they contained themselves, they felt that that would not be good. But then there is a point beyond which you cannot do anything. The bowels moved, the bladder emptied itself; they dirtied each other and they hated even more. They closed their eyes, they did not want to see each other. And this for twenty-four hours – a marathon! And after twenty-four hours they were released. It is said they never saw each other's faces again. They escaped the moment they were released from the palace. They escaped in different directions; they never saw each other's faces again. The whole thing became so ugly. Marriages become ugly because they follow this principle of that wise man.

There should be a rhythm of coming together and going apart, being together and being alone. If you can come together freely and move away again, that's how hunger and satiety are created. If you go on eating twenty-four hours a day there will be no hunger and no satiety. Eat and then you fast! The English word for the morning food, breakfast, is good. It means breaking the fast; the whole night you fasted. You have to fast if you want to enjoy food. This is the hidden harmony of opposites.

*Cool things become warm, the warm grows cool.*
*The moist dries, the parched becomes moist.*

*It is by disease that health is pleasant....*

So sometimes it is very, very good to be ill. Nothing wrong about it. A healthy person is bound to fall ill sometimes. But you have different conceptions; you think a healthy person should never be ill – that is absolutely foolish. It is not possible. Only a dead person is never ill. A healthy person has to be ill sometimes. Through illness he attains to health again, and then the health is fresh. Passing through illness, passing through the opposite, it again becomes new. Have you ever watched? After a long fever, when you are getting well you have a freshness, a virginity; the whole body seems to be rejuvenated.

If you remain healthy for seventy years continuously, your health will be like an illness, a death, because it was never rejuvenated, never made fresh. The opposite always gives freshness. It will be stale if you are never ill; your health will become like a burden. Sometimes falling ill is beautiful. I am not saying to remain in bed forever; that too would be bad. Always ill is bad. Anything that becomes a permanent thing is bad. Anything that moves and flows into the other is good, it is alive.

Because of such statements, Aristotle called Heraclitus a little defective – defective in character, defective in his physiology, somehow biologically defective. ...Because who will say that illness is good? Aristotle is logical. He says health is good, illness is bad; one has to avoid illness, and if you can avoid it completely, that will be the best thing. That's what science is doing all over the world – trying to remove illness completely. It follows Aristotle. But I say to you, the more science tries to avoid illness, the more new diseases arise.

There are many new diseases which were never there in the world before. Because you close one door to illness, another has to be opened immediately by nature – because without illness no health is possible; you are doing a foolish thing. You close one door; now no more malaria, no more plague – two doors have to be opened somewhere else. And if you are mad about closing doors – and science is closing all the doors – then more dangerous diseases will arise, because if you close a million doors of illnesses, then nature has to open a very, very great door so that it balances the millions of doors. Then cancer comes in. You cure diseases and you create incurable diseases. Cancer is a new phenomenon; it was never before in the world – and it is incurable. Why is it incurable? – because nature is defending its law. You go on curing every disease so something incurable has to be created, otherwise man will be dead. Without illness nobody will be healthy. And this is going to happen. It seems some day cancer will be cured, then nature will immediately create something more incurable.

And remember: in this fight science cannot win and should not win. Nature should always be the winner. Nature is more wise than all your scientists put together.

Look: go to a primitive community where no medicine exists, where no doctors are, no science to cure them. They are less ill and more healthy. Illness is common but not incurable. And there are a few primitive communities still alive which don't believe in medicine at all. They don't really do anything, or whatsoever they do is just to console the patient, in fact. Mantras, magical tricks – they are not medicines: they are just to help the patient to pass time –

because nature cures itself. It is said that if you take a medicine for a common cold, it will be cured in seven days; if you don't take, then in a week.

Nature cures itself. In fact, nature cures. One has to give time; patience is needed. The English word for an ill person, patient, is beautiful. It means patience is needed; one has to wait. In fact, the function of the doctor is to help the patient to be patient. By giving medicine he is consoled. He thinks: "Now something is being done and soon I will be cured." He is helped in waiting. The doctor cannot do anything else. That's why so many "pathies" work – homeopathy, allopathy, ayurveda – thousands of pathies work; even naturopathy works. Naturopathy means not doing anything, or doing something which is actually nothing. That's why even Satya Sai Baba succeeds. Consolation is needed – the work is done by nature itself.

Heraclitus is not defective, Aristotle is defective. Something is lacking in Aristotle's physiology and biology. But the whole Western mind has followed Aristotle. And if you go to the very logical end, which is to make the human body completely healthy, without any disease, the logical end will be to have plastic parts. This heart, natural heart, is bound to be ill sometimes, tired, wearied, needs rest. A plastic heart needs no rest; it is never tired. And if something goes wrong you can simply change the part. You can go to the garage and simply change the part, you can carry spare parts with you. Sooner or later, the whole body – if Aristotle succeeds to the very end, and Heraclitus is not listened to and not taken back into the human consciousness – if. Aristotle goes on and on, the logical end will be a plastic body with spare parts; not blood flowing in the veins, but some chemical which can be immediately pumped out and refilled.

But what type of man will be there? Of course no illness, but no health either. Imagine that type of man yourself: that you have all things plastic – plastic kidneys and plastic hearts and plastic everything, plastic skin, and inside you plastic – will you be healthy? Will you ever be able to feel a wellbeing? No, you will not be ill, that's right. The mosquitoes will not affect you – you can meditate without being disturbed, they cannot bite. But you will be enclosed in a shell and cut off from nature completely. No need to breathe, because the whole thing can be run by a battery. Just imagine yourself completely encapsulated in a mechanical phenomenon – will you ever be healthy? You will never be ill, that's right, but you will never be healthy. And whenever you fall in love you will not be able to put your hand on your heart, because there is nothing but plastic. This is going to happen if Heraclitus is not listened to. Aristotle is defective, not Heraclitus. Aristotle is wrong, not Heraclitus.

*It is by disease that health is pleasant;*
*by evil that good is pleasant....*

More and more difficult he becomes. We can even agree, reluctantly, that okay, without illness there will be no health – but then he says it is by evil that good is pleasant, by the Devil that God is pleasant, by the sinners that saints are so beautiful. If sinners disappear, the saints disappear. And if there is really a saint, he is bound to be a sinner also. There are only two possibilities to do this. One is that I become a saint and you become a sinner. This is what religions have done. Just a division of labor – you do the work of the sinner and I do the work of a saint. But in a better world, in a more logos-oriented world – not logical – is it good to force somebody else to be a sinner and force myself to be a saint? Is it good to be a saint at somebody else's cost? No, it is not. Then in a better world the saint will be the sinner also. Of course, he will sin in a very saintly way, that's right – but this becomes more and more difficult. Then he will be like Gurdjieff: a sinner and saint both.

Gurdjieff is a turning-point in the history of human consciousness. After Gurdjieff, the concept of saint should be completely different; it can never be the same, the old. Gurdjieff stands at a crisis point from where a new saint is to arise. That's why Gurdjieff was very much misunderstood – because the concepts were that a saint should be a saint, and he was both.... It was difficult to understand: "How can a man be both? Either you are a saint or you are a sinner." So, many types of rumors go around about Gurdjieff. Some think that he was the most devilish person possible, a devil's agent. And some think he was the greatest sage ever born. He was both, and both types of rumor are true, but both are wrong also. Followers think that he was a sage and they try to hide the sinner part because they also cannot comprehend how he could be both. So they simply say that that is a rumor, that these are people who don't understand who are talking. And then there are people who are against him. They cannot believe in his sage part because, they say, "How can such a sinner be a sage? Impossible! Both cannot exist in one man." And this is the whole point, that they both exist in one man.

You can do only one thing: you can suppress one and pretend the other. You can suppress one in the unconscious and the other you can bring to the surface, but then your saint will be skindeep and your sinner will be very, very deep in the roots. Or you can do just the opposite: you can bring the sinner to the skin and suppress the saint – the criminals are doing that. The one possibility is that I suppress my

sinner, but that sinner will affect somebody somewhere, because we are one.

Says Heraclitus: "Private intelligence is false." We are one. Consciousness is a community, we exist in one net. And if I suppress my sinner, somewhere at some weaker link the sinner will pop up. Ram is a saint; then the sinner pops up in Ravana. They are both together, one phenomenon. Jesus is a saint; then Judas, the disciple who loved him most, becomes the sinner.

Saints are responsible for sinners, and sinners help saints to be saints.

But this is not good. If I suppress something in my consciousness so deep that it moves into the collective unconscious...because this is how the mind is: the conscious mind is just the first layer which looks private, appears private. Then there is a deeper layer of unconsciousness; that, too, has a certain flavor of privacy because it is so near the conscious mind. Then there is a third layer of collective unconsciousness which is not private at all, which is public, which is in fact universal.

So if I suppress something, then first it goes into my unconscious and creates trouble for me. If I suppress it really deep, and go on suppressing it, and use methods and tricks to suppress it so much that it simply drops from my unconscious also and moves into the collective unconscious, then somewhere, somebody, a weakling, will get it. Because I force it too much, somewhere it has to pop up to the surface. Then I am Ram and somebody becomes a Ravana. Then I am a Christ and somebody becomes a Judas. Just the other day one sannyasin who is here wrote me a letter saying, "You are Christ and I am a Judas." But I can tell him that that is not possible – I am both. With Christ it was possible, not with me. I don't allow that possibility.

Then what type of saint do I have in my mind? A saint who does not suppress the opposite but uses it, who is not against anything but makes a new arrangement of things. In his greater harmony even evil becomes good. In that harmony he uses even discarded parts. And it is a great art to be both together. It is the greatest art, because then you have to seek the hidden harmony between the opposites – then you are neither this nor that, but both. Even poison can be used as elixir, but then you have to be very, very careful. Much awareness is needed to use poison as elixir, to use evil as good, to use the Devil as God. This is also what Heraclitus means by the hidden harmony. He says:

*...by evil that good is pleasant;*
*by hunger, satiety; by weariness, rest.*
*It is one and the same thing...*

...the good and the bad, the illness and health, the sinner and the saint.

*It is one and the same thing to be living or dead,*
*awake or asleep, young or old.*
*The former aspect in each case becomes the latter,*
*and the latter again the former,*
*by sudden unexpected reversal.*

It is a wheel – yin and yang, good and bad, male and female, day and night, summer and winter. It is a wheel; everything moves into the other and comes back to itself again. It is an eternal recurrence.

*It throws apart*
*and then brings together again.*

We have met before, now we are meeting again. We have met before! Then nature throws apart; then the nature brings together again. That is the meaning of the first fragment: *Into the same rivers we step and do not step.* We are meeting again but we are not the same. We have met before....

This idea caught hold of one of the greatest geniuses of this century, the past century, in fact – Friedrich Nietzsche. It possessed him so totally that he became completely mad – the idea of recurrence, eternal recurrence. He says that everything has happened before, is happening again, will happen again...not exactly the same, but still the same. Looks very weird if you think about it, that you have listened to me before also many times – and you are listening again. Looks very weird, strange; you feel uncomfortable with the very idea. But it is so, because nature brings people together and takes them apart just to bring them together again.

No departure is ultimate. No coming together is final. Coming together is just a preparation for going apart. Going apart is again just a preparation for coming together. And it is beautiful! – it is beautiful.

*Into the same rivers we step and do not step.*

*It throws apart*
*and then brings together again.*

*All things come in their due seasons.*

This is the peak of Heraclitus' consciousness. Let it go deep in you. Let it circulate in your blood and in your heart. Let it become a beat.

*All things come in their due seasons.*

Many things are implied. One: you need not make much effort. Even making much effort may be a barrier because nothing can come before its season – all things come in their due seasons. Too much effort can be dangerous. Too much effort may be an effort to bring things when the season is not ripe. That doesn't mean don't make any effort...because if you don't make any effort, then they may not come even in their due season. Just the right amount of effort is needed. What does a farmer do? He watches the seasons in the sky: now it is time to sow, he sows – never before it, never after it. A farmer simply watches for the right moment, then he sows; then he waits, then he sings. Then in the night he sleeps and watches – and waits. Whatsoever is to be done, he does it, but there is no hurry.

That's why countries which have lived long with agriculture are never in a hurry. Countries which have become technological are always in a hurry – because with technology you can bring things without their season. Countries which are agriculturist and have remained agriculturist for thousands of years, are never in a hurry, they are not time conscious. That's why in India it happens every day that somebody says, "I will be coming at five," and never comes. Or he says, "I will be coming at five sharp," and comes in the night at ten. And you cannot believe what type of...no time consciousness really.

A farmer doesn't divide in hours. He says, "I will be coming in the evening." The evening can mean anything – four o'clock, six o'clock, eight o'clock. He says, "I will come in the morning." The morning can mean anything – he may come at four o'clock in the morning or ten o'clock in the morning. He doesn't divide it by hours. He cannot. He cannot because he has to live by the seasons. The year is divided not in months but in seasons – summer, winter – and he has to wait. He cannot be in a hurry. With the seeds what can you do? They don't listen. You cannot send them to schools, you cannot teach them. And they don't bother, they are not in any hurry; they simply wait in the earth. And when the time comes, they sprout and they grow on their own. They don't bother about you, that you are in a hurry, or whether something can be done. You cannot persuade them, you cannot talk to them – they take their own time. A farmer becomes a deep awaiting.

Become like a farmer. If you are sowing seeds of enlightenment, of understanding, of meditation, be like a farmer, not like a technician. Don't be in a hurry. Nothing can be done about it. Whatsoever can be done, you do, and wait.

Don't do too much. Doing too much may become a subtle undoing. Your very effort may become a barrier.

*All things come in their due seasons.*

And then don't ask for the result. They come in their due season. If it happens today it is okay. If it doesn't happen, a man of understanding, intelligence, clarity, knows that the time is not ripe. When the time is ripe, it will happen. He waits; he is not childish.

Childishness consists of asking for things immediately. If a child wants a toy in the middle of the night, he wants it immediately. He cannot follow and understand that one has to wait for the morning to come; shops are closed. He thinks these are just excuses. He wants it immediately, right now. He thinks that these are tricks to divert his mind, that it is midnight and shops are not open – what is the relevance? Why are shops not open at midnight? What is wrong with midnight? And he knows that by the morning he will have forgotten the whole thing. And these people are tricky: if he goes to sleep, by the morning he will have forgotten. He wants it immediately. And a country which is juvenile, a civilization which is juvenile and childish, also wants everything immediately – instant coffee, instant love, instant meditation also. That's what Maharishi Mahesh Yogi is doing: instant, right now – you do ten minutes, and within fifteen days you are enlightened.... Looks foolish.

No, nature doesn't follow you or your demands. Nature follows its own course. This is the meaning: *All things come in their due seasons*. Wait. Make the effort and wait. And don't ask for the result to come immediately. If you ask, your very asking will delay the phenomenon more and more. If you can wait, wait patiently, passively, still alert, watching, just like a farmer, you will attain to it. If you are in a hurry you will miss. If you are very time conscious you cannot move into meditation – because meditation is timelessness. And always remember: whenever you are ready, it will happen. And the readiness comes in its due season.

A young man comes to me and he says, "I am very, very tense." A young man has to be tense. He says, "I would like to be detached" – but this is asking for something out of season. A young man has to be attached. Unless you suffer attachment you can never grow towards detachment. And if you force detachment you will make a mess of your life because when the right time was there for attachment you missed it. Then you tried to pretend and force detachment. Then when the time of detachment comes, when you become old, the suppressed part is still hanging around you like a haze and then you see that death is reaching – you

become afraid. The suppressed part says, "Then when will there be a time for me? I wanted to love, I wanted to be attached, I wanted to be involved and committed to some relationship – now there is no time!" Then the suppressed part forces itself up and an old man becomes foolish and he starts asking for relationships. He has missed everything. He has missed all seasons.

Remember: Be in step with the season.

When it is time to be tense, be tense! What is wrong in it?...because if you are not tense how will you be able to rest? If you are not angry how will you be in compassion? If you don't fall in love, how will you rise out of it? Everything in its due season. It comes by itself. It has always been so and it will always be so. Existence is vast and you cannot force your own ways on it. You have to watch where it is going and you have to follow.

This is the difference between an ignorant man and a wise man. An ignorant man is always pushing the river according to his idea. A wise man has no ideas of his own. He is simply watching where nature flows; he flows with it. He has no ego to push; he has no conflict with nature. He is not trying to conquer nature; he understands the foolishness of it, that it cannot be conquered. How can the part conquer the whole? No – he surrenders, he becomes a shadow. He moves wherever nature moves. He is like a white cloud moving in the sky, not knowing where he is going but unworried...unworried because wherever the winds take him, that will be the goal. The goal is not a fixed phenomenon. Wherever nature leads you, if you allow nature, if you remain in a letgo, wherever it leads it will be blissful.

Everywhere is the goal, you only have to allow it. Every moment is the peak, you have to allow it. Just allowing – let go, surrender, and then you can rest assured: *All things come in their due seasons*.

# ABOUT OSHO

MOST OF US LIVE OUT our lives in the world of time, in memories of the past and anticipation of the future. Only rarely do we touch the timeless dimension of the present – in moments of sudden beauty, or sudden danger, in meeting with a lover or with the surprise of the unexpected. Very few people step out of the world of time and mind, its ambitions and competitiveness, and begin to live in the world of the timeless. And of those who do, only a few have attempted to share their experience. Lao Tzu, Gautam Buddha, Bodhidharma...or more recently, George Gurdjieff, Raman Maharshi, J. Krishnamurti – they are thought by their contemporaries to be eccentrics or madmen; after their death they are called "philosophers." And in time they become legends – not flesh-and-blood human beings, but perhaps mythological representations of our collective wish to grow beyond the smallness and trivia, the meaninglessness of our everyday lives.

Osho is one who has discovered the door to living His life in the timeless dimension of the present – He has called Himself a "true existentialist" – and He has devoted His life to provoking others to seek this same door, to step out of the world of past and future and discover for themselves the world of eternity.

Osho was born in Kuchwada, Madhya Pradesh, India, on December 11, 1931. From His earliest childhood, His was a rebellious and independent spirit, insisting on experiencing the truth for Himself rather than acquiring knowledge and beliefs given by others.

After His enlightenment at the age of twenty-one, Osho completed His academic studies and spent several years teaching philosophy at the University of Jabalpur. Meanwhile, He traveled throughout India giving talks, challenging

orthodox religious leaders in public debate, questioning traditional beliefs, and meeting people from all walks of life. He read extensively everything He could find to broaden His understanding of the belief systems and psychology of contemporary man. By the late 1960s Osho had begun to develop His unique dynamic meditation techniques. Modern man, He said, is so burdened with the outmoded traditions of the past and the anxieties of modern-day living that he must go through a deep cleansing process before he can hope to discover the thought-less, relaxed state of meditation.

In the early 1970s, the first Westerners began to hear of Osho. By 1974 a commune had been established around Him in Poona, India, and the trickle of visitors from the West was soon to become a flood. In the course of His work, Osho has spoken on virtually every aspect of the development of human consciousness. He has distilled the essence of what is significant to the spiritual quest of contemporary man, based not on intellectual understanding but tested against His own existential experience.

He belongs to no tradition – "I am the beginning of a totally new religious consciousness," He says. "Please don't connect me with the past – it is not even worth remembering."

His talks to disciples and seekers from all over the world have been published in more than six hundred volumes, and translated into over thirty languages. And He says, "My message is not a doctrine, not a philosophy. My message is a certain alchemy, a science of transformation, so only those who are willing to die as they are and be born again into something so new that they cannot even

imagine it right now...only those few courageous people will be ready to listen, because listening is going to be risky.

"Listening, you have taken the first step towards being reborn. So it is not a philosophy that you can just make an overcoat of and go bragging about. It is not a doctrine where you can find consolation for harassing questions. No, my message is not some verbal communication. It is far more risky. It is nothing less than death and rebirth."

Osho left His body on January 19, 1990, as a result of poisoning by US government agents while held incognito in custody on technical immigration violations in 1985.

His huge commune in India continues to be the largest spiritual growth center in the world attracting thousands of international visitors who come to participate in its meditation, therapy, bodywork and creative programs, or just to experience being in a buddhafield.

# VIGYAN BHAIRAV TANTRA

Shiva's one hundred and twelve meditation techniques made relevant to twenty-first century man. "Though the oldest in the world," Osho tells us, "nothing need be added to them. They constitute the whole science of transforming the mind." Osho then promptly adds to them, giving us his rich and lighthearted commentaries, resulting in two exquisitely designed volumes of over 600 pages each.

Complete in a single box, they come with a deck of one hundred and twelve giant full color cards, each one distinctively illustrated by one of a group of five artists. Pick a card at random, alone or with a friend, and it will lead to a particular meditation method in the book. Disciples' questions on that method are answered by Osho in the same chapter.

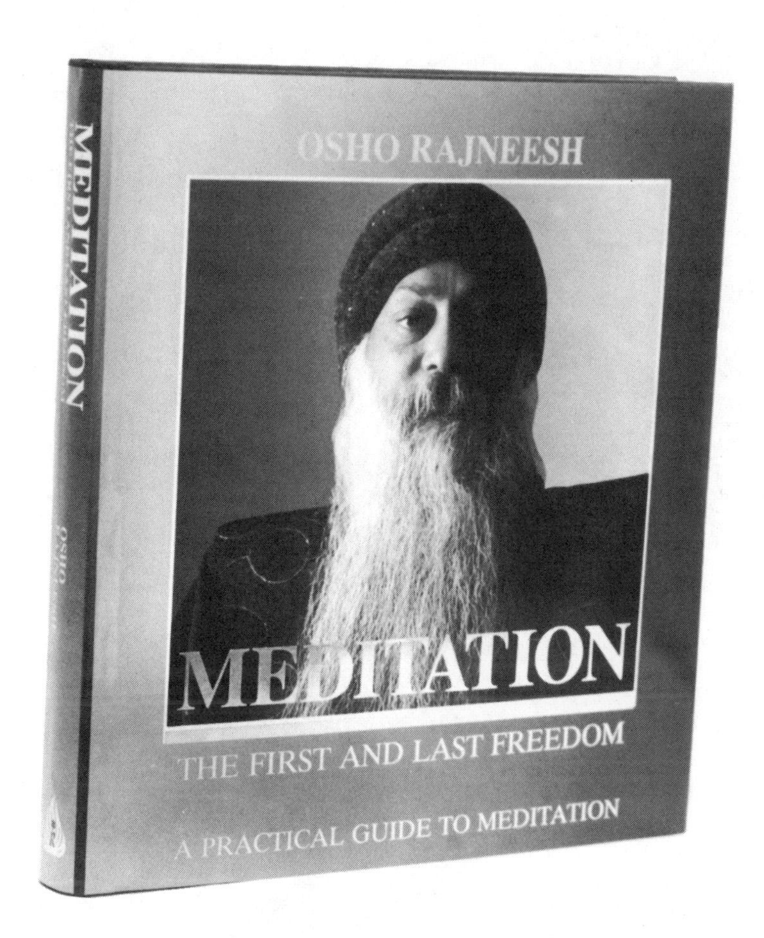


## MEDITATION: THE FIRST AND LAST FREEDOM

A seeker's practical handbook to meditation straight from the enlightened master. Techniques specially devised by Osho for the twenty-first century man. From meditating while smoking to reaching the ultimate state of emptiness by talking one hour of gibberish, ninety different ways to connect with your inner being. Plus just about everything else Osho has ever said about meditation and the problems confronting meditators. In a beautifully bound hardback, covering two hundred and eighty pages.

# NOW READ THE MAGAZINE

news and developments, thoughtful editorials, music reviews, regular supplements updating the Osho Multiversity Program, a regular Insanities column, horoscopes – and more!

For subscription details, please write to:

Osho Times International
Tao Publishing Pvt Ltd
50 Koregaon Park
Poona 411001
India

# BOOKS BY OSHO
## ENGLISH LANGUAGE EDITIONS

**Buddha and Buddhist Masters**

The Dhammapada (Series 1–12) *The Way of the Buddha*
The Diamond Sutra *The Vajrachchedika Prajnaparamita Sutra*
The Discipline of Transcendence (Volumes 1–4) *On the Sutra of 42 Chapters*
The Heart Sutra *The Prajnaparamita Hridayam Sutra*
The Book of Wisdom (Volumes 1&2) *Atisha's Seven Points of Mind Training*

**Indian Mystics**

***The Bauls***

The Beloved (Volumes 1&2)

***Kabir***

The Divine Melody
Ecstasy: The Forgotten Language
The Fish in the Sea is Not Thirsty
The Great Secret
The Guest
The Path of Love
The Revolution

***Krishna***

Krishna: The Man and His Philosophy

**Jesus and Christian Mystics**

Come Follow Me (Volumes 1–4) *The Sayings of Jesus*
I Say Unto You (Volumes 1&2) *The Sayings of Jesus*
The Mustard Seed *The Gospel of Thomas*
Theologia Mystica *The Treatise of St. Dionysius*

**Jewish Mystics**

The Art of Dying
The True Sage

**The Mantra Series**

Satyam-Shivam-Sundram *Truth-Godliness-Beauty*
Sat-Chit-Anand *Truth-Consciousness-Bliss*
Om Mani Padme Hum *The Sound of Silence: The Diamond in the Lotus*
Hari Om Tat Sat *The Divine Sound: That is the Truth*
Om Shantih Shantih Shantih *The Soundless Sound: Peace, Peace, Peace*

**Master and Disciple**

Be Still and Know
Come, Come, Yet Again Come
The Goose is Out!
The Great Pilgrimage: From Here to Here
The Invitation
My Way: The Way of the White Clouds
The Razor's Edge
Walk Without Feet, Fly Without Wings and Think Without Mind
The Wild Geese and the Water
YAA-HOO! The Mystic Rose
Zen: Zest, Zip, Zap and Zing

**Meditation**

And Now, and Here (Volumes 1&2)
In Search of the Miraculous (Volumes 1&2)
Meditation: The First and Last Freedom
The Orange Book *Meditation Techniques*
The Perfect Way
Vigyan Bhairav Tantra (Series 1&2) *The Book of the Secrets – A New Commentary*

**Osho's Vision for the World**

The Golden Future
The Hidden Splendor
The New Dawn
The Rebel
The Rebellious Spirit

**Personal Glimpses**

Books I Have Loved
Glimpses of a Golden Childhood
Notes of a Madman

**Sufism**

Just Like That
The Perfect Master (Volumes 1&2)
The Secret
Sufis: The People of the Path (Volumes 1&2)
Unio Mystica (Volumes 1&2) *The Hadiqa of Hakim Sanai*
Until You Die
The Wisdom of the Sands (Volumes 1&2)

**Tantra**

Tantra, Spirituality and Sex *Excerpts from The Book of the Secrets*
Tantra: The Supreme Understanding *Tilopa's Song of Mahamudra*
The Tantra Vision (Volumes 1&2) *The Royal Song of Saraha*
Vigyan Bhairav Tantra (Series 1&2) *The Book of the Secrets – A New Commentary*

**Tao**

The Empty Boat *The Stories of Chuang Tzu*
The Secret of Secrets (Volumes 1&2) *The Secret of the Golden Flower*
Tao: The Golden Gate (Volumes 1&2)
Tao: The Pathless Path (Volumes 1&2) *The Stories of Lieh Tzu*
Tao: The Three Treasures (Volumes 1–4) *The Tao Te Ching of Lao Tzu*
When the Shoe Fits *The Stories of Chuang Tzu*

**The Upanishads**

I Am That *Isa Upanishad*
Philosophia Ultima *Mandukya Upanishad*
The Supreme Doctrine *Kenopanishad*
That Art Thou *Sarvasar Upanishad, Kaivalya Upanishad, Adhyatma Upanishad*
The Ultimate Alchemy (Volumes 1&2) *Atma Pooja Upanishad*
Vedanta: Seven Steps to Samadhi *Akshya Upanishad*

**Western Mystics**

Guida Spirituale *On the Desiderata*
The Hidden Harmony *The Fragments of Heraclitus*
The Messiah (Volumes 1&2) *Commentaries on Kahlil Gibran's The Prophet*
The New Alchemy: To Turn You On *Mabel Collins' Light on the Path*
Philosophia Perennis (Volumes 1&2) *The Golden Verses of Pythagoras*
Zarathustra: A God That Can Dance *Commentaries on Friedrich Nietzsche's Thus Spake Zarathustra*
Zarathustra: The Laughing Prophet *Commentaries on Friedrich Nietzsche's Thus Spake Zarathustra*

**Yoga**

Yoga: The Alpha and the Omega (Volumes 1–10) *The Yoga Sutras of Patanjali* Volumes 1–3 also available as:
Yoga: The Science of the Soul (Volumes 1–3)

**Zen**

***Poona 1974-1981***

Ah, This!
Ancient Music in the Pines
And the Flowers Showered
Dang Dang Doko Dang
The First Principle
The Grass Grows By Itself
Nirvana: The Last Nightmare
No Water, No Moon
Returning to the Source
Roots and Wings
The Search *The Ten Bulls of Zen*
A Sudden Clash of Thunder
Walking in Zen, Sitting in Zen
Zen: The Path of Paradox (Volumes 1–3)
Zen: The Special Transmission

**Zen**

***The Mystery School 1986-1989***

Christianity, the Deadliest Poison, and Zen, the Antidote to All Poisons
Communism and Zen Fire, Zen Wind
God is Dead: Now Zen is the Only Living Truth
I Celebrate Myself: God is No Where; Life is Now Here
No Mind: The Flowers of Eternity
One Seed Makes the Whole Earth Green
The Zen Manifesto
Zen: The Mystery and the Poetry of the Beyond

The World of Zen *A boxed set of 5 volumes, containing:* *
- Live Zen
- This. This. A Thousand Times This.
- Zen: The Quantum Leap from Mind to No-Mind
- Zen: The Solitary Bird, Cuckoo of the Forest
- Zen: The Diamond Thunderbolt

Zen: All the Colors of the Rainbow *A boxed set of 5 volumes, containing:* *
- The Miracle
- Turning In
- The Original Man
- The Language of Existence
- The Buddha: The Emptiness of the Heart

**Each volume is also available individually*

**Zen Masters**

Bodhidharma: The Greatest Zen Master *Commentaries on the Teachings of the Messenger of Zen from India to China*
The Great Zen Master Ta Hui *Reflections on the Transformation of an Intellectual to Enlightenment*
Hsin Hsin Ming: The Book of Nothing *Discourses on the Faith-Mind of Sosan*
Kyōzan: A True Man of Zen

Osho Rajneesh: The Present Day Awakened One Speaks on the Ancient Masters of Zen *A boxed set of 7 volumes, containing:* *
- Dōgen, the Zen Master: A Search and a Fulfillment
- Ma Tzu: The Empty Mirror
- Hyakujō: The Everest of Zen, with Bashō's Haikus
- Nansen: The Point of Departure
- Jōshū: The Lion's Roar

Rinzai: Master of the Irrational
Isan: No Footprints in the Blue Sky
The Sun Rises in the Evening *Sutras of Yoka Daishi*
Take it Easy (Volumes 1&2) *Poems of Ikkyu*
This Very Body the Buddha *Hakuin's Song of Meditation*
The White Lotus *The Sayings of Bodhidharma*
Yakusan: Straight to the Point of Enlightenment

**Each volume is also available individually*

**Darshan Diaries – Intimate Talks between Master and Disciple**

Hammer on the Rock *(December 10, 1975 – January 15, 1976)*
Above All Don't Wobble *(January 16 – February 12, 1976)*
Nothing to Lose But Your Head *(February 13 – March 12, 1976)*
Be Realistic: Plan For a Miracle *(March 13 – April 6, 1976)*
Get Out of Your Own Way *(April 7 – May 2, 1976)*
Beloved of My Heart *(May 3 – 28, 1976)*
The Cypress in the Courtyard *(May 29 – June 27, 1976)*
A Rose is a Rose is a Rose *(June 28 – July 27, 1976)*
Dance Your Way to God *(July 28 – August 20, 1976)*
The Passion for the Impossible *(August 21 – September 18, 1976)*
The Great Nothing *(September 19 – October 11, 1976)*
God is Not for Sale *(October 12 – November 7, 1976)*
The Shadow of the Whip *(November 8 – December 3, 1976)*
Blessed are the Ignorant *(December 4 – 31, 1976)*
The Buddha Disease *(January 1977)*
What Is, Is, What Ain't, Ain't *(February 1977)*
The Zero Experience *(March 1977)*
For Madmen Only (Price of Admission: Your Mind) *(April 1977)*
This is It *(May 1977)*
The Further Shore *(June 1977)*
Far Beyond the Stars *(July 1977)*
The No Book (No Buddha, No Teaching, No Discipline) *(August 1977)*
Don't Just Do Something, Sit There *(September 1977)*
Only Losers Can Win in This Game *(October 1977)*
The Open Secret *(November 1977)*
The Open Door *(December 1977)*
The Sun Behind the Sun Behind the Sun *(January 1978)*
Believing the Impossible Before Breakfast *(February 1978)*
Don't Bite My Finger, Look Where I'm Pointing *(March 1978)*
Let Go! *(April 1978)*
The 99 Names of Nothingness *(May 1978)*
The Madman's Guide to Enlightenment *(June 1978)*
Don't Look Before You Leap *(July 1978)*
Hallelujah! *(August 1978)*
God's Got a Thing About You *(September 1978)*
The Tongue-Tip Taste of Tao *(October 1978)*
The Sacred Yes *(November 1978)*
Turn On, Tune In, and Drop the Lot *(December 1978)*
Zorba the Buddha *(January 1979)*
Won't You Join the Dance? *(February 1979)*
You Ain't Seen Nothin' Yet *(March 1979)*
The Shadow of the Bamboo *(April 1979)*
Just Around the Corner *(May 1979)*
Snap Your Fingers, Slap Your Face & Wake Up! *(June 1979)*
The Rainbow Bridge *(July 1979)*
Don't Let Yourself Be Upset by the Sutra, Rather Upset the Sutra Yourself *(August/September 1979)*
The Sound of One Hand Clapping *(March 1981)*

**Early Discourses and Writings**

A Cup of Tea *Letters to Disciples*
Dimensions Beyond the Known
From Sex to Superconsciousness
I Am the Gate
The Long and the Short and the All
The Psychology of the Esoteric

**Interviews with the World Press**

The Last Testament (Volume 1)

**Talks in America**

From Bondage to Freedom *Answers to the Seekers of the Path*
From Darkness to Light *Answers to the Seekers of the Path*
From Death to Deathlessness *Answers to the Seekers of the Path*
From the False to the Truth *Answers to the Seekers of the Path*
The Rajneesh Bible (Volumes 1–4)

**The World Tour**

Beyond Enlightenment *Talks in Bombay*
Beyond Psychology *Talks in Uruguay*
Light on the Path *Talks in the Himalayas*
The Path of the Mystic *Talks in Uruguay*
The Rajneesh Upanishad *Talks in Bombay*
Sermons in Stones *Talks in Bombay*
Socrates Poisoned Again After 25 Centuries *Talks in Greece*
The Sword and the Lotus *Talks in the Himalayas*
The Transmission of the Lamp *Talks in Uruguay*

**Compilations**

At the Feet of the Master
Beyond the Frontiers of the Mind
Bhagwan Shree Rajneesh On Basic Human Rights
The Book *An Introduction to the Teachings of Bhagwan Shree Rajneesh*
Series I from A – H
Series II from I – Q
Series III from R – Z
Death: The Greatest Fiction

The Greatest Challenge: The Golden Future
I Teach Religiousness Not Religion
Jesus Crucified Again, This Time in Ronald Reagan's America
A Must for Morning Contemplation
A Must for Contemplation Before Sleep
The New Man: The Only Hope for the Future
Priests and Politicians: The Mafia of the Soul
The Rebel: The Very Salt of the Earth
Sex: Quotations from Bhagwan Shree Rajneesh

**Gift Books of Osho Quotations**

Gold Nuggets
More Gold Nuggets
Words from a Man of No Words

**Photobiographies**

Shree Rajneesh: A Man of Many Climates, Seasons and Rainbows *Through the Eye of the Camera*
This Very Place The Lotus Paradise *Bhagwan Shree Rajneesh and His Work 1978–1984*

**Books about Osho**

Bhagwan: The Buddha For The Future *(by Juliet Forman)*
Bhagwan Shree Rajneesh: The Most Dangerous Man Since Jesus Christ *(by Sue Appleton)*
Bhagwan: The Most Godless Yet The Most Godly Man *(by Dr. George Meredith)*
Bhagwan: One Man Against the Whole Ugly Past of Humanity *The World Tour and Back Home Again to India (by Juliet Forman)*
Bhagwan: Twelve Days That Shook The World *(by Juliet Forman)*
The Choice is Ours *(by George Meredith)*
Was Bhagwan Shree Rajneesh Poisoned by Ronald Reagan's America? *(by Sue Appleton)*

**OTHER PUBLISHERS**

**NEW ZEALAND**

After Middle Age: A Limitless Sky *(Hazard Press)*

**UNITED KINGDOM**

The Art of Dying *(Sheldon Press)*
The Book of the Secrets *(Volume 1, Thames & Hudson)*
Dimensions Beyond the Known *(Sheldon Press)*
The Hidden Harmony *(Sheldon Press)*
Meditation: The Art of Ecstasy *(Sheldon Press)*
The Mustard Seed *(Sheldon Press)*
Neither This Nor That *(Sheldon Press)*
No Water, No Moon *(Sheldon Press)*
Roots and Wings *(Routledge & Kegan Paul)*
Straight to Freedom *(Original title: Until You Die, Sheldon Press)*
The Supreme Understanding *(Original title: Tantra: The Supreme Understanding, Sheldon Press)*
The Supreme Doctrine *(Routledge & Kegan Paul)*
Tao: The Three Treasures *(Volume 1, Wildwood House)*

**Books about Osho**

The Way of the Heart: The Rajneesh Movement *by Judith Thompson and Paul Heelas, Department of Religious Studies, University of Lancaster (Aquarian Press)*

**UNITED STATES OF AMERICA**

And the Flowers Showered *(De Vorss)*
The Book of the Secrets *(Volumes 1–3, Harper & Row)*
Dimensions Beyond the Known *(Wisdom Garden Books)*
The Grass Grows By Itself *(De Vorss)*
The Great Challenge *(Grove Press)*
Hammer on the Rock *(Grove Press)*
I Am the Gate *(Harper & Row)*
Journey Toward the Heart *(Original title: Until You Die, Harper & Row)*
Meditation: The Art of Ecstasy *(Original title: Dynamics of Meditation, Harper & Row)*
Mojud, The Man with the Inexplicable Life *Excerpts from The Wisdom of the Sands (Ansu Publishing Co., Ltd.)*
The Mustard Seed *(Harper & Row)*
My Way: The Way of the White Clouds *(Grove Press)*
Nirvana: The Last Nightmare *(Wisdom Garden Books)*
Only One Sky *(Original title: Tantra: The Supreme Understanding, Dutton)*
The Psychology of the Esoteric *(Harper & Row)*
Roots and Wings *(Routledge & Kegan Paul)*
The Supreme Doctrine *(Routledge & Kegan Paul)*
When the Shoe Fits *(De Vorss)*
Words Like Fire *(Original title: Come Follow Me,Volume 1, Harper & Row)*

**Books about Osho**

The Awakened One: The Life and Work of Bhagwan Shree Rajneesh *by Vasant Joshi (Harper & Row)*
Dying for Enlightenment *by Bernard Gunther (Harper & Row)*
Rajneeshpuram and the Abuse of Power *by Ted Shay, Ph.D. (Scout Creek Press)*
Rajneeshpuram, the Unwelcome Society *by Kirk Braun (Scout Creek Press)*
The Rajneesh Story: The Bhagwan's Garden *by Dell Murphy (Linwood Press, Oregon)*

## FOREIGN LANGUAGE EDITIONS

Books by Osho have been translated and published in the following languages:

Chinese
Czech
Danish
Dutch
Finnish
French
German
Greek
Gujrati
Hebrew
Hindi
Italian
Japanese
Korean
Marathi
Nepali
Polish
Portuguese
Punjabi
Russian
Serbo-Croat
Sindhi
Spanish
Swedish
Tamil
Telugu
Urdu

## AUDIO/VIDEO

The discourses in this book are available on audio and video tape. Most of the other books listed are also available in audio or video format. For information about these and tapes for Osho's meditations, contact your local distributor.

# WORLDWIDE DISTRIBUTION CENTERS FOR THE WORKS OF OSHO

## EUROPE

**Belgium**

Osho Indu Distribution
Coebergerstraat 40
B 2018 Antwerpen

**Denmark**

Osho RISK Bookstore
Boegballevej 3
DK 8740 Braedstrup

**Finland**

Unio Mystica Shop for Meditative Books and Tapes
P.O. Box 186
Albertinkatu 10
00121 Helsinki 12

**Germany**

The Rebel Publishing House GmbH*
Venloer Strasse 5-7
5000 Cologne 1

**Italy**

News Services Corporation
Via Teulie 14
I 20136 Milano

**Netherlands**

Osho Publikaties Nederland
Vianenstraat 48
NL 1106 DD Amsterdam

**Norway**

Osho Devananda Meditation Center
P.O. Box 177 Vinderen
N 0319 Oslo 3

**Spain**

Distribuciones "El Rebelde"
"Es Serralet"
E 07192 Estellencs
Mallorca - Baleares

**Sweden**

Osho Madhur Meditation Center
Fridhemsgatan 41
S-112 46 Stockholm

**Switzerland**

Osho Mingus Meditation Center
Asylstrasse 11
CH 8032 Zurich

OSHO PURNIMA DISTRIBUTION
"GREENWISE"
VANGE PARK ROAD
VANGE, BASILDON
ESSEX, SS16 5LA
Tel: 01268 584141

## AUSTRALIA

Osho Meditation & Healing Centre
22 Alexandra Road
East Fremantle, WA 6158

## NEW ZEALAND

Rebel Books Mail Order
P.O. Box 193
Papakura N.Z.

## AMERICA

**U.S.A.**

Chidvilas Inc.
P.O. Box 17550
Boulder, CO 80308

Ansu Publishing Co., Inc.
19023 SW Eastside Rd.
Lake Oswego, OR 97034

Osho Viha Meditation Center
P.O. Box 352
Mill Valley, CA 94942

Osho Nartano Distribution
P.O. Box 51171
Levittown,
Puerto Rico 00950-1171

Also available in bookstores nationwide at Walden Books

**Brazil**

Osho Jyotsana Meditation Center
Rua Moura Brasil 58/101
Rio de Janeiro, RJ CEP 22231

**Canada**

Publications Osho
c/o Swami Prem Bruno
1120 Paquette
Brossard, P.Que. J4W 2T2

**ASIA**

**India**

Sadhana Foundation*
17 Koregaon Park
Poona 411 001, MS

**Japan**

Osho Eer Neo-Sannyas Commune
Mimura Building 6-21-34
Kikuna, Kohoku-ku
Yokohama 222

*All books available AT COST PRICE

## OSHO MEDITATION CENTERS AND COMMUNES

There are many Osho Meditation Centers throughout the world which can be contacted for information about the teachings of Osho and which have His books available as well as audio and video tapes of His discourses. Centers exist in practically every country.

## FOR FURTHER INFORMATION CONTACT

Osho Commune International
17 Koregaon Park, Poona 411 001, India